MILLENNIAL HOUSE

GINGKO PRESS

MILLENNIAL
HOUSE

ISBN 978-1-58423-525-5

First Published in the United States of America by
Gingko Press by arrangement with
Sandu Publishing Co., Ltd.

Text edited by Gingko Press.

Gingko Press, Inc.
1321 Fifth Street
Berkeley, CA 94710 USA
Tel: (510) 898 1195
Fax: (510) 898 1196
Email: books@gingkopress.com
www.gingkopress.com

Copyright © 2013 by Sandu Publishing
First published in 2013 by Sandu Publishing

Sponsored by Design 360°
– Concept and Design Magazine

Edited and produced by
Sandu Publishing Co., Ltd.
Book design, concepts & art direction by
Sandu Publishing Co., Ltd.
sandu.publishing@gmail.com
www.sandupublishing.com

Cover project by Renato D'Ettorre Architects

All rights reserved. No part of this publication
may be reproduced or transmitted in any form or
by any means, electronic or mechanical, including
photocopy, recording or any information storage
and retrieval system, without prior permission in
writing from the publisher.

Printed and bound in China

PREFACE
/
BY
DAVID JAMESON

Habitable Art

"The highest and most beautiful things in life are not to be heard about, nor read about, nor seen but, if one will, are to be lived."

- Søren Kierkegaard

Architecture is a material and social art that is the most profound of all the arts because it is viscerally experiential. Dwellings conceived as art can produce an unexpected set of relationships and opportunities that become manifested as social and spatial events. It is the experiential quality of these events that, when precisely crafted and well positioned, can produce extraordinarily beautiful meanings that are recognized within the participant or community.

The meaning of the works revealed in *Millennial House* is conveyed within each project as moments of complexity, diversity, beauty, and richness. Within these moments, architecture emerges as an art form that is critically engaged with the visual, social, and historical culture of which it is an active part.

The work of my studio is rooted in the distillation of an elemental architecture. The operation of the work is formed by repositioning and braiding each project's diverse pressures into a unique situational aesthetic. Exploring notions of reflectivity and interstitial space, the resultant spatial logic of the work is to be "lived," yet formed with specificity to the conceptual genesis of each project. Tectonically, the work is conceived as an intertwining of the the refined and the raw.

David Jameson

CONTENTS

| / 008 / | **Godiva House**
Empty Space Architecture |
|---|---|
| / 014 / | **Private House in Sassuolo**
Enrico Iascone Architetti |
| / 020 / | **h.3. House in Athens**
314 Architecture Studio |
| / 024 / | **Wissioming2**
Robert M. Gurney Architect |
| / 030 / | **House in Estoril**
Frederico Valsassina Arquitectos |
| / 036 / | **House in Lemesos**
Skinotechniki |
| / 042 / | **Ipês House**
Studio MK27 |
| / 048 / | **L23 House**
Pitágoras Arquitectos |
| / 054 / | **Casa Guanábanos**
Taller Héctor Barroso |
| / 058 / | **House in Conceição**
Vitor Vilhena Arquitectura |
| / 064 / | **Casa La Palma**
Miguel Ángel Aragonés |
| / 068 / | **House M**
monovolume architecture + design |
| / 072 / | **Aboo Makhado**
Nico van der Meulen Architects |
| / 076 / | **Bridge House**
123DV |
| / 080 / | **Family House J20**
DAR612 |
| / 084 / | **Browne Street House**
Shaun Lockyer Architects |
| / 090 / | **G1 House**
Arch. Gabriel Rivera +
Arch. Cristina Vargas |
| / 094 / | **W House**
IDIN Architects |
| / 098 / | **Azuris**
Renato D'Ettorre Architects |
| / 102 / | **Photographer's Weekend House**
General Design Co., Ltd. |
| / 106 / | **Garden Tree House**
Hironaka Ogawa & Associates |
| / 112 / | **Casa Almare**
Elías Rizo Arquitectos |
| / 118 / | **House in Hiyoshi**
EANA |
| / 124 / | **House in Shimoda**
EANA |
| / 130 / | **Hye Ro Hun**
IROJE KHM Architects |
| / 136 / | **Can Manuel d'en Corda**
Daniel Redolat +
Marià Castelló Architects |
| / 142 / | **House on the Cliff**
Fran Silvestre Arquitectos |
| / 148 / | **Colunata House**
Mário Martins Atelier |
| / 152 / | **House in Travanca**
Nelson Resende Arquitecto |
| / 158 / | **Rieteiland House**
Hans van Heeswijk Architects |
| / 164 / | **YAK01**
Ayutt and Associates Design |
| / 172 / | **The Curving House**
JOHO Architecture |
| / 178 / | **LA House**
Studio Guilherme Torres |
| / 184 / | **Villa SSK**
Takeshi Hirobe Architects |
| / 188 / | **Maracanã House**
Terra e Tuma Arquitetos Associados |
| / 192 / | **Whistler Residence**
BattersbyHowat Architects |
| / 198 / | **Fieldview House**
Blaze Makoid Architecture |
| / 202 / | **House VMVK**
dmvA |
| / 208 / | **Aalen-Zochental House**
L/A Liebel/Architekten BDA |
| / 212 / | **House in Ayukawa**
Dai Nagasaka/Mega |
| / 216 / | **105 V**
Shaun Lockyer Architects |
| / 222 / | **Tusculum St. Residence**
Smart Design Studio |
| / 226 / | **House in Quinta Patino**
Frederico Valsassina Arquitectos |

Godiva House
Godiva House is intended to reflect a unique way of living.

Empty Space Architecture
Cascais, Portugal
400sqm

The house consists of two rectangular volumes connected by a central quadrangular volume. The two rectangular volumes are rotated according to the municipal alignment rules. The house was designed to be used by someone with reduced mobility and to be as sustainable as possible.

The interior and exterior spaces that make up this modernist architectural piece have a constant and ever-present dialogue.

The interior spaces, regardless of their function, adjoin the garden. The garden was designed as if it were an interior space although it has no roof.

The interior is flooded with natural light. The light changes throughout the day and the play of light and shadows enrich the architectural piece.

The house is intended to reflect a unique way of living.

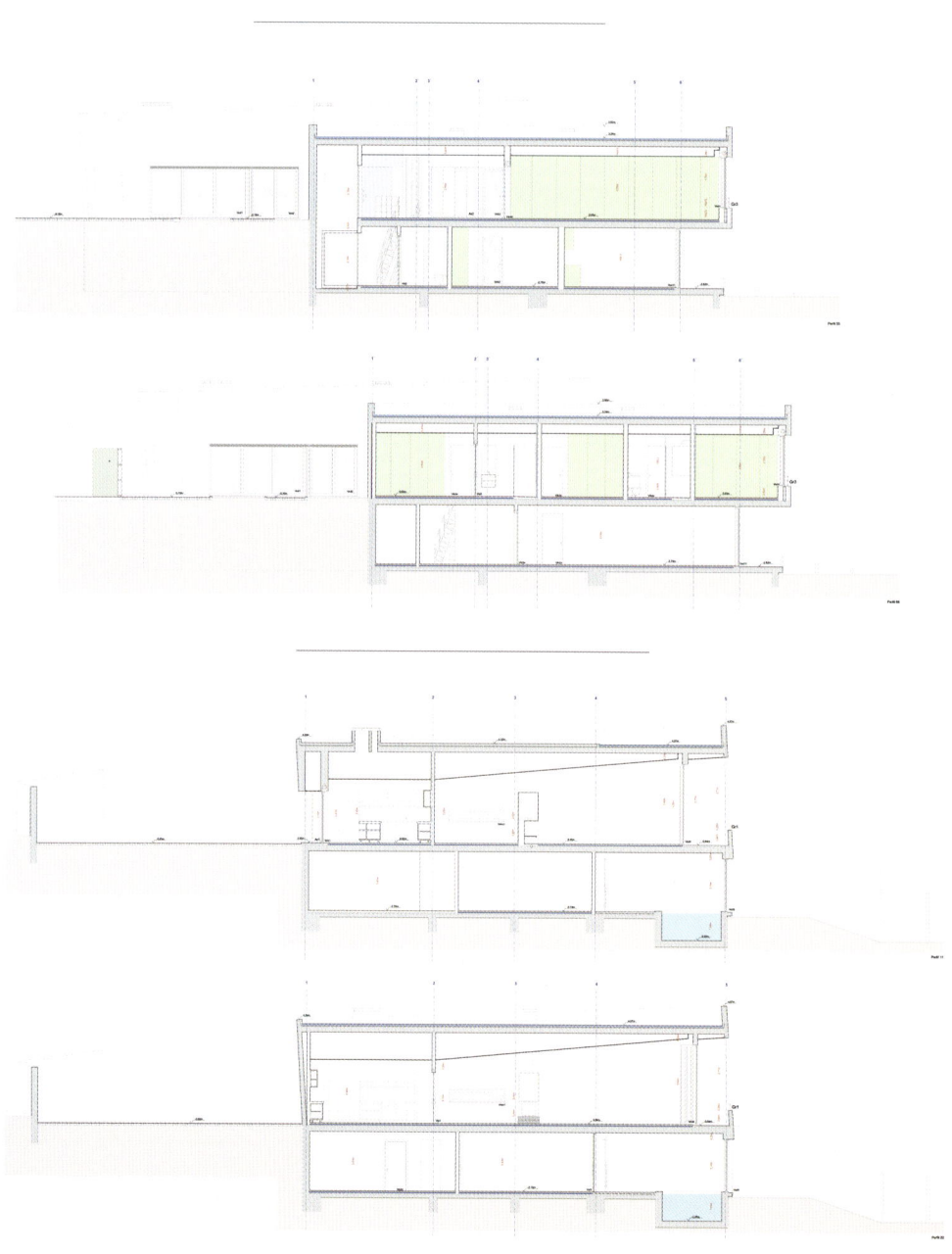

Empty Space Architecture

Godiva House

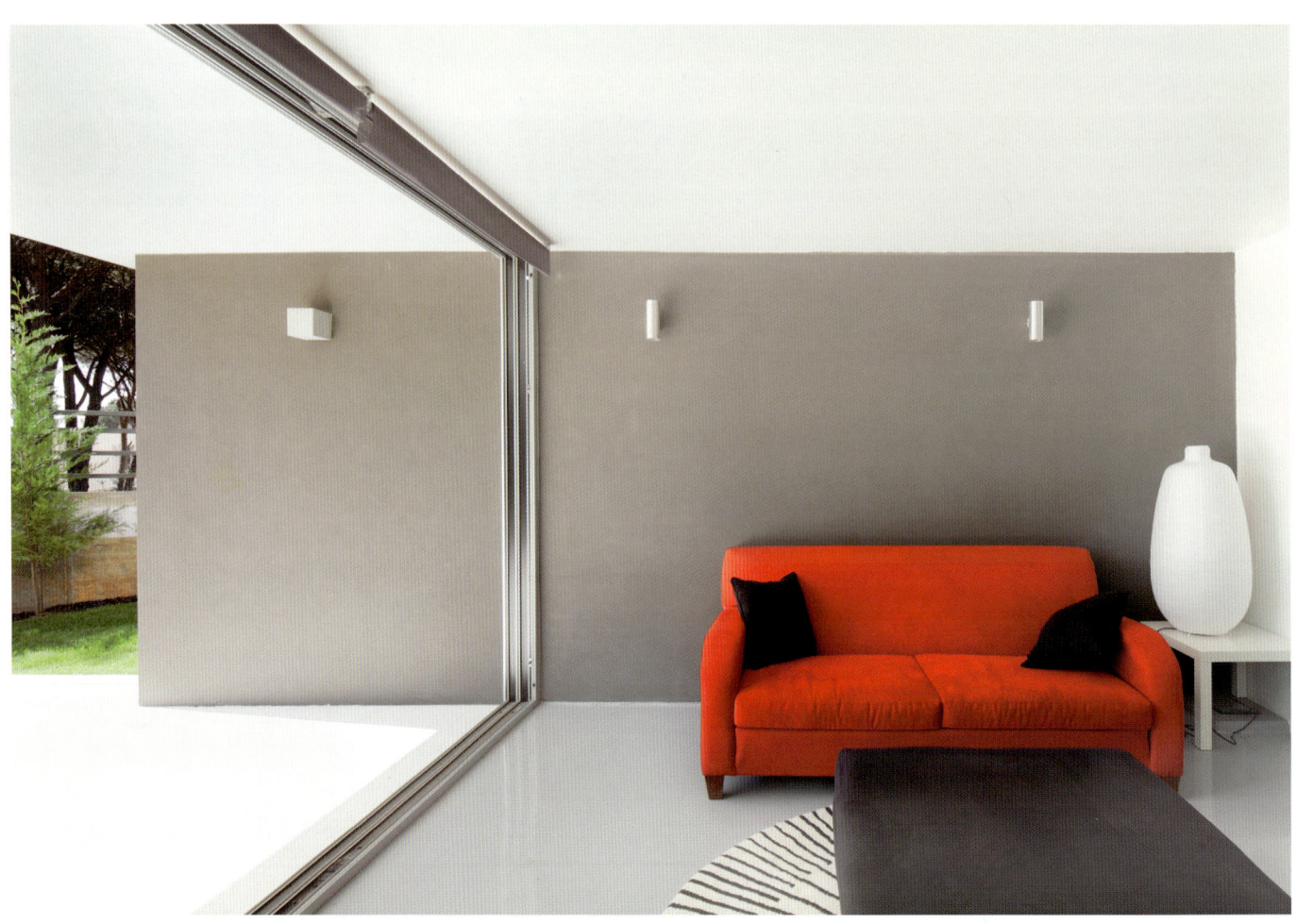

Empty Space Architecture

Private House in Sassuolo

The **Private House in Sassuolo** has thermal insulation and moisture control that enabled it to obtain class A energy certification.

Enrico Iascone Architetti
Modena, Italy
1600sqm

The house is located in an extensive residential area outside Sassuolo, Modena's ceramic manufacturing heartland. It stands amid other detached houses surrounded by small gardens on a plot once occupied by a detached house.

The high-end design used prefabricated wooden elements for the aboveground stories that sit atop a concrete underground level. The resulting thermal insulation and humidity control made it possible for the structure to obtain class A energy certification. Using joint-mounted prefabricated wooden elements increased on-site safety and cut overall worksite time considerably.

The whole architecture is a play on opposites: the large monolithic volume has glazed windows on its more secluded sides that give glimpses into the deep interiors and provide views of the outside.

The ventilated walls are clad with extra-thin laminam ceramic slabs. Their gray-black shade lends materiality and elegance to the structure.

The windows and door frames are made of burnished bronze. The laminam ceramic slabs cover both the walls and roof. The roof is also covered with a photovoltaic film. With this project we have tried to show how technology and sustainability can be successfully combined with quality architecture.

To the east, wooden terraces with glass parapets mediate the daylight that enters the interior. Both natural and artificial light are defining factors of the interior spatial design. LED strip lighting set above the windows creates a break between the interior and exterior and makes the house gleam like a diamond.

Enrico Iascone Architetti

Private House in Sassuolo

Enrico Iascone Architetti

Private House in Sassuolo

Enrico Iascone Architetti

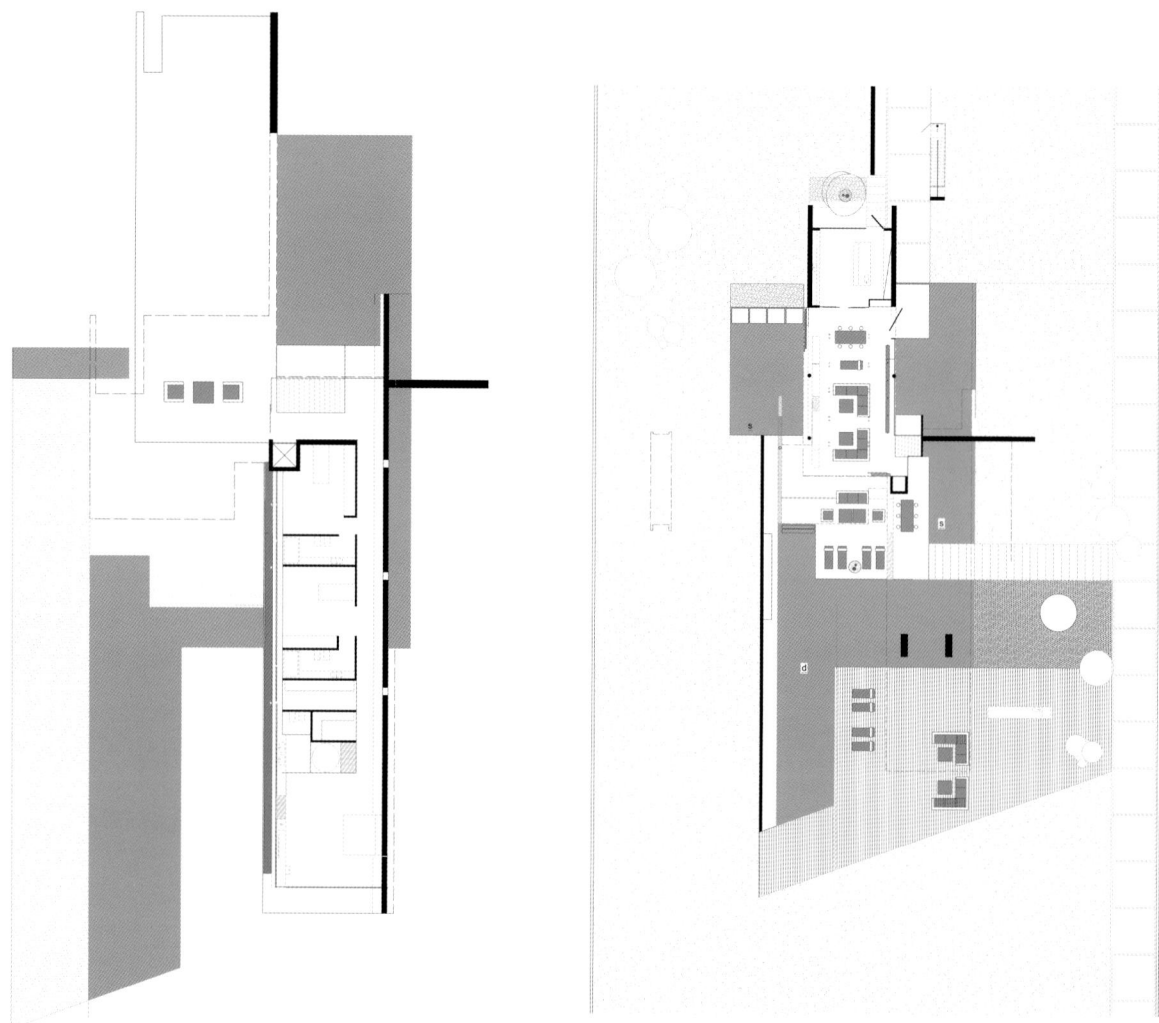

h.3. House in Athens
A coil fan that uses geothermal energy makes the cooling and heating systems of **h.3. House in Athens** energy efficient.

314 Architecture Studio
Athens, Greece
1000sqm

Located on a 700sqm plot, the house was designed to reflect the owner's love of yachts.

The ponds that surround the house have a cooling effect. The water for the lakes and pool comes from a well. Rainwater is collected through a drainage system and is then distilled and used for irrigation. The bioclimatic housing design allows the sun to warm cold spaces in the winter. In the summer, the ventilation system blows warm air out. A coil fan that uses geothermal energy makes the cooling and heating systems energy efficient.

The rooms are covered with a spiral that heats the pool water with the help of the solar panels located at the rear side of the plot. Photovoltaic panels have been fitted at the rear side of the plot to produce electric power.

The house was constructed from eco-friendly materials. The furniture was designed with the owner's needs in mind. The design objective was to create a luxurious and ergonomic environment with clean lines and a minimalist aesthetic. The sculptures by John Aspras give the house an abstract feel.

314 Architecture Studio

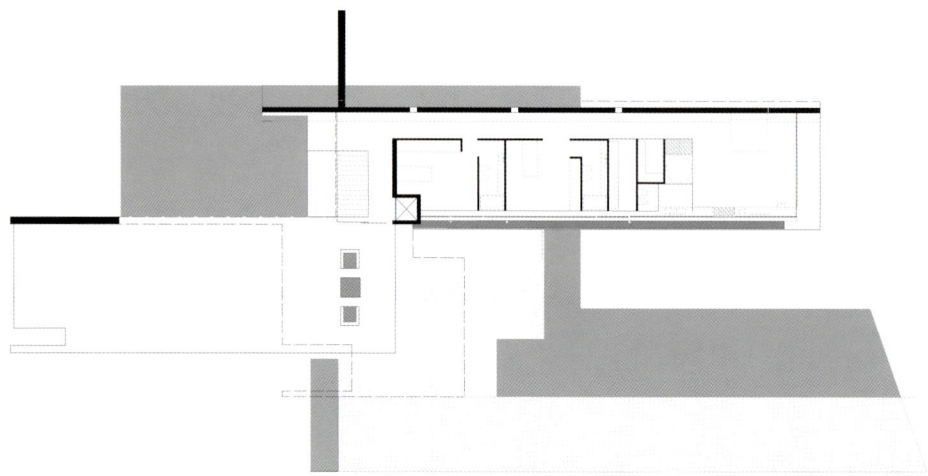

h.3. House in Athens

314 Architecture Studio

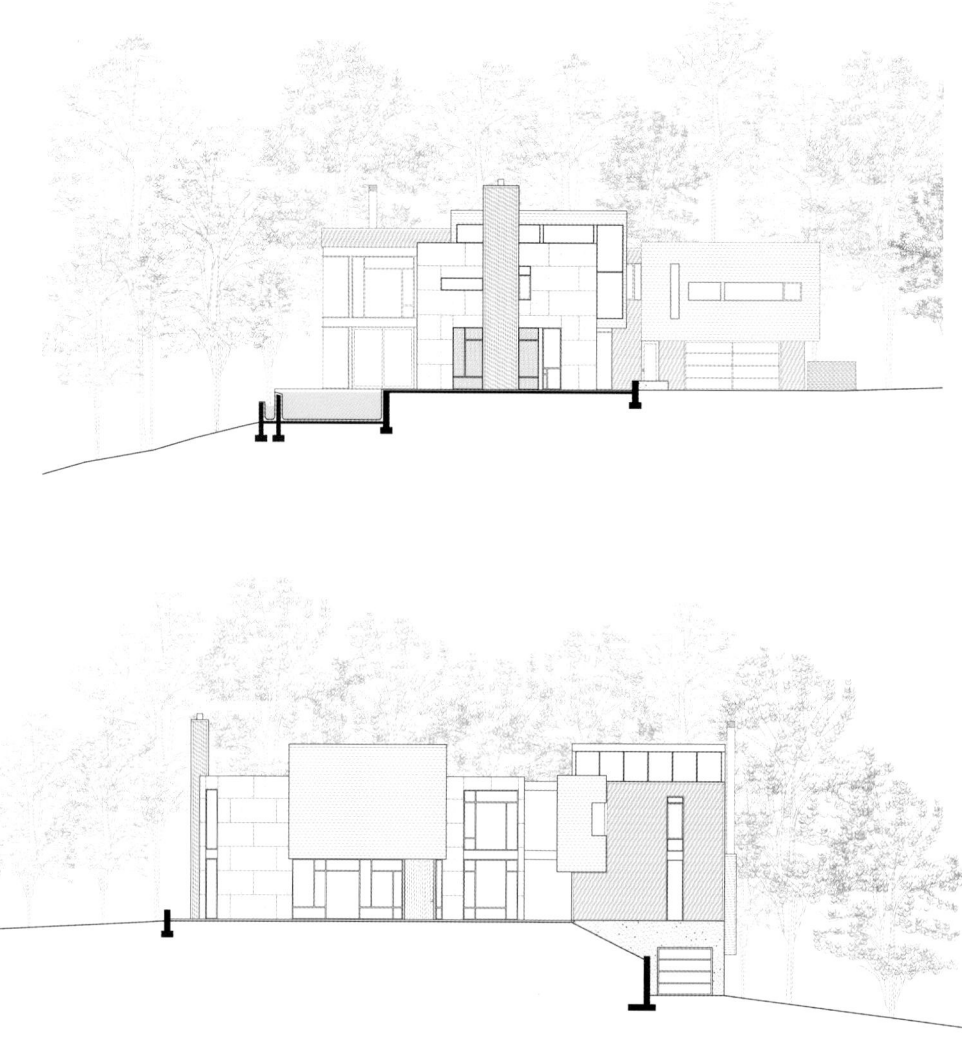

Wissioming2
Wissioming2 is designed to provide spaces that are organized to integrate its inherently picturesque site.

Robert M. Gurney Architect
Bethesda, MD, USA
767sqm

Located in Glen Echo, Maryland, just outside of Washington, DC, this new house is situated on a sloping, wooded lot with distant views of the Potomac River. The house was positioned to preserve a number of mature trees and is oriented toward the river views and south facing slope. The house is organized into two volumes connected by glass bridges that span a reflecting pool that separates the volumes. Secondary volumes intersect and overlap the two larger structures, making the composition more dynamic. Material changes in the various elements intensify the relationships. Expanses of glass open to a terrace organized around a swimming pool with two infinity edges that reinforce the connection with the wooded landscape.

The interiors are painted with light. Walls constructed with slender, steel window frames composed in Mondrian inspired patterns combine with translucent panels, wenge and white oak millwork, and Pompeii Scarpaletto stone to define the interior spaces. White terrazzo flooring is juxtaposed with the black window frames and the two unify the volumes on the main floor.

The house is designed to provide spaces that are organized to integrate its inherently picturesque site such that the architecture becomes subservient to the landscape that surrounds it.

Robert M. Gurney Architect

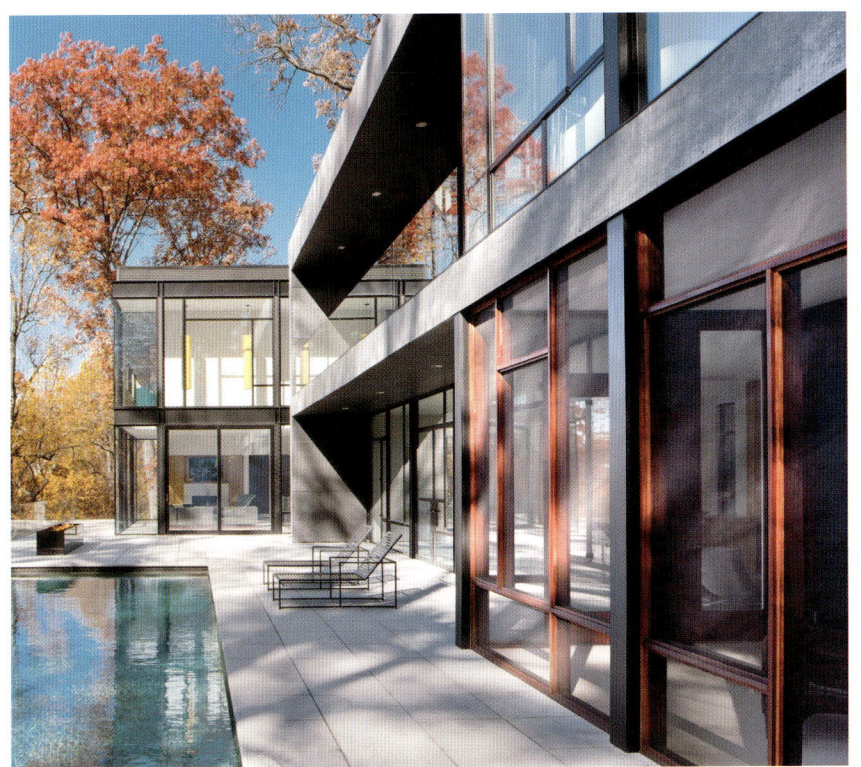

Robert M. Gurney Architect

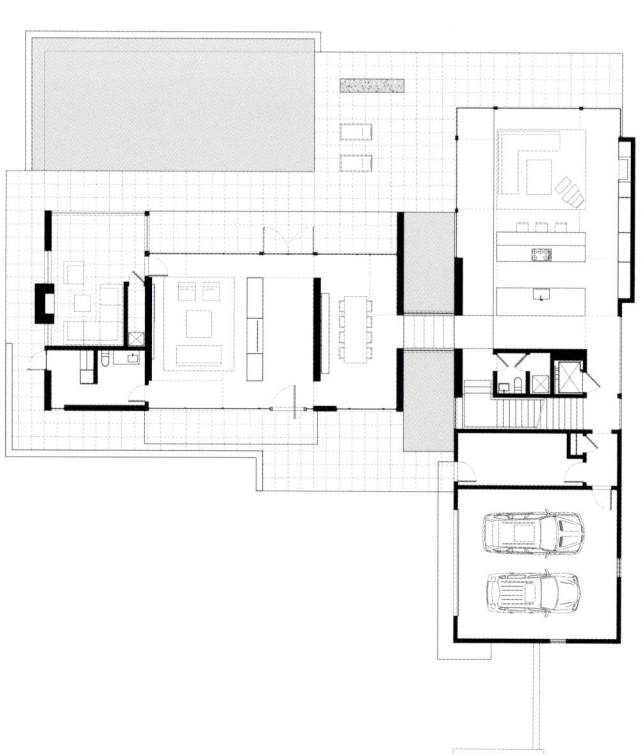
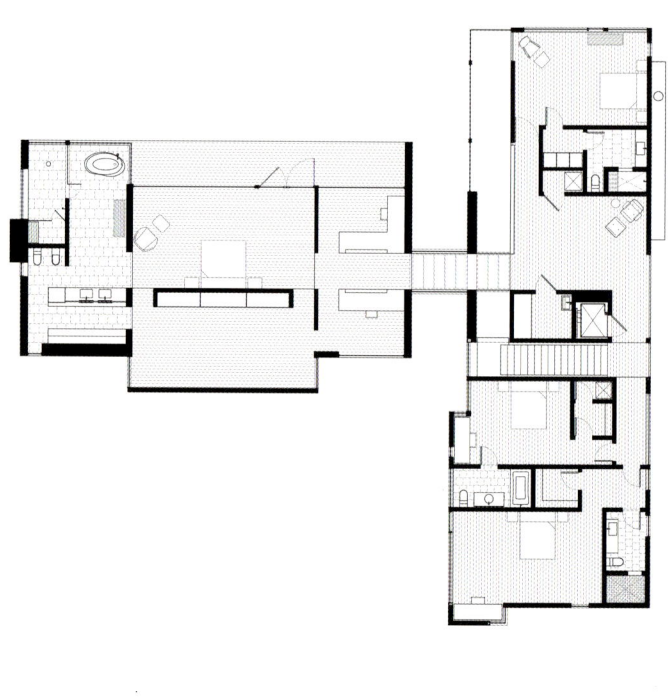

Wissioming2

Robert M. Gurney Architect

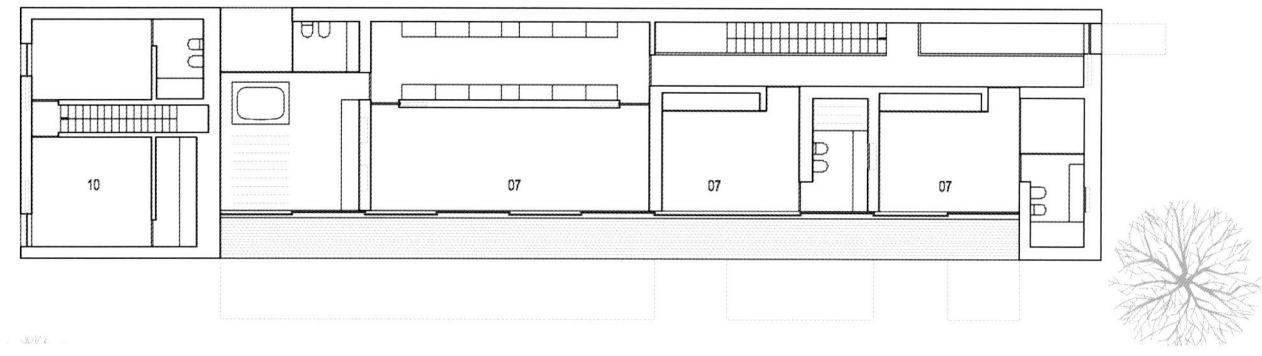

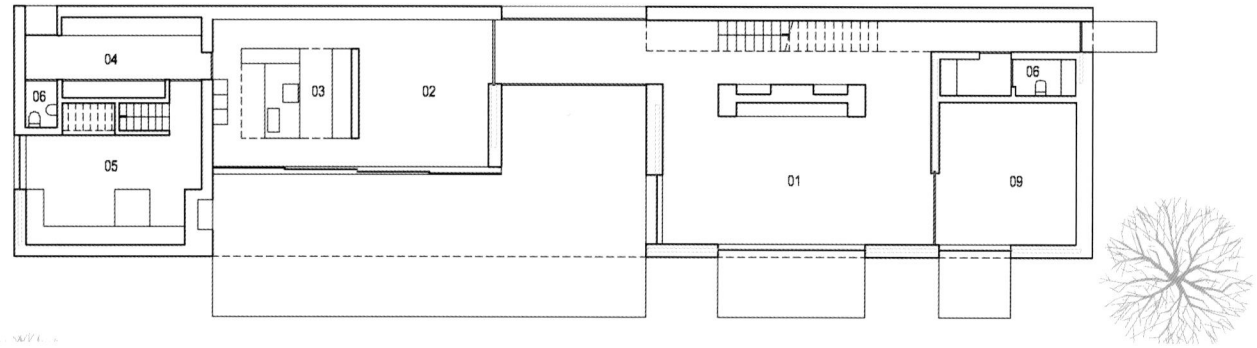

House in Estoril
The natural and artificial harmonize and establish the spatiality of House in Estoril.

Frederico Valsassina Arquitectos
Estoril, Portugal
562.9sqm

Located in one of Estoril's residential neighborhoods, the house stands in a plot where greenery dominates. The natural and artificial harmonize and establish the spaciality of the house and its surroundings.

The object of this renovation was to overcome the irregularity of the original house through simplicity. Thus, the designers created massive monolithic volumes. The choice of materials was intended to enhance the effect.

The new floor plan fuses the social spaces and makes them more open and exposed. The service area, on the other hand, is more closed off.

The main entrance is located on the north side, off of the garden. There is another garden located immediately to the south. A series of interconnected spaces with a rhythm defined by a lack of visual obstacles lies between the gardens. The circulation space pierces the house and provides access to the upper floor through a dematerialized stairway.

The upper level houses the bedrooms. In order to give the floor as much natural light as possible, we included large windows and courtyards in the design.

The lack of formal commitment between the parts is not only a catalyst for the dynamics of the whole, but also makes the house flexible.

Frederico Valsassina Arquitectos 31

House in Estoril

Frederico Valsassina Arquitectos

House in Estoril

Frederico Valsassina Arquitectos

35

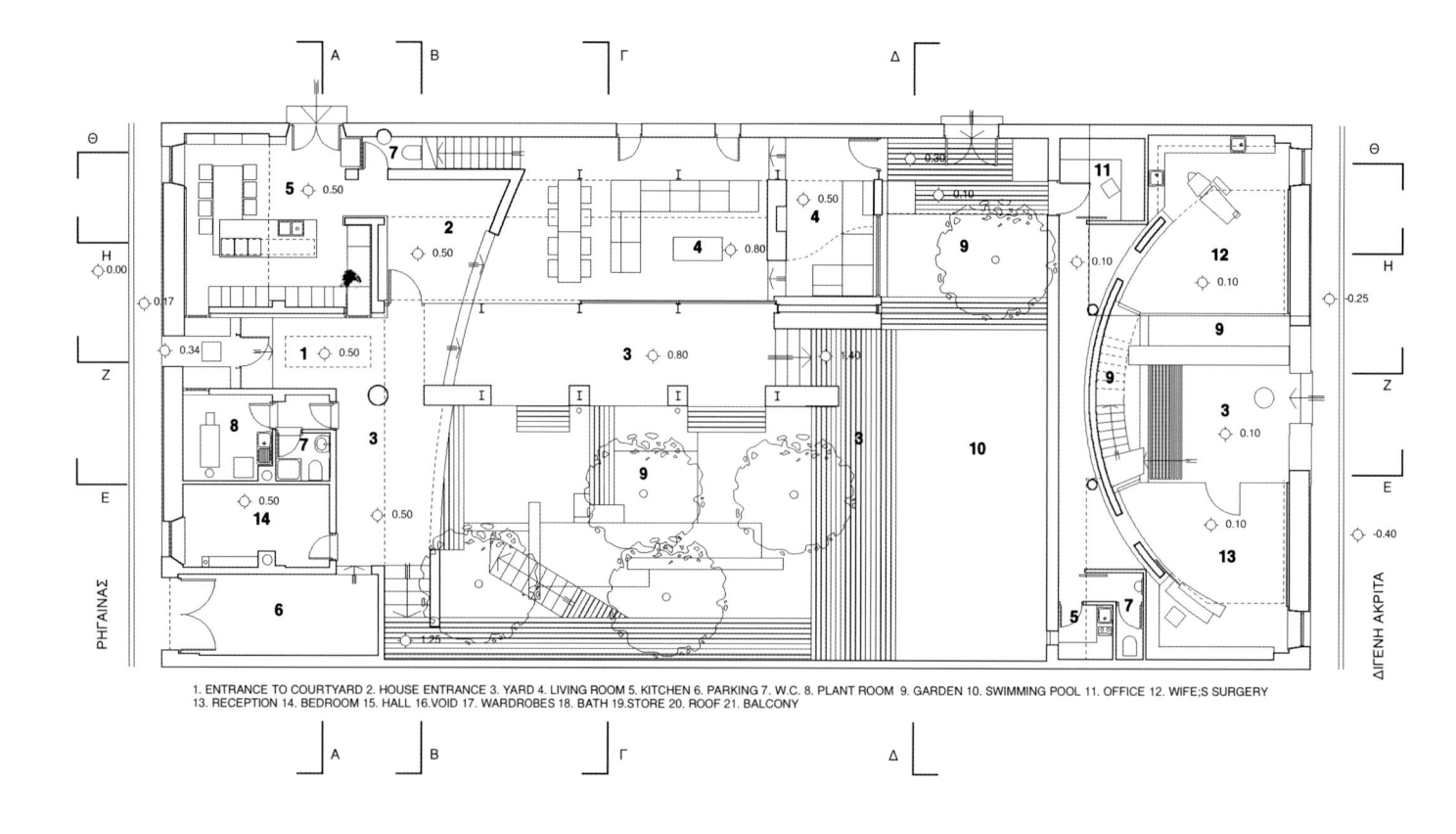

1. ENTRANCE TO COURTYARD 2. HOUSE ENTRANCE 3. YARD 4. LIVING ROOM 5. KITCHEN 6. PARKING 7. W.C. 8. PLANT ROOM 9. GARDEN 10. SWIMMING POOL 11. OFFICE 12. WIFE;S SURGERY 13. RECEPTION 14. BEDROOM 15. HALL 16.VOID 17. WARDROBES 18. BATH 19.STORE 20. ROOF 21. BALCONY

House in Lemesos
House in Lemesos does not have a conventional cooling system. Instead, it is cooled by a combination of elements.

Skinotechniki
Limassol, Cyprus
500sqm

The Lemesos House was built between two narrow streets in the old part of Cyprus.

The project was to create a family home for a couple and their four boys. For convenience and privacy, the clients wanted their work space to be located within the same plot but to have a separate entrance.

The 55-75cm thick walls are made out of aerated concrete blocks. Their thermal resistance is much greater than that of traditional adobe walls.

In Lemesos, cooling takes up 70% of the total energy consumed in modern buildings. This house does not have a conventional cooling system. Rather, it is cooled by a combination of elements. The first is its numerous ceiling fans. Secondly, the shaded skylights and a hallway that rises through the house draw hot air out through the stack effect principle. Large trees in the internal garden provide shade. Evaporated water from the fish ponds and pool in the internal garden provides additional cooling. At night the cooler air from the mountains sinks through the open skylights.

The main bedroom has its own special geothermic cooling system. A small fan draws air out of the bedroom through an underground pipe. The chilled air is then circulated back into the bedroom.

The children's bedrooms face west. However, the rooms are not hot at night because they are constructed from steel and wood, which do not store or emit heat. The idea for the construction of these rooms comes from traditional Lemesos houses, which often have bedrooms made of lightweight materials on the first floor.

The house is heated by a diesel boiler. In addition to the boiler, 8 racks of 20 solar-heated vacuum tubes heat the under-floor heating system.

Skinotechniki

House in Lemesos

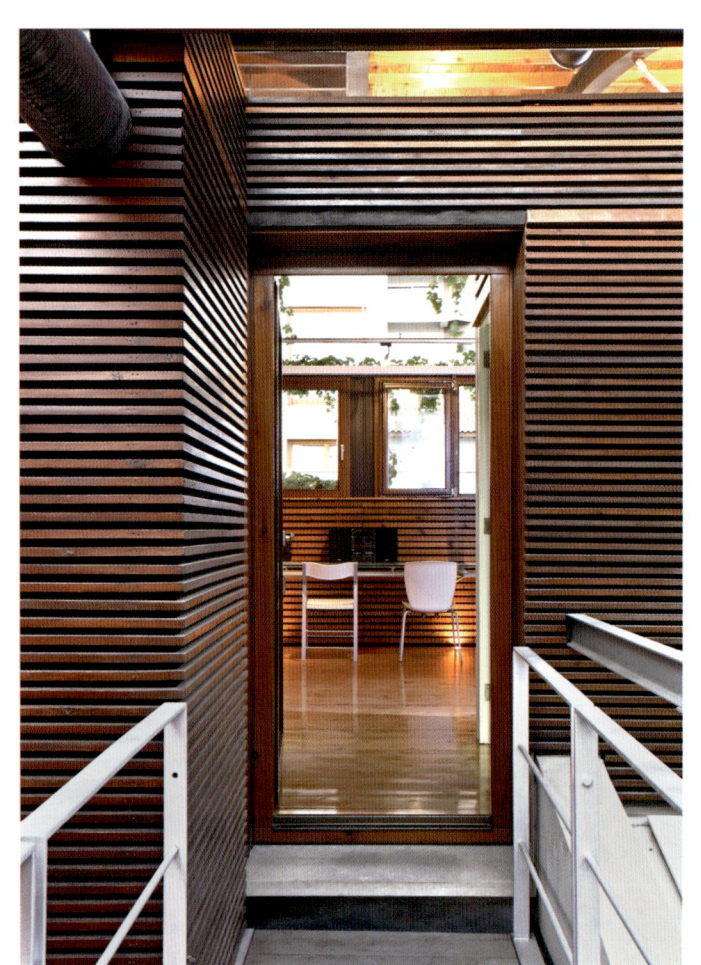

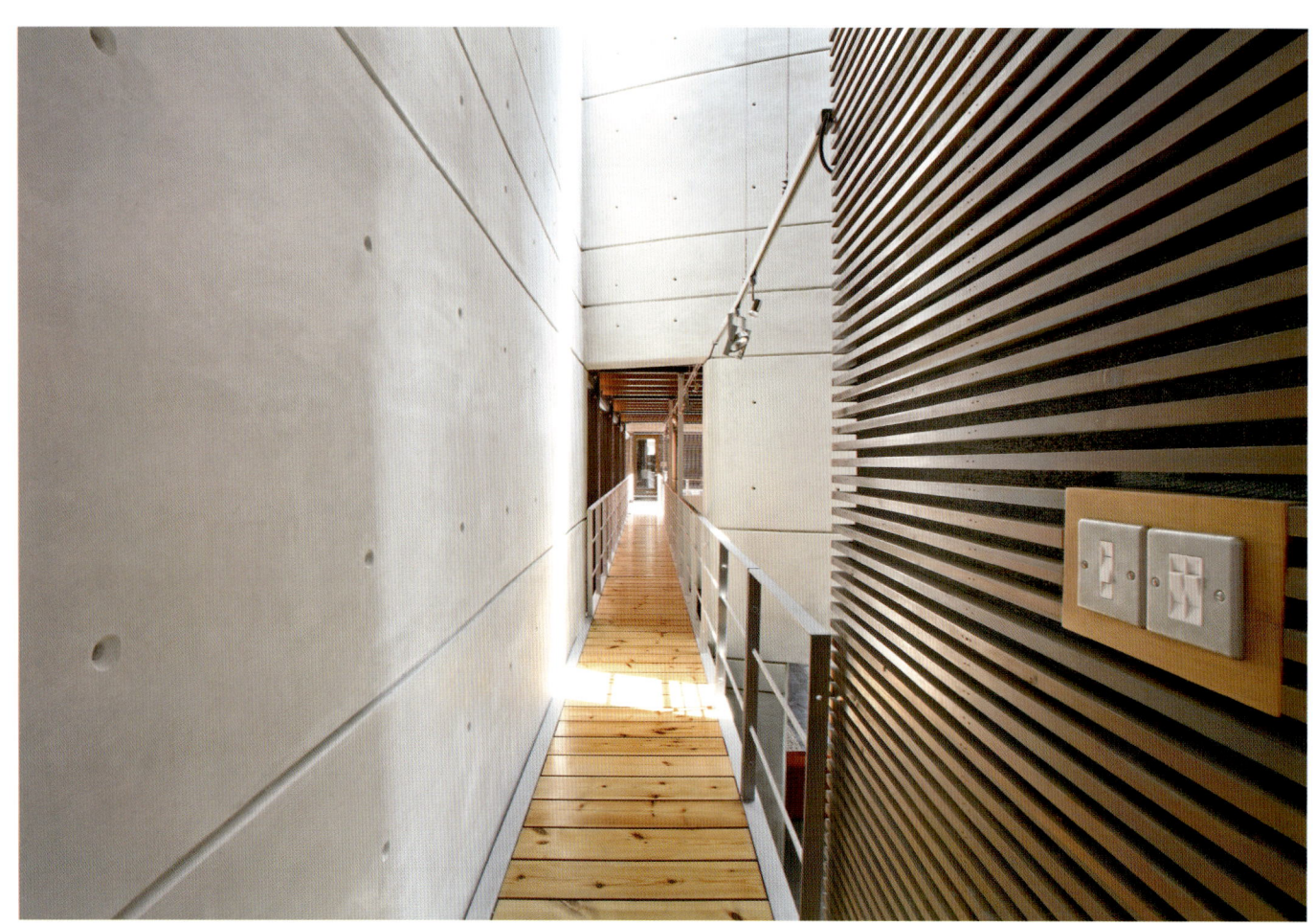

Skinotechniki

House in Lemesos

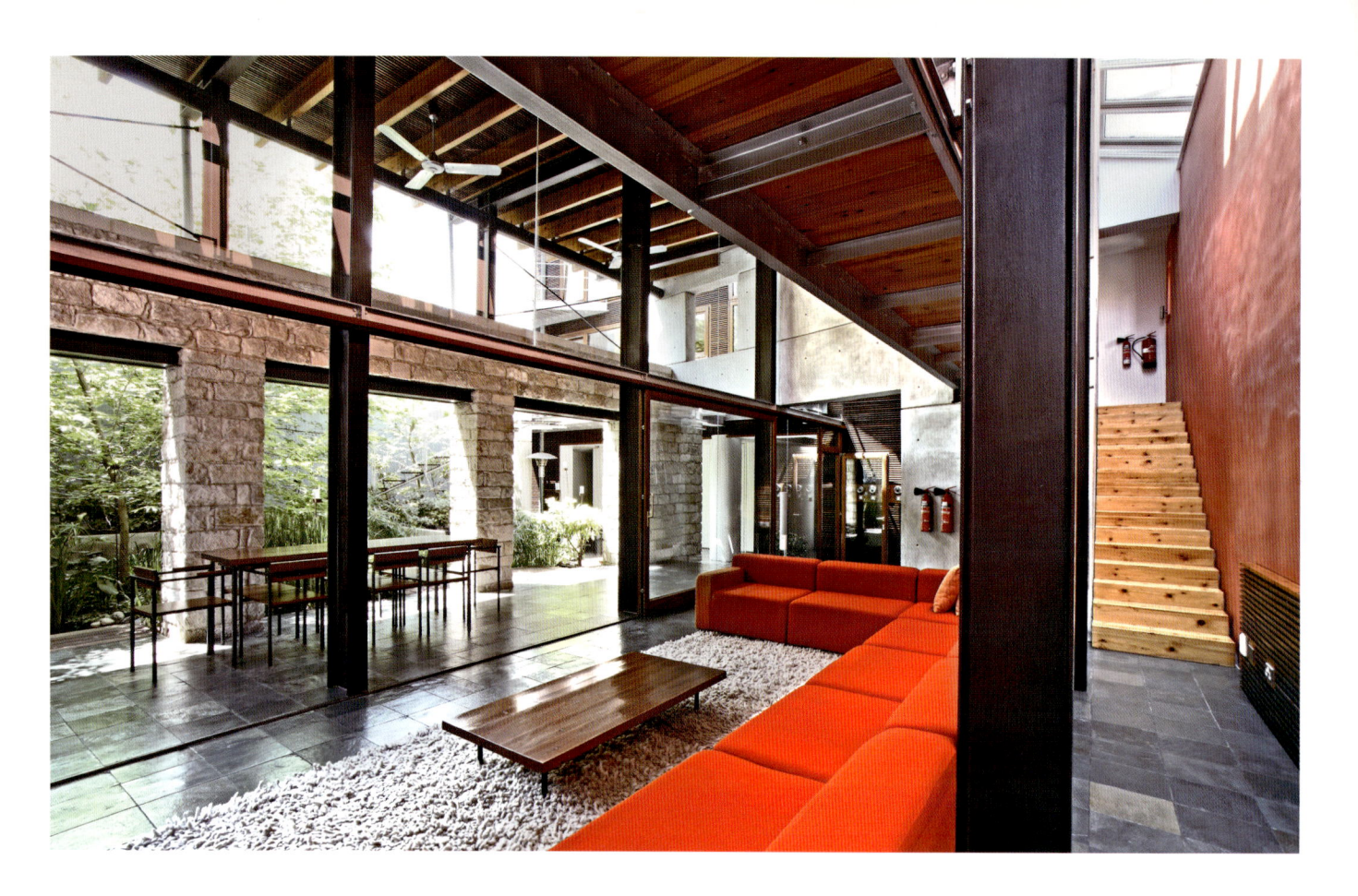

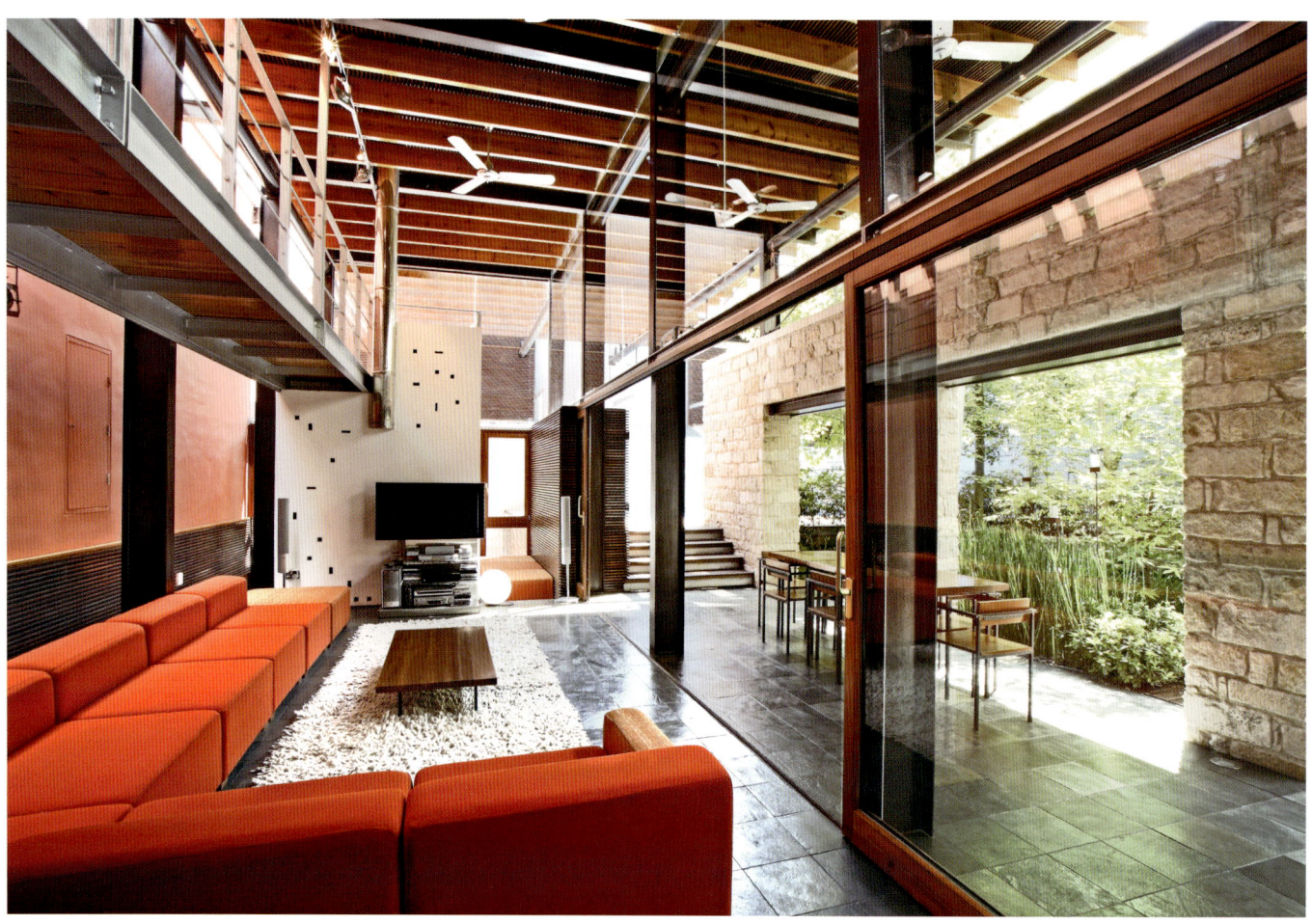

Skinotechniki

Ipês House

Concrete was used throughout the upper volume of Ipês House. The concrete volume looks like it is floating above the glass volume below.

Studio MK27
São Paulo, Brasil
1343sqm

Ten years ago, when Studio MK27 tried to do a project using exposed concrete, many builders said that it was practically impossible. During a period in the 90s, the use of the material declined sharply. It was used only occasionally and in experimental projects.

What makes concrete interesting is that it creates a type of x-ray of the construction it's used in. Its surface will be imprinted with knots in the wood and even the smallest defects. It is liquid stone. The experience of constructing in raw concrete during the last ten years has shown StudioMK27 the impracticality of making an absolutely perfect material. Ipês House is a reflection of our experience working with this material.

Concrete was used throughout the upper volume. The unique construction makes the concrete volume look as though it is a large box floating above the glass volume below. The living room doors open onto the veranda, thus blurring the division between the interior and exterior. The main entrance was constructed with pivoting panels that open onto the front garden. Inside, a long irregularly-shaped sofa wriggles around the room, constructing a space with no hierarchy among the different orientations.

The bedrooms, located on the top floor, are lit by a wooden block on the concrete wall of the façade. The wooden panels help regulate the temperature and make it possible to control the lighting.

The structure of the house incorporates large spans that accentuate the idea of a floating box. The raw concrete references modern buildings in terms of functionality and aesthetics. The grand spans and brute material express a sobriety while the concrete reveals the passage of time and the life of the building.

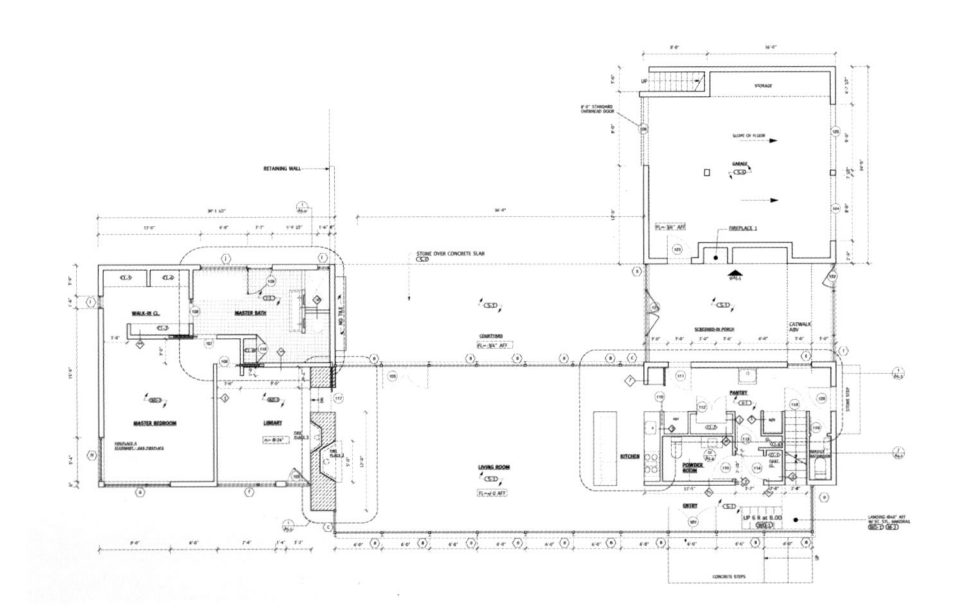

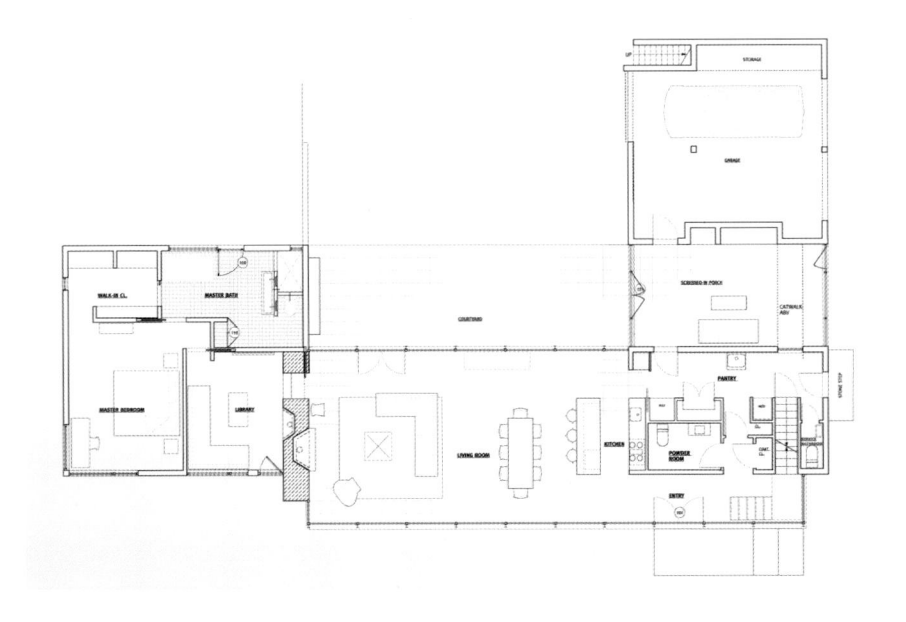

Studio MK27

Ipês House

Studio MK27

Ipês House

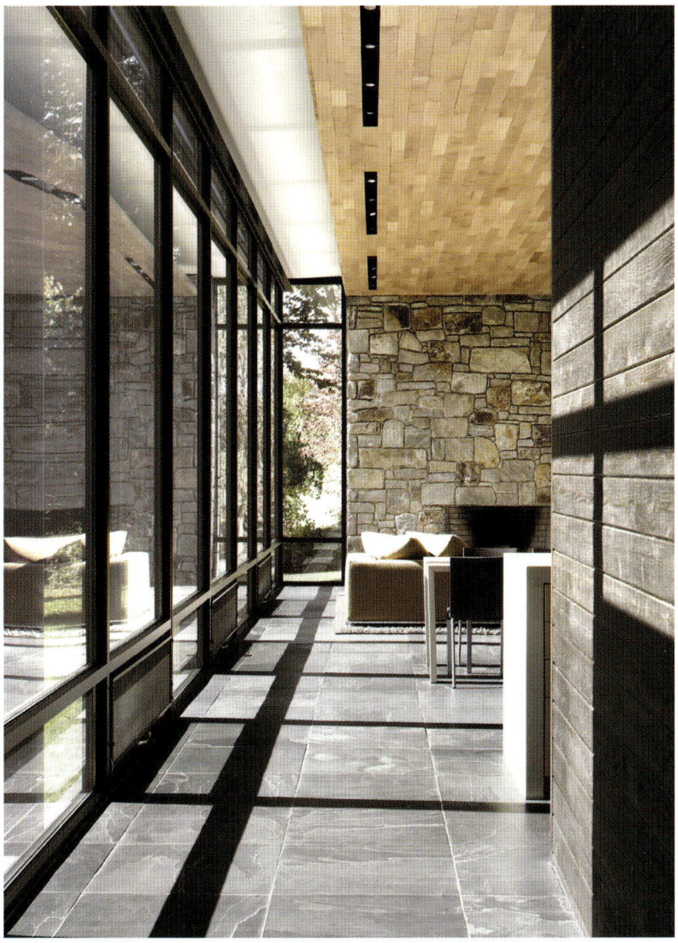

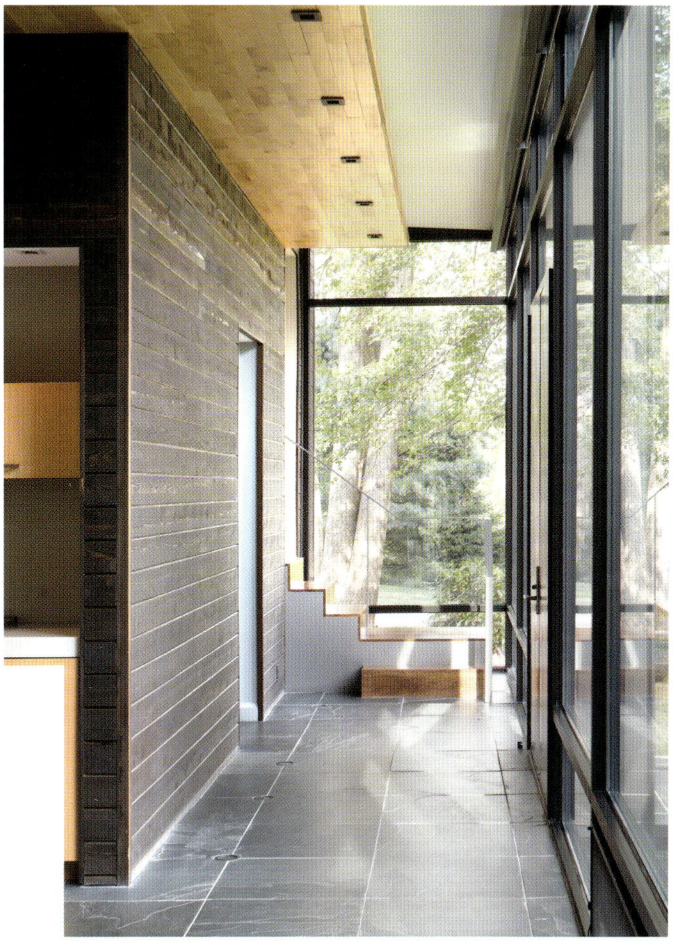

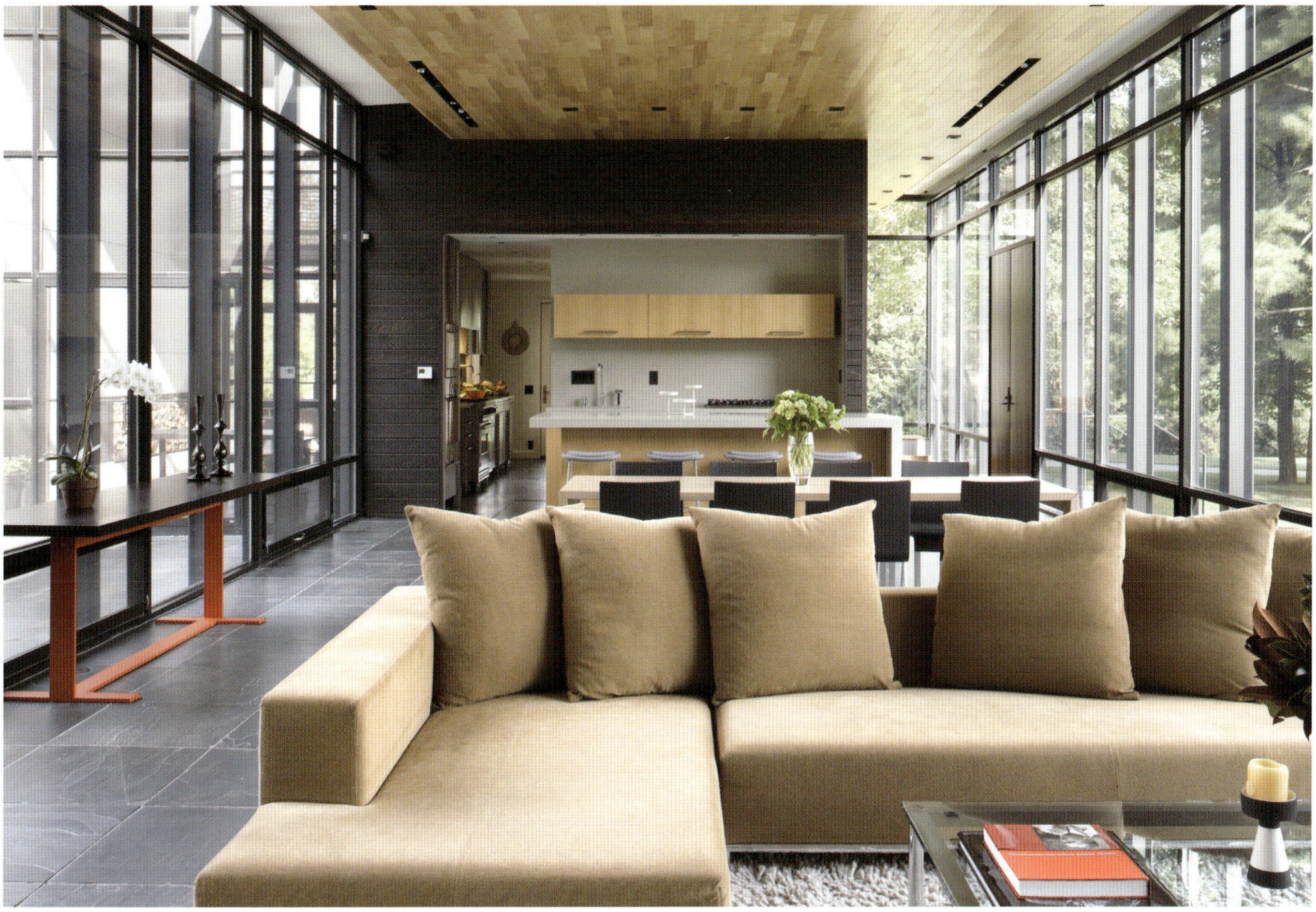

L23 House
L23 House is located on an elevated point in the city and faces west.

Pitágoras Arquitectos
Guimarães, Portugal
535sqm

The house is located on an elevated point in the city and faces west. The house is delimited on the east side by a concrete wall that erupts from the ground. Behind the concrete wall, a slope leads to a platform on the first floor where the main entrance is located.

The main entrance opens onto a hall with a staircase that leads to the second floor. The bedrooms, living room, and gym are distributed on both sides of the hall.

The bedrooms are connected to a balcony located over the patio. The second floor houses common areas, including a small gym that connects to the indoor pool on the first floor.

The first floor is made up of two volumes. One houses the pool and locker room, and the other houses social and service areas. The patio acts as an exterior extension of these spaces.

Pigmented concrete defines this structural volume. Anthracite zinc was used to cover some of the façades.

Basalt cubes were used for the external decks that provide car access and wood panels for the walkways. The external casings were made from black aluminum. Porous concrete was used in order to create a totally uniform surface for the exterior.

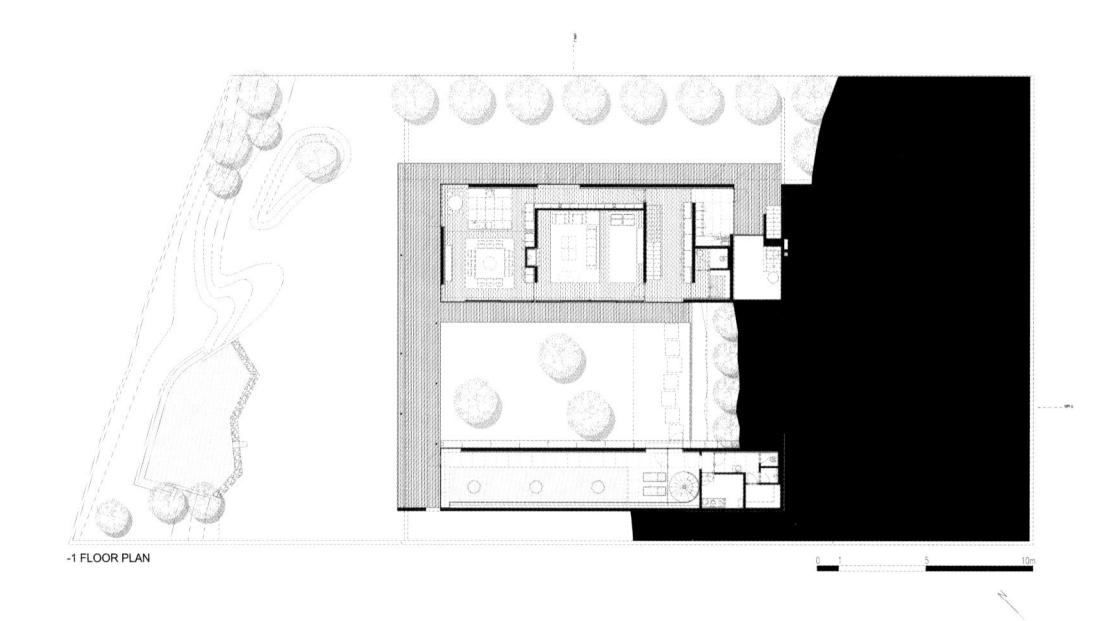

-1 FLOOR PLAN

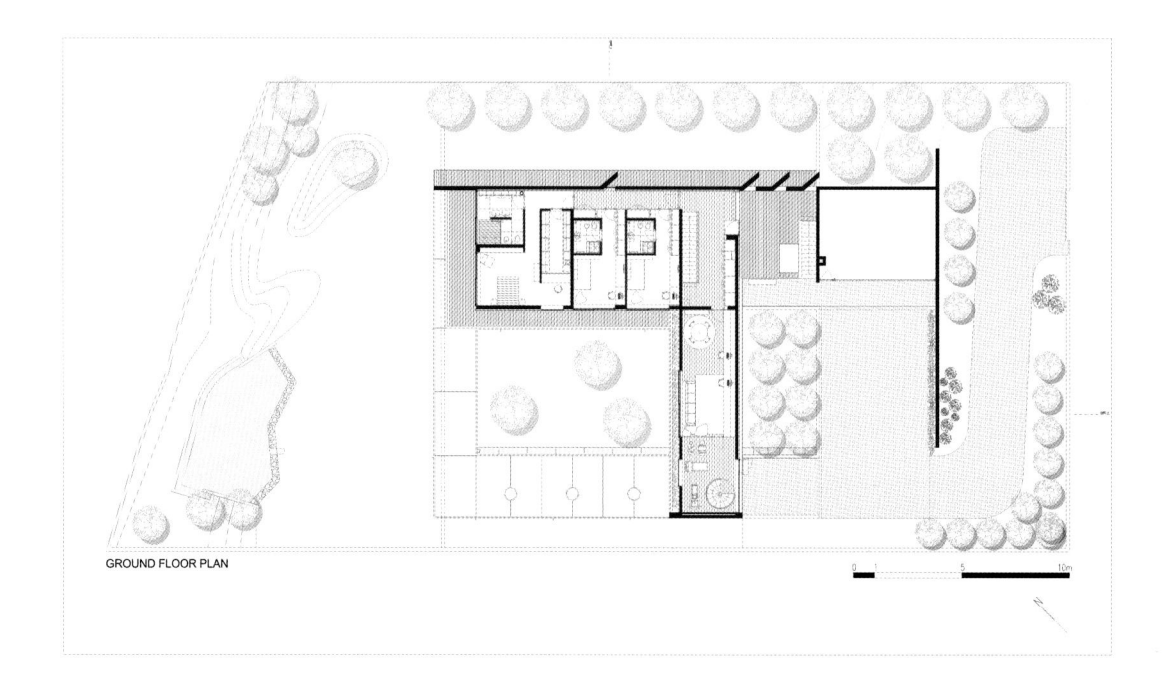

GROUND FLOOR PLAN

Pitágoras Arquitectos

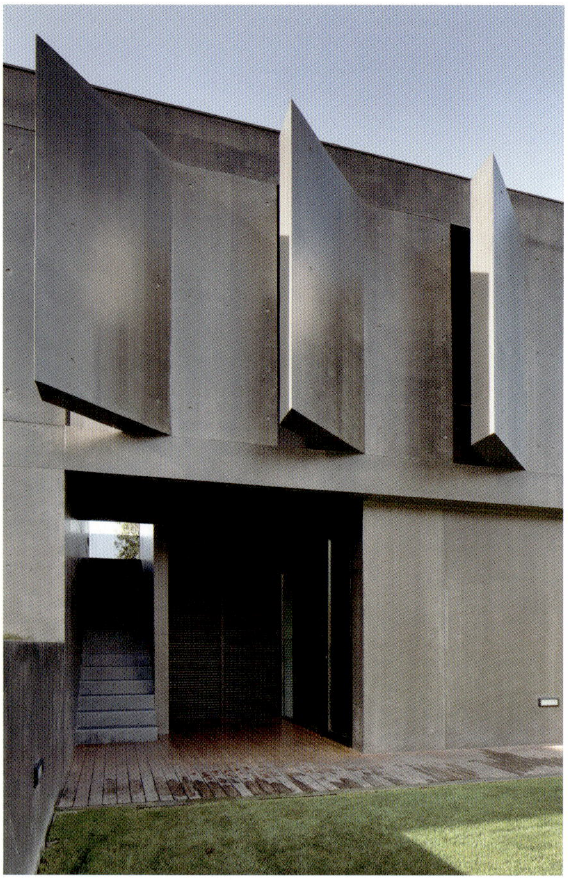

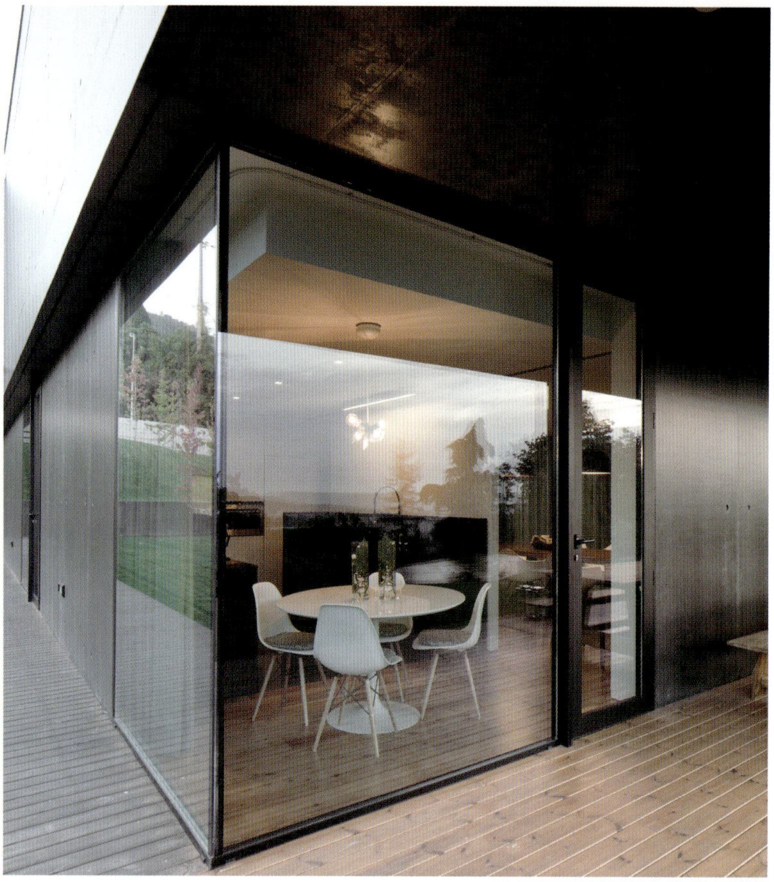

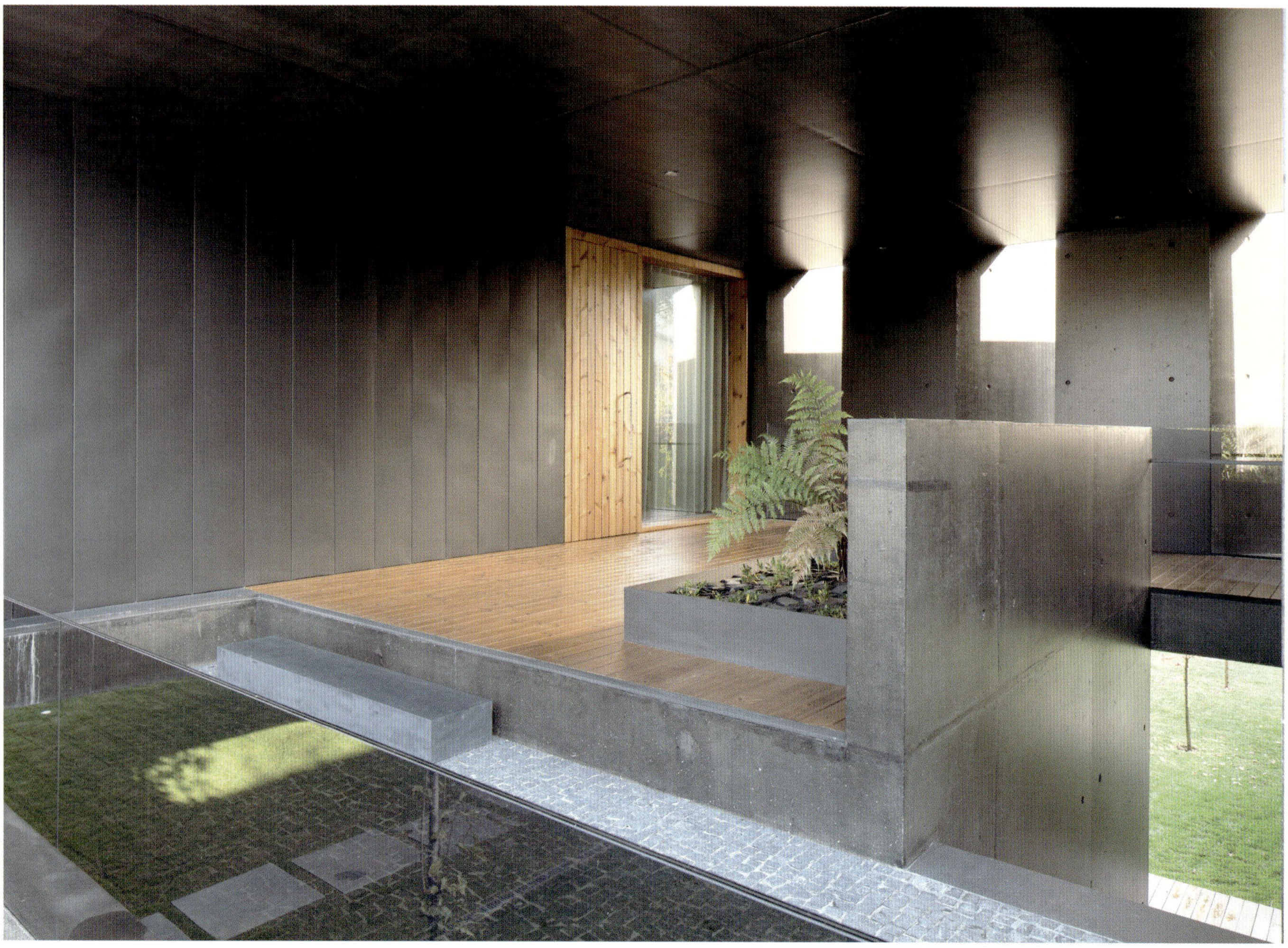

Pigmented concrete defines the structural volume. Anthracite zinc was used to cover some of the façades.

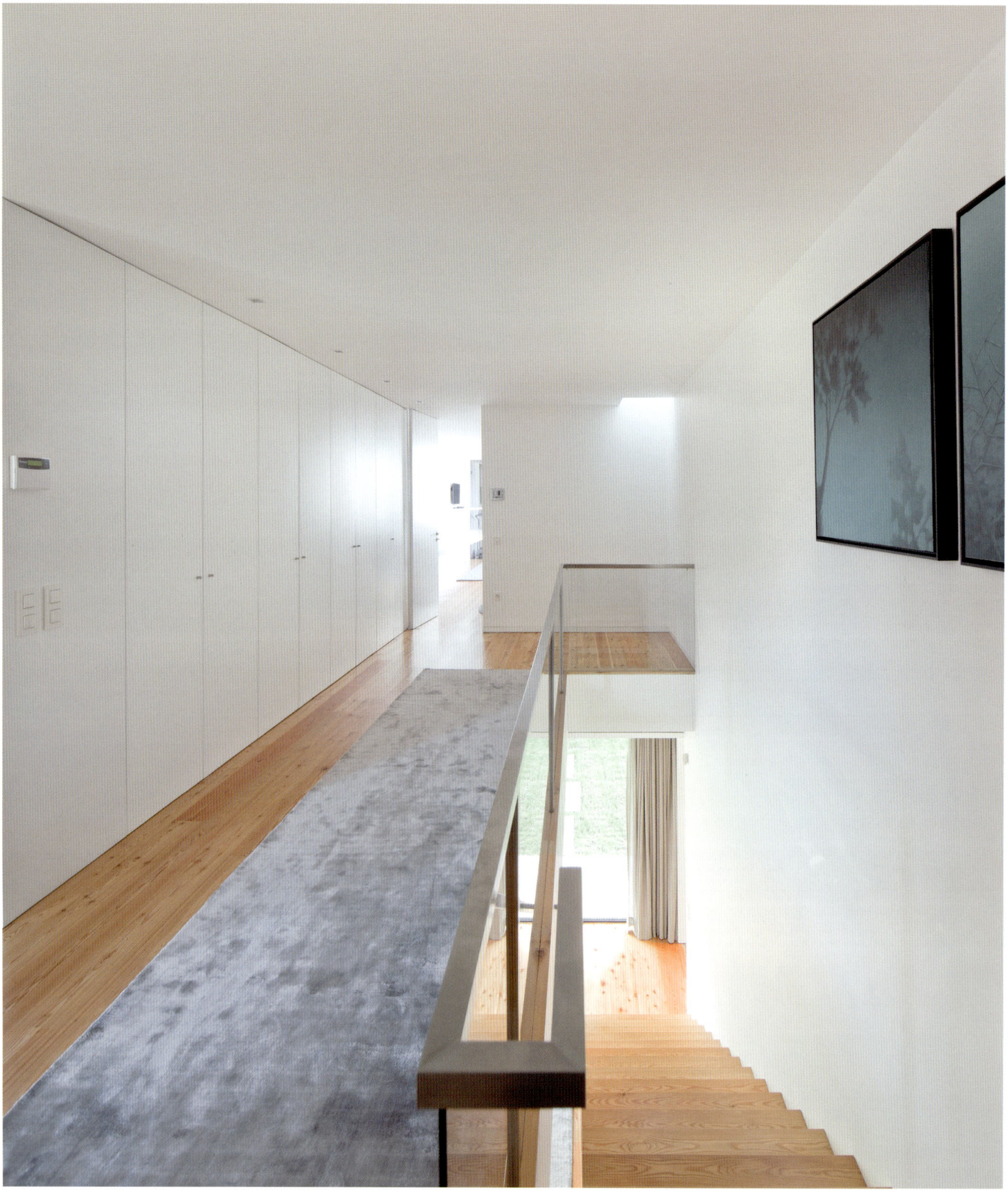

Pitágoras Arquitectos

Casa Guanábanos

At the end of the day, all the spaces of Casa Guanábanos speak the same language trough their texture and light.

Taller Héctor Barroso
Mexico City, Mexico
610sqm

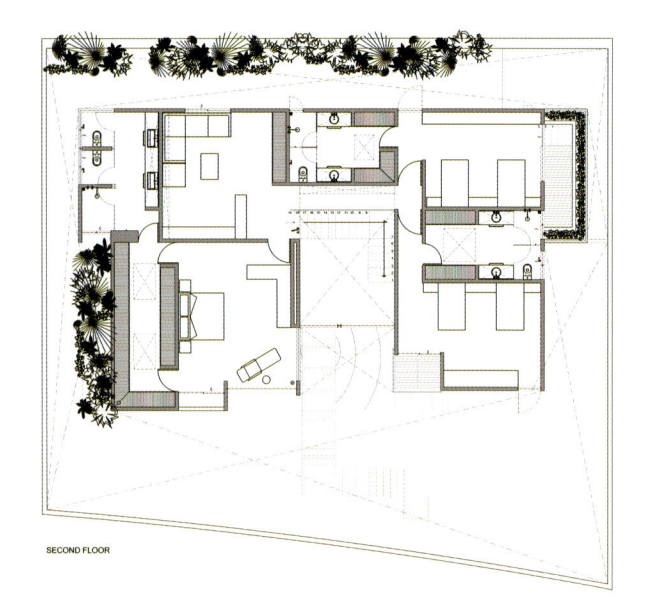

The goal of this project was to design a house that was fully integrated with its immediate surroundings and incorporated natural light as much as possible.

The project is based on the communication between the interior and the exterior. One of the goals was to break down the boundaries between the two areas by connecting them visually and spatially. Another important design factor was the light. By connecting the interior and exterior, the designers ensured that the resulting spaces would be filled with natural light and be well ventilated.

The idea behind the choice of materials for the house was to highlight the connection between the inside and outside. The designers decided on silk georgette marble and used it on the entire house. The material provides a natural texture and successfully connects the house to its surroundings. A very visible example of this implementation is the foyer.

Light is one of the elements that best define all of the spaces. Each room is naturally illuminated and surrounded by a garden. The many windows provide a view of the foliage that the texture of the materials used for both the interior and exterior mimic. The wooden floors and marble walls create a continuity between the interior and exterior of the house. At the end of the day, all the spaces speak the same language through their texture and light.

SECOND FLOOR

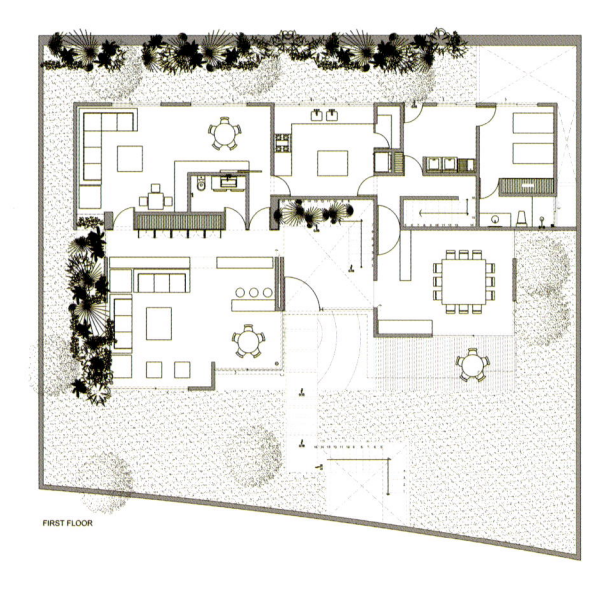

FIRST FLOOR

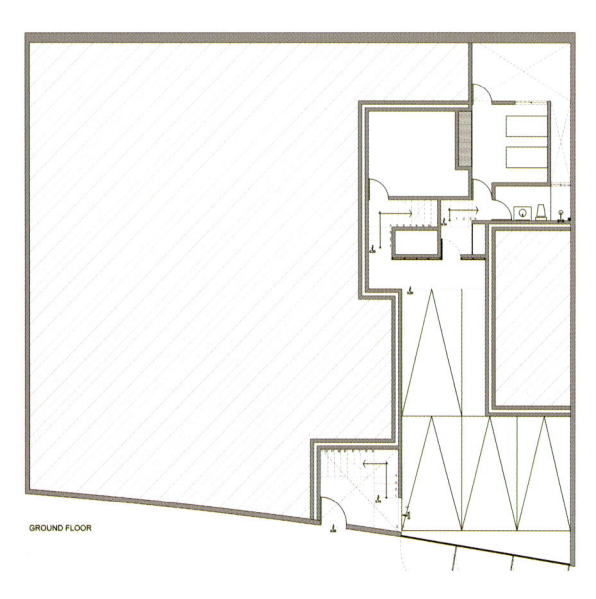

GROUND FLOOR

Taller Héctor Barroso

SECTION F

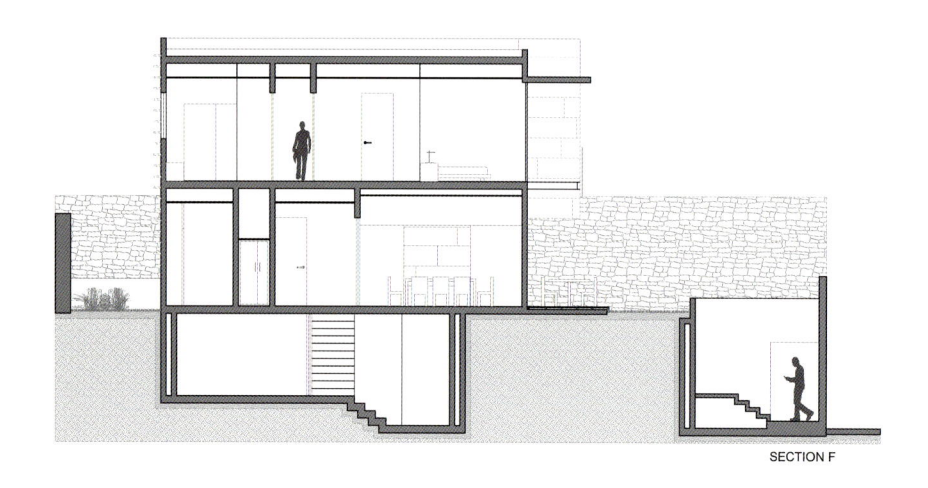

Casa Guanábanos

SECTION D

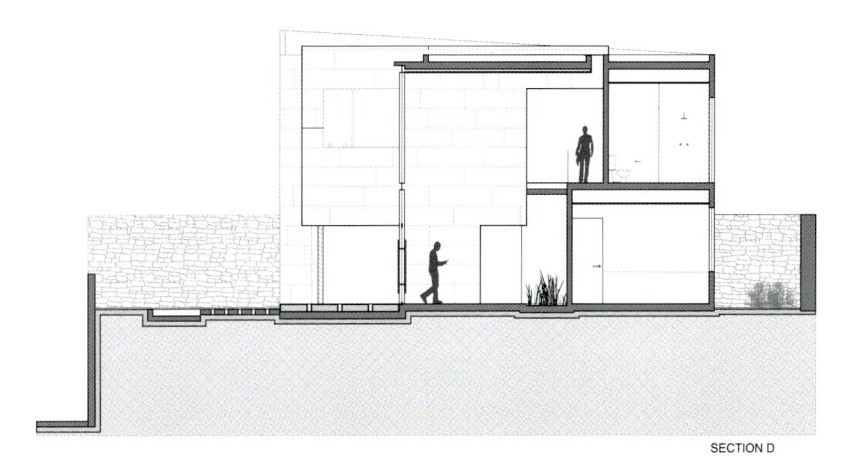

Taller Héctor Barroso

House in Conceição

House in Conceição references vernacular Algarve architecture through its simple geometry, flat roof, and color.

Vitor Vilhena Architectura
Tavira, Portugal
400sqm

This house features a seating area designed to connect the space with the landscape outside. The area is covered with solar glass in order to protect and control the environment inside.

The house is made up of volumes with distinct identities. It includes a volume that is an industrial and commercial space as well as one with a contemporary language that references vernacular Algarve architecture through its simple geometry, flat roof, and color.

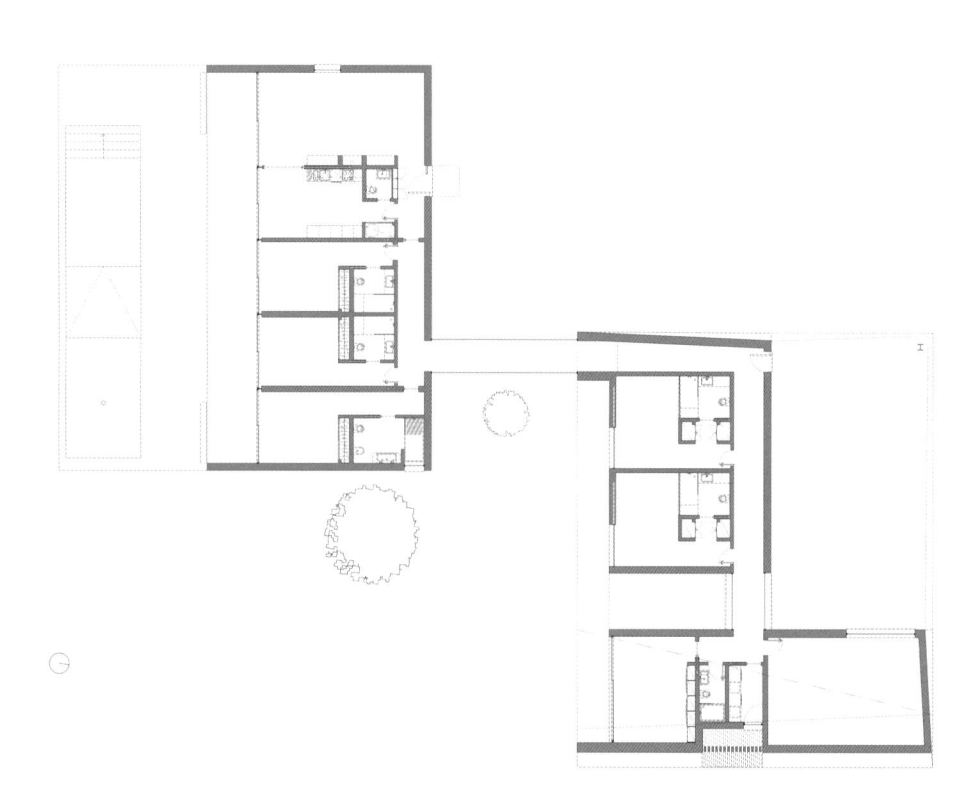

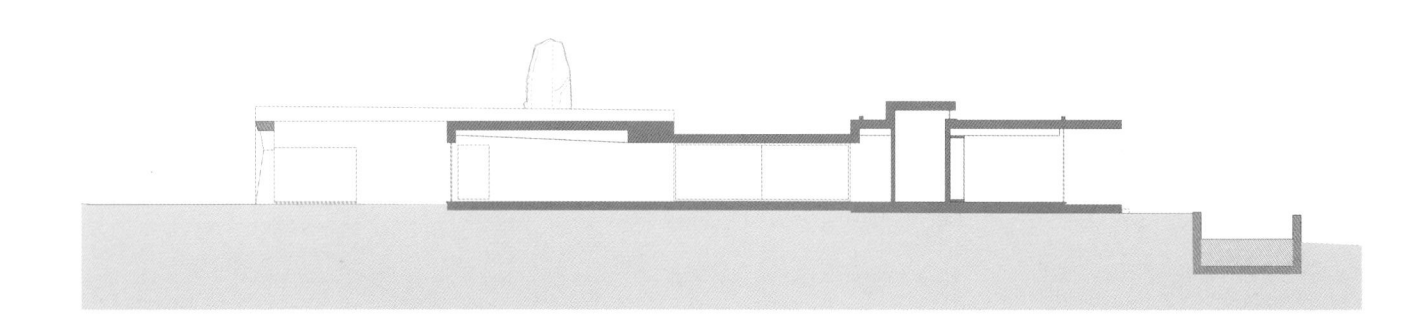

Vitor Vilhena Architectura

House in Conceição

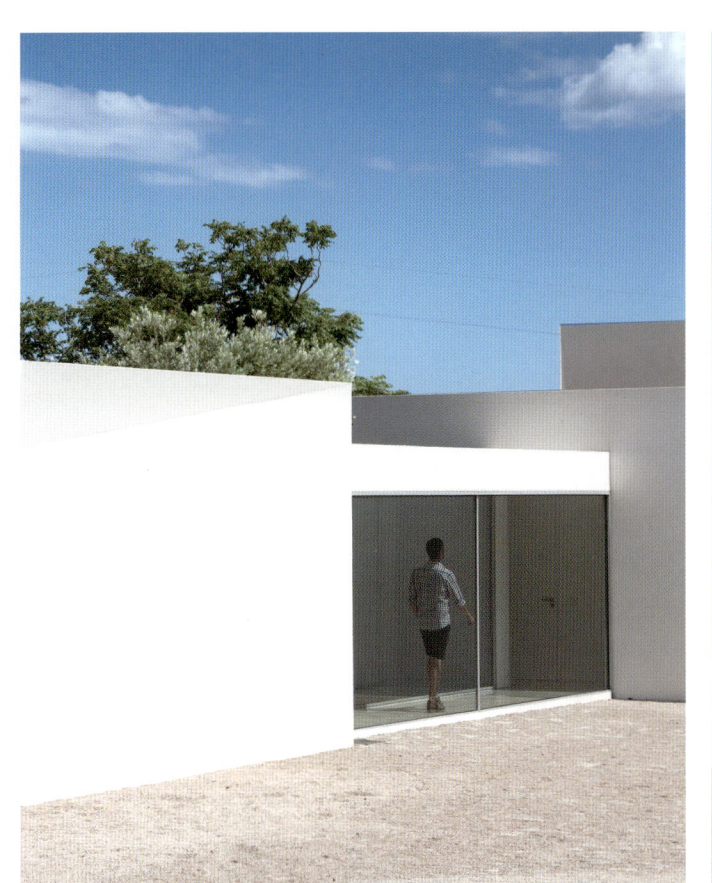

Vitor Vilhena Architectura 61

House in Conceição

Vitor Vilhena Architectura

Casa La Palma
Light is the focal point of Casa La Palma.

Miguel Ángel Aragonés
Mexico City, Mexico
1200sqm

For architects, the sun is both the starting point and guiding principle behind all projects. Casa La Palma was designed to showcase the intense sunlight Mexico enjoys. The house's bright white exterior acts as a canvas, reflecting the light as it changes according to the hour and season. Light cascades into the interior spaces through the expansive windows. The interior of the house is finished in the same bright white as the exterior, smoothing the transition between the two spaces. The minimalist aesthetic of the house and its furnishings allows light to remain the uncontested focal point of both the interior and exterior.

Miguel Ángel Aragonés

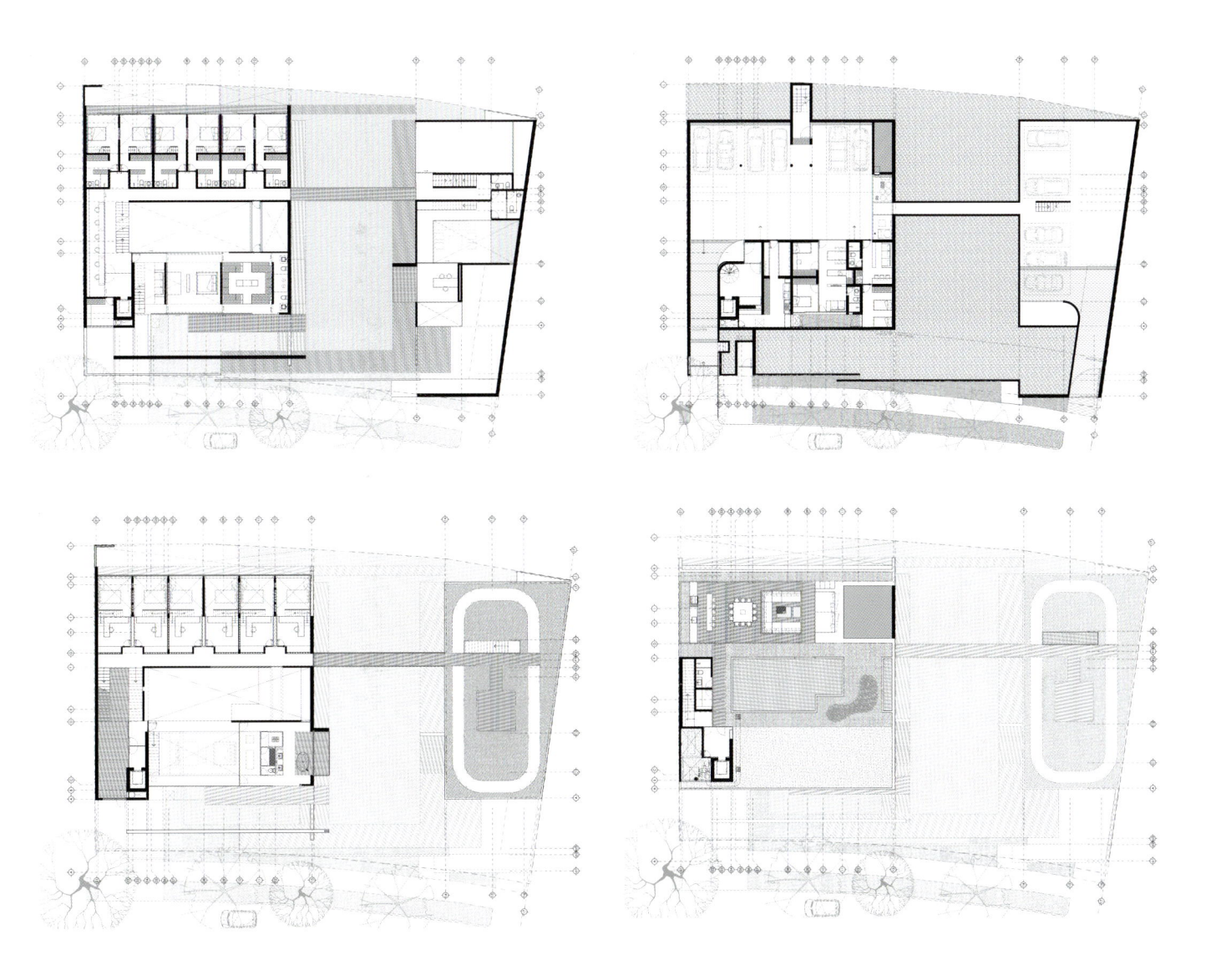

Casa La Palma

Miguel Ángel Aragonés

House M

The concept of **House M** was to play with transparent and solid surfaces.

**monovolume
architecture + design
Meran, Italy
360sqm**

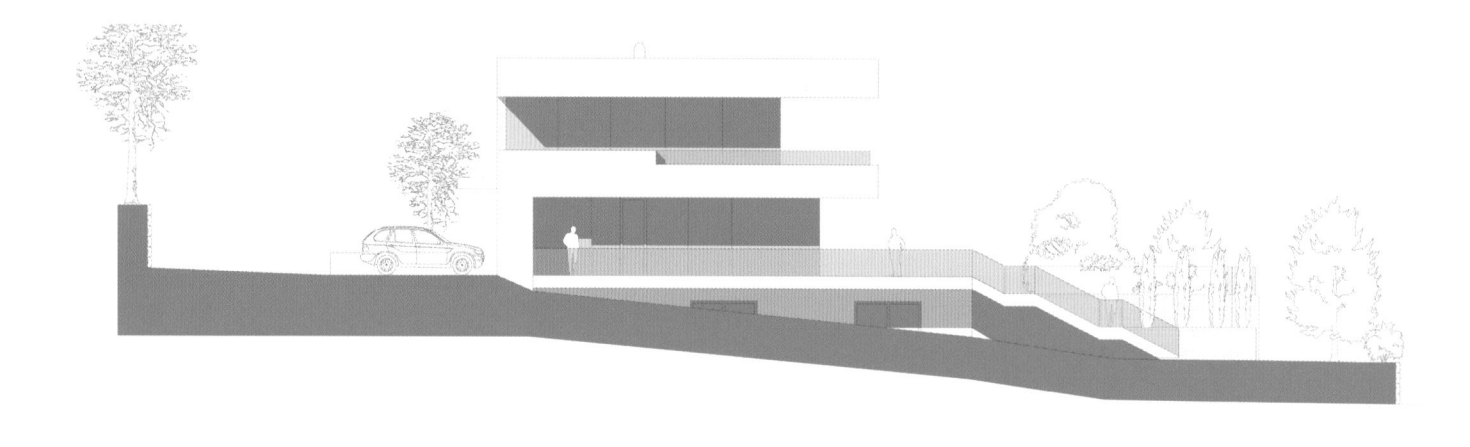

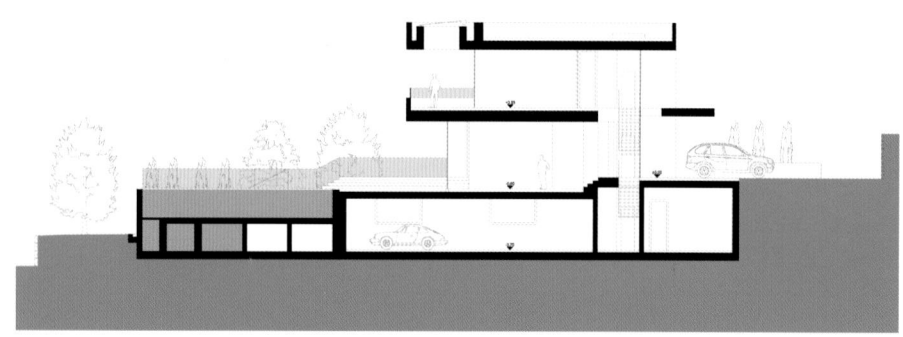

Haus M_Längsschnitt BB_M 1:100

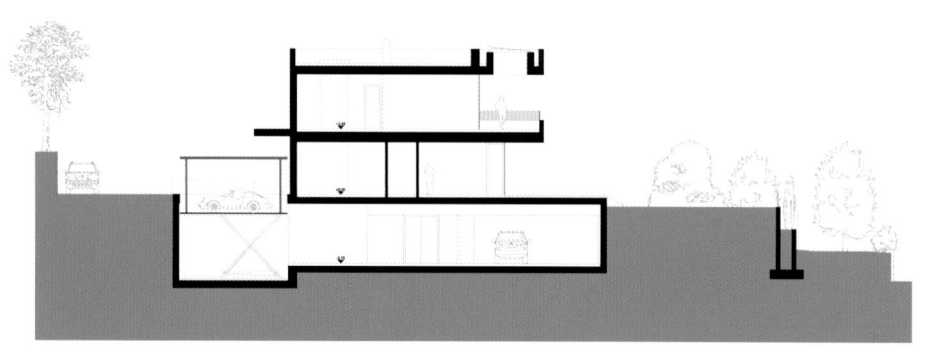

Haus M_Längsschnitt AA_M 1:100

The house is located in the quiet area of Obermais in the center of Meran. The concept of the design was to play with transparent and solid surfaces. The interior melts together with the outside space. The terrain flows through the building and is echoed by the pool and the meadow area. Because of its refined external design and the arrangement, the whole space is unified and has seamless transitions.

The first floor follows the slightly sloping ground with a staircase that leads to a large garden area. Because of engineering considerations, the building was designed as a compact volume with one sub level and two upper floors. The house is constructed from concrete and features upgraded insulation. The glass used for the façade, doors, and windows has three layers.

monovolume architecture + design

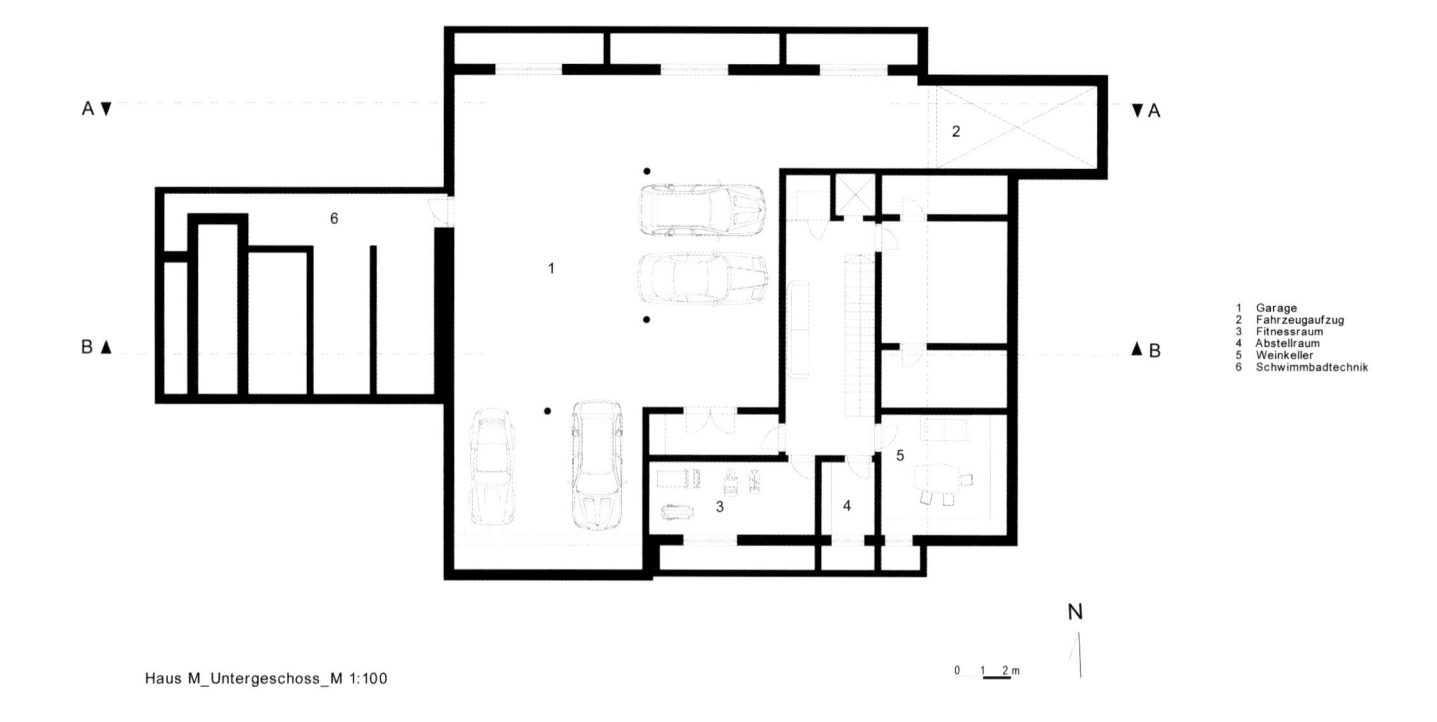

Haus M_Untergeschoss_M 1:100

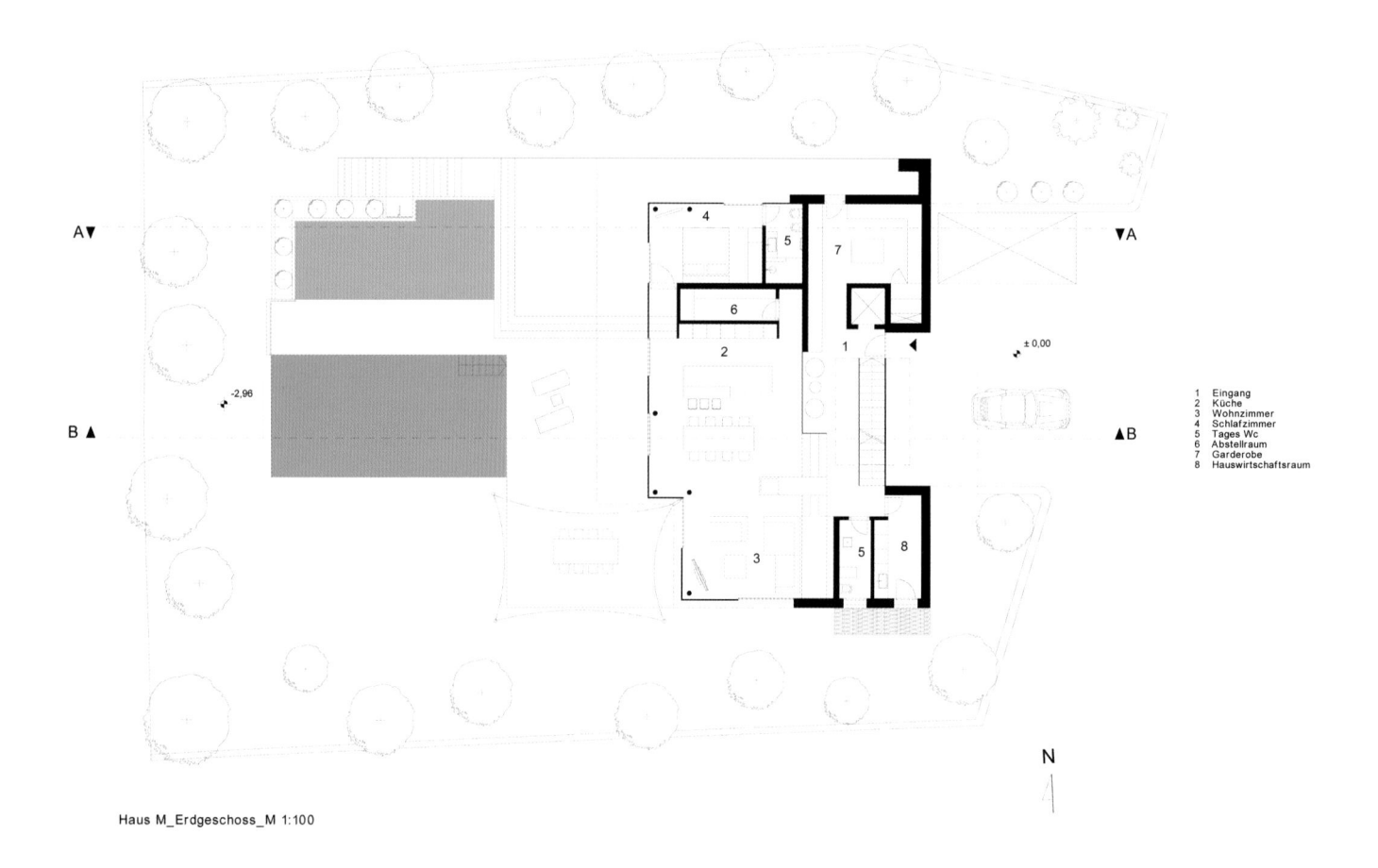

1 Garage
2 Fahrzeugaufzug
3 Fitnessraum
4 Abstellraum
5 Weinkeller
6 Schwimmbadtechnik

Haus M_Erdgeschoss_M 1:100

1 Eingang
2 Küche
3 Wohnzimmer
4 Schlafzimmer
5 Tages Wc
6 Abstellraum
7 Garderobe
8 Hauswirtschaftsraum

monovolume architecture + design

71

Aboo Makhado

Aboo Makhado required special treatment because of the excessive heat in the Tropic of Capricorn.

Nico van der Meulen Architects
Johannesburg, South Africa
494sqm

The existing single storey 343sqm building was turned into a two story 494sqm house.

The internal alterations were extensive. The designers used various forms of steel, added double volume areas, and used large expanses of glass to allow as much natural light in as possible without inundating the house with sun all year round. The sun is let into the house only during the winter. The house cools down quickly in the evening due to its lightweight and well insulated structure. The water features and pool help create a natural cooling system.

The existing living room was opened up to create a double volume area. We used frameless folding doors to enable the house to become a veranda. A staircase highlighted by designer lighting connects the lower and upper areas. A concrete block measuring 6 cubic meters anchors the staircase and allows it to float.

Vast expanses of glass were incorporated into the bedroom wing, which is accessed through a bridge that spans the swimming pool. Glass sliding doors are situated on both sides of the bedroom wing to enable cross draught ventilation at all times. The glass sliding doors were fitted with steel horizontal shutters for sun control.

The use of exterior louvers influenced the design of the horizontal grooves on the plaster wall of the dining room. The grooves, low ledges, and built-in fireplace add interest and character to an otherwise boring wall. The paint colors were carefully chosen to complement each other and the rusted corten steel adds creative interest.

The staircase leading up to the first floor is further enhanced by the hanging pendant lights that lead the eye up toward the double volume ceiling.

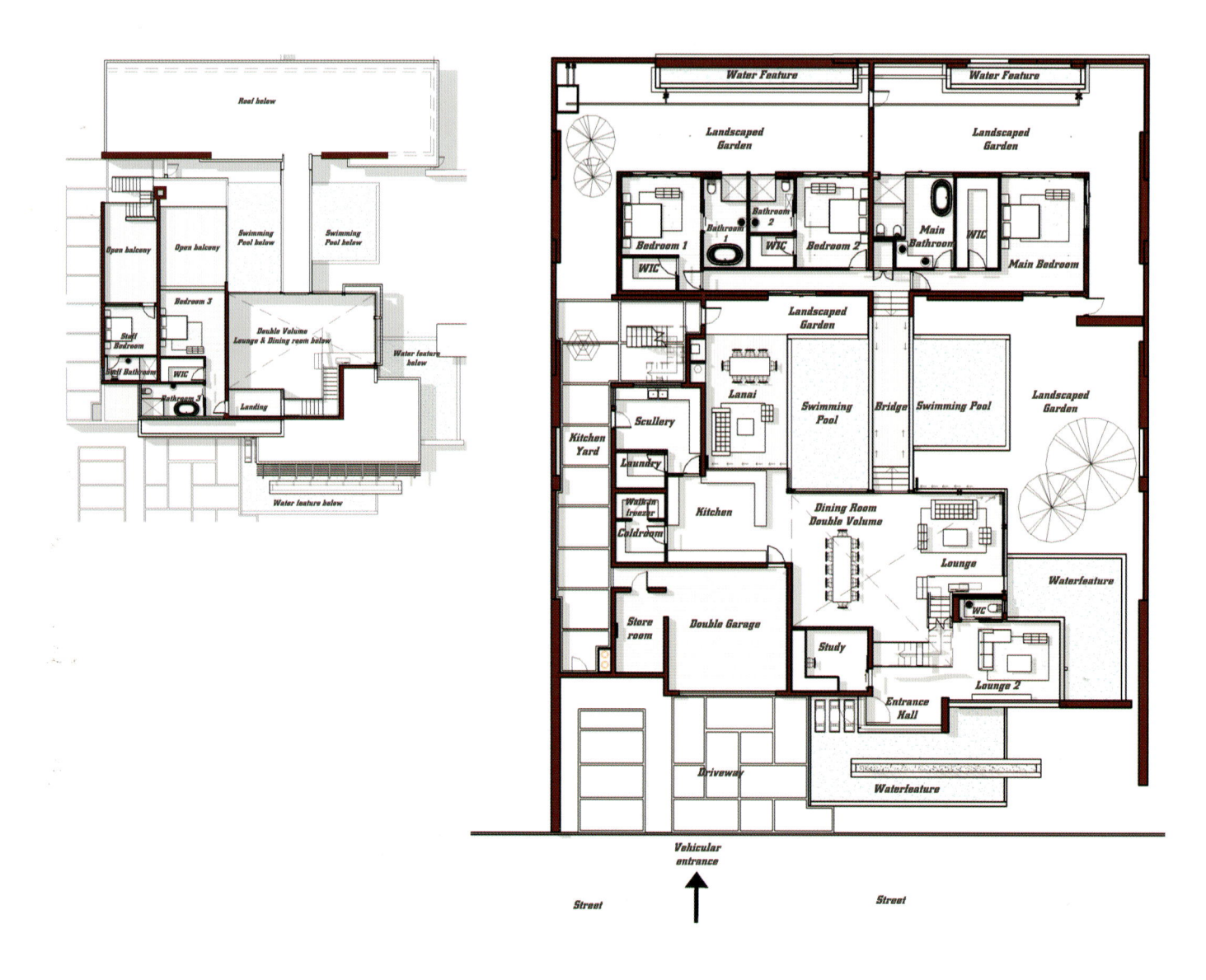

Nico van der Meulen Architects

Aboo Makhado

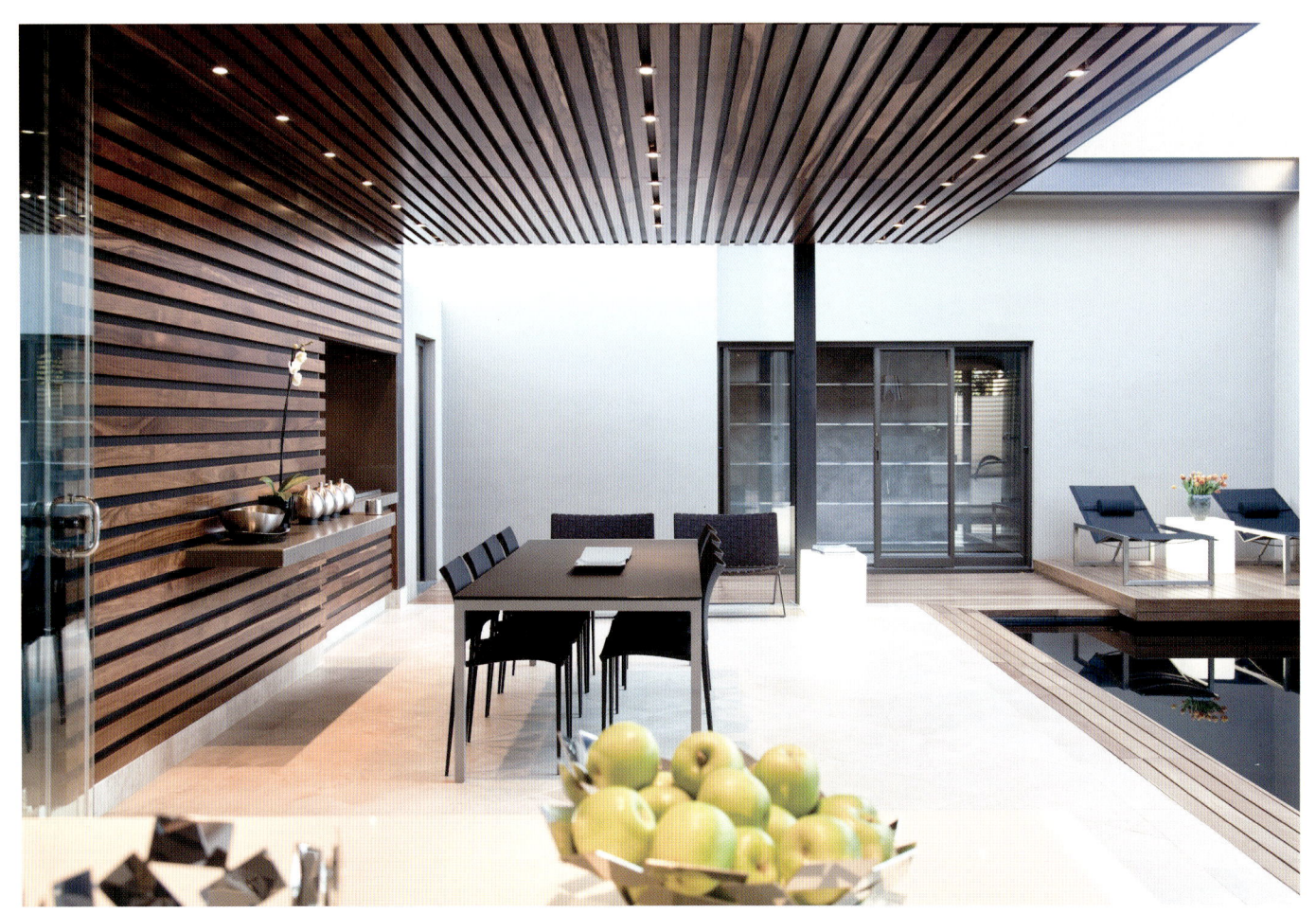

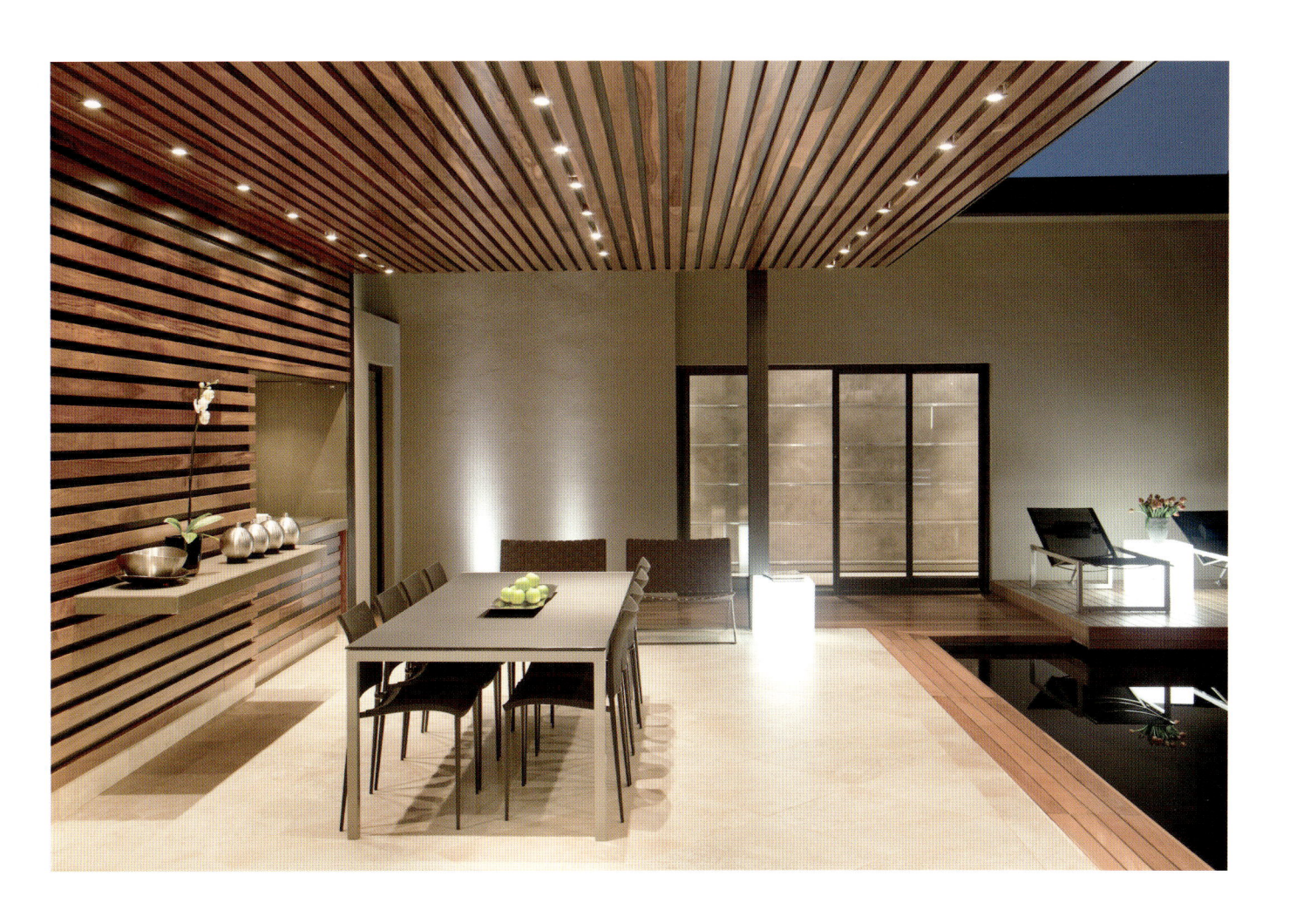

Nico van der Meulen Architects

Bridge House

Bridge House is designed to be self-sufficient and generate its own power. Water is sourced from a private well and rainwater is collected and reused.

123DV
Rotterdam, the Netherlands
825sqm

The villa is set in a newly developed estate in the unique, tree-lined landscape of the Dutch Achterhoek, where unexpected scenes of rural beauty are always just around the bend.

The lower floor is mostly buried beneath two grassy mounds. There is a large open space in front of the house that stylishly frames the park, most of which is open to walkers. The park blends into the landscape around it. The landscape architect for this project carefully restored the property to its original state with rows of trees throughout the landscape. To make the soil less fertile, the top layer was removed throughout the property. In the interest of sustainability, this soil was reused to form a raised area beneath the house. The result is a traditional Dutch terp dwelling, a house with a cellar located on top of a hill.

Sustainability also inspired the design of the house. The villa is self-sufficient. At any time, the occupants can go off the grid without losing their energy supply. Water is drawn from a private well and rainwater is collected and reused. The house also features solar panels, thermal energy storage for roof and floor heating, a septic tank, shielded power cables, and heat-mirror glass. This unique glass acts as an efficient and environmentally friendly awning, cooling the house and keeping out excess heat.

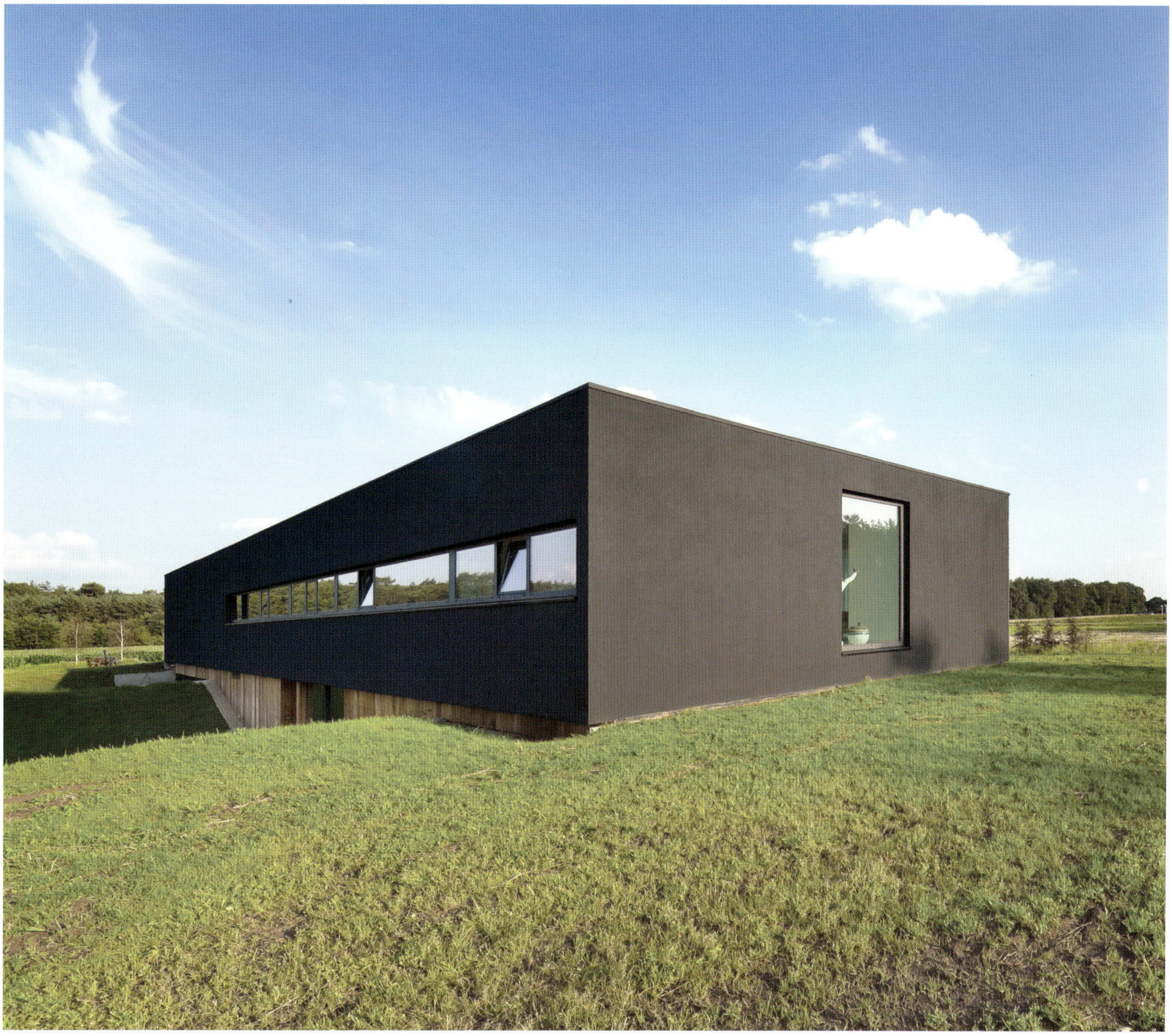

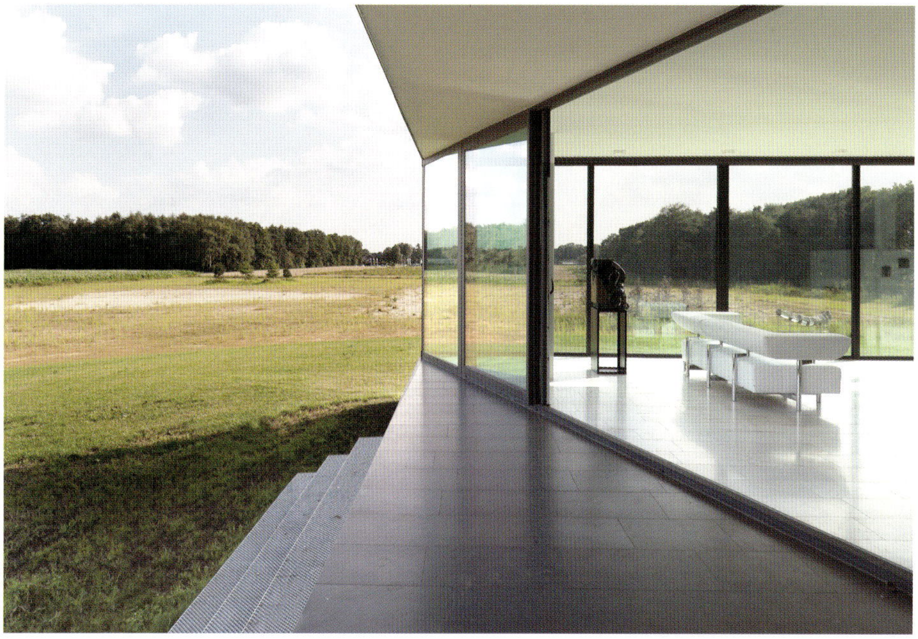

The living rooms and bedrooms are all located on the upper floor, which also includes a large lounge and dining room with glazed walls on two sides.

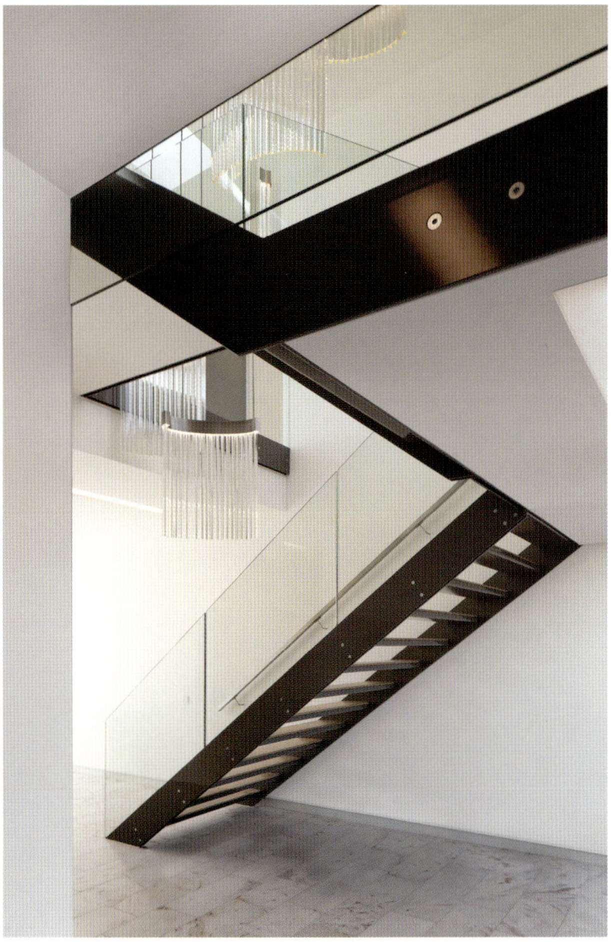

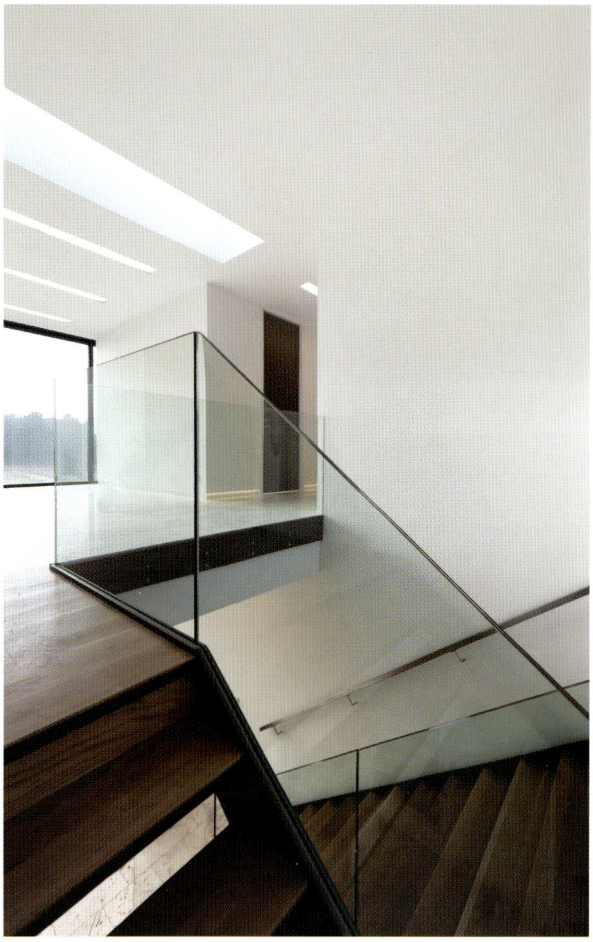

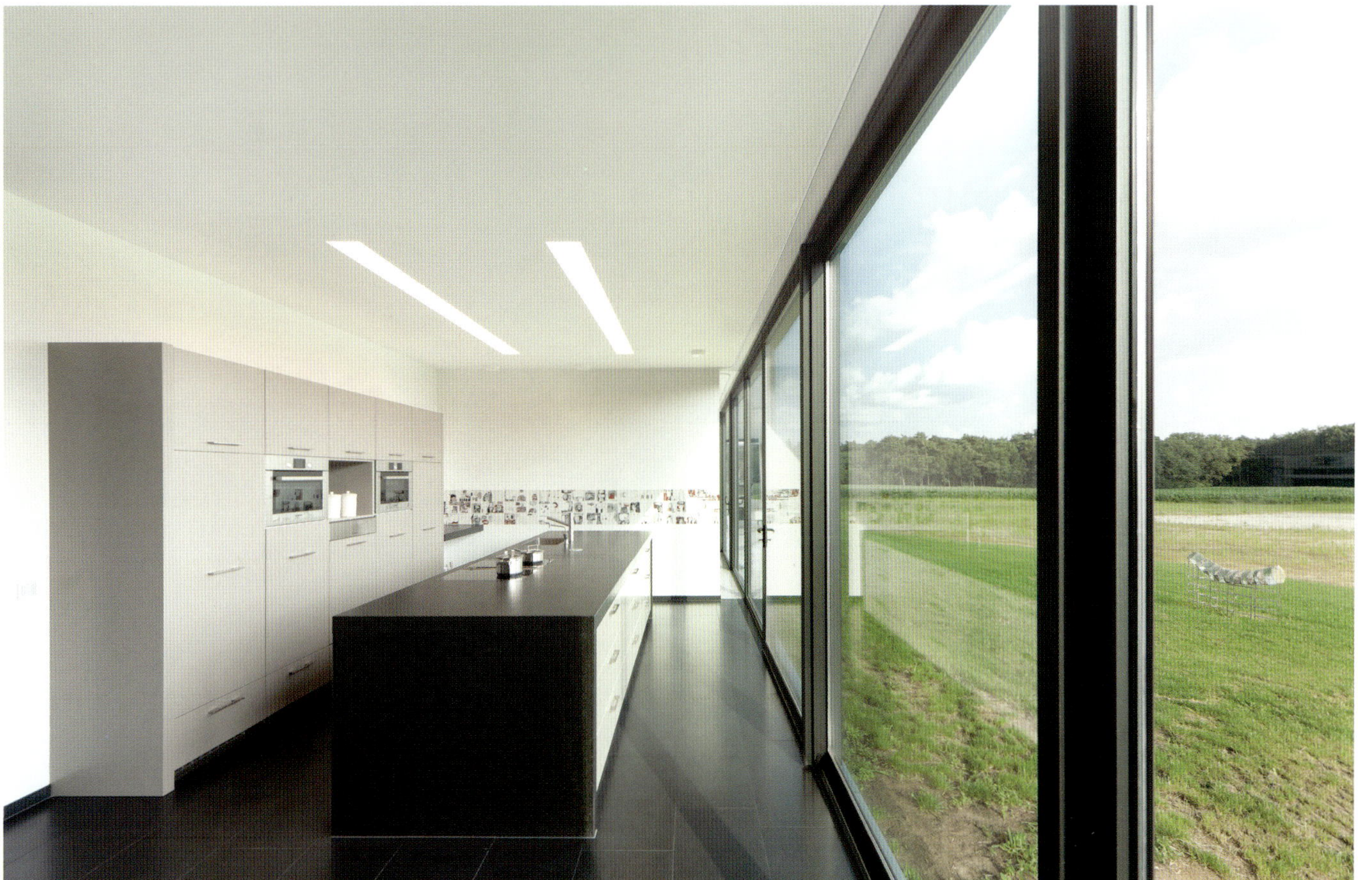

Family House J20

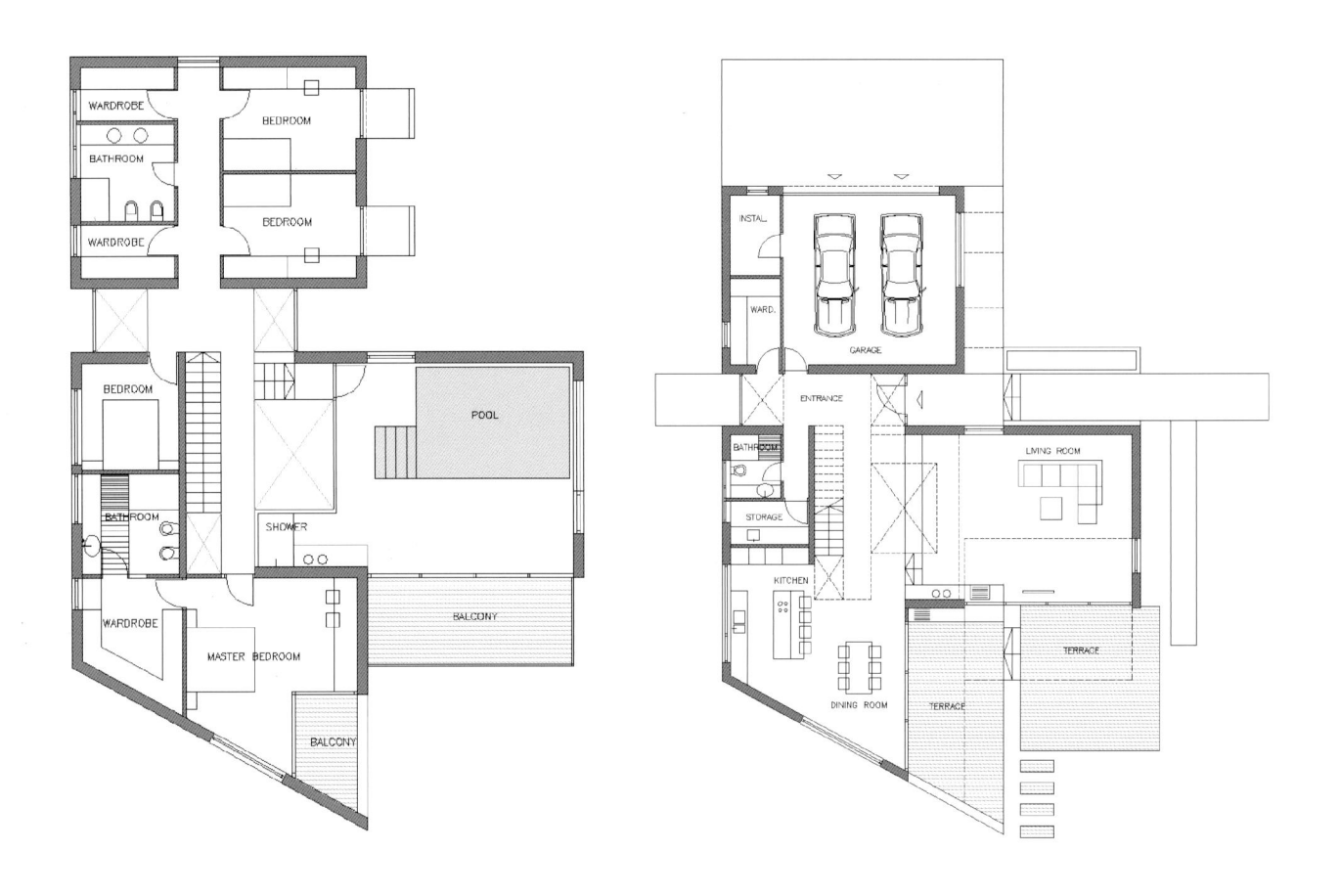

Family House J20 is a design with an indoor pool for a young family of four.

DAR612
Zagreb, Croatia
400sqm

This family house with a pool, located on a gentle slope, is designed as a juxtaposition of two elements: a primary longitudinal wing with a white finish, and a perpendicular element covered in a dark wood coating. The T-shaped floor plan enables the house to be oriented toward both the south and the west. A two story-high entry divides the house into two segments connected by a wooden bridge: the eastern segment is a secondary space with a garage on the ground floor and children's area on the first floor; the western segment contains the main living spaces and parents' quarters on the upper floor. The pool, located above the living room, is visible from the rest of the house. The stairs and the bridge, designed as a steel structure with wooden cladding, are the core of the house and functionally connect the spaces, create a dynamic flow, and visually unify the interior.

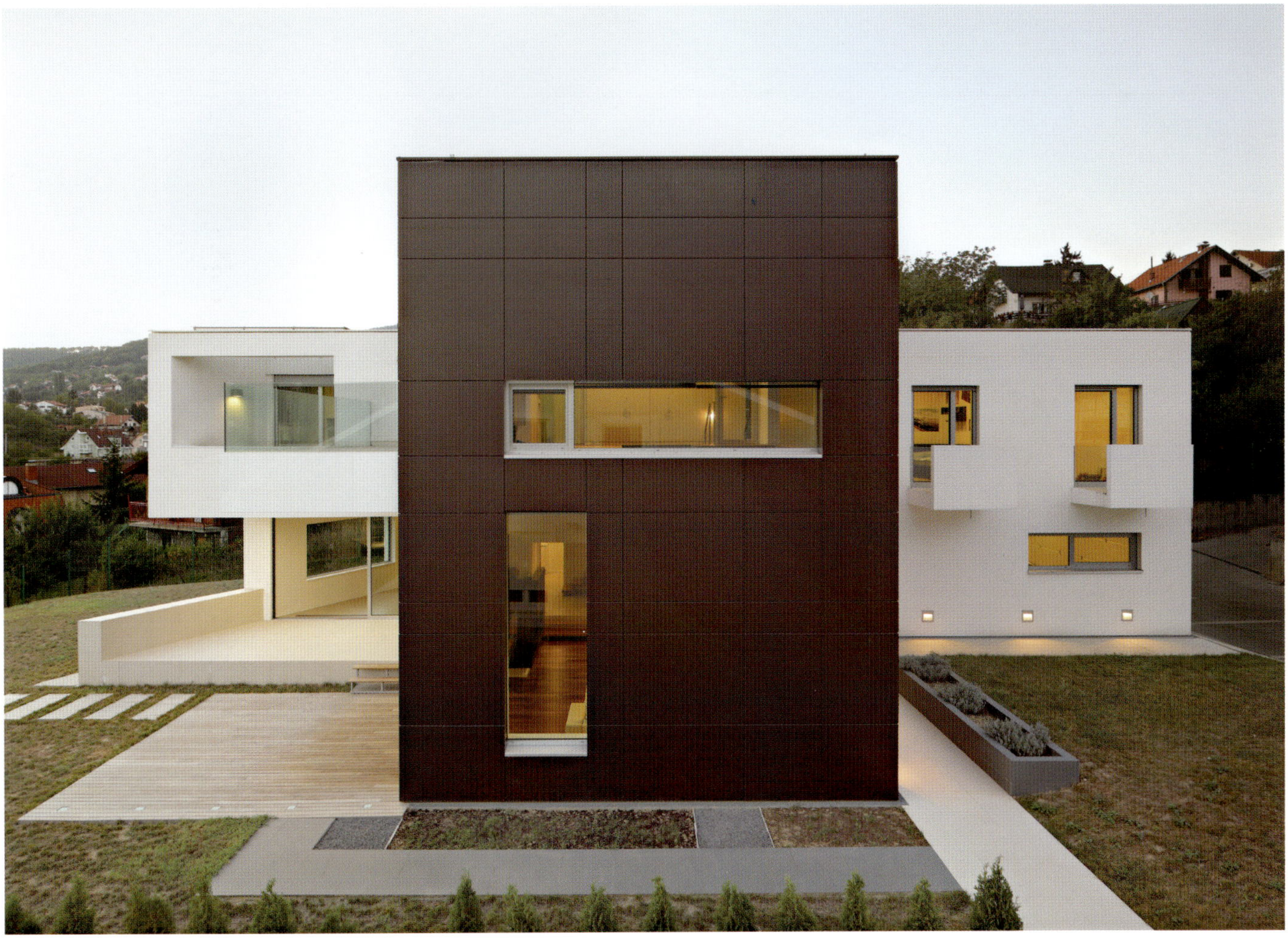

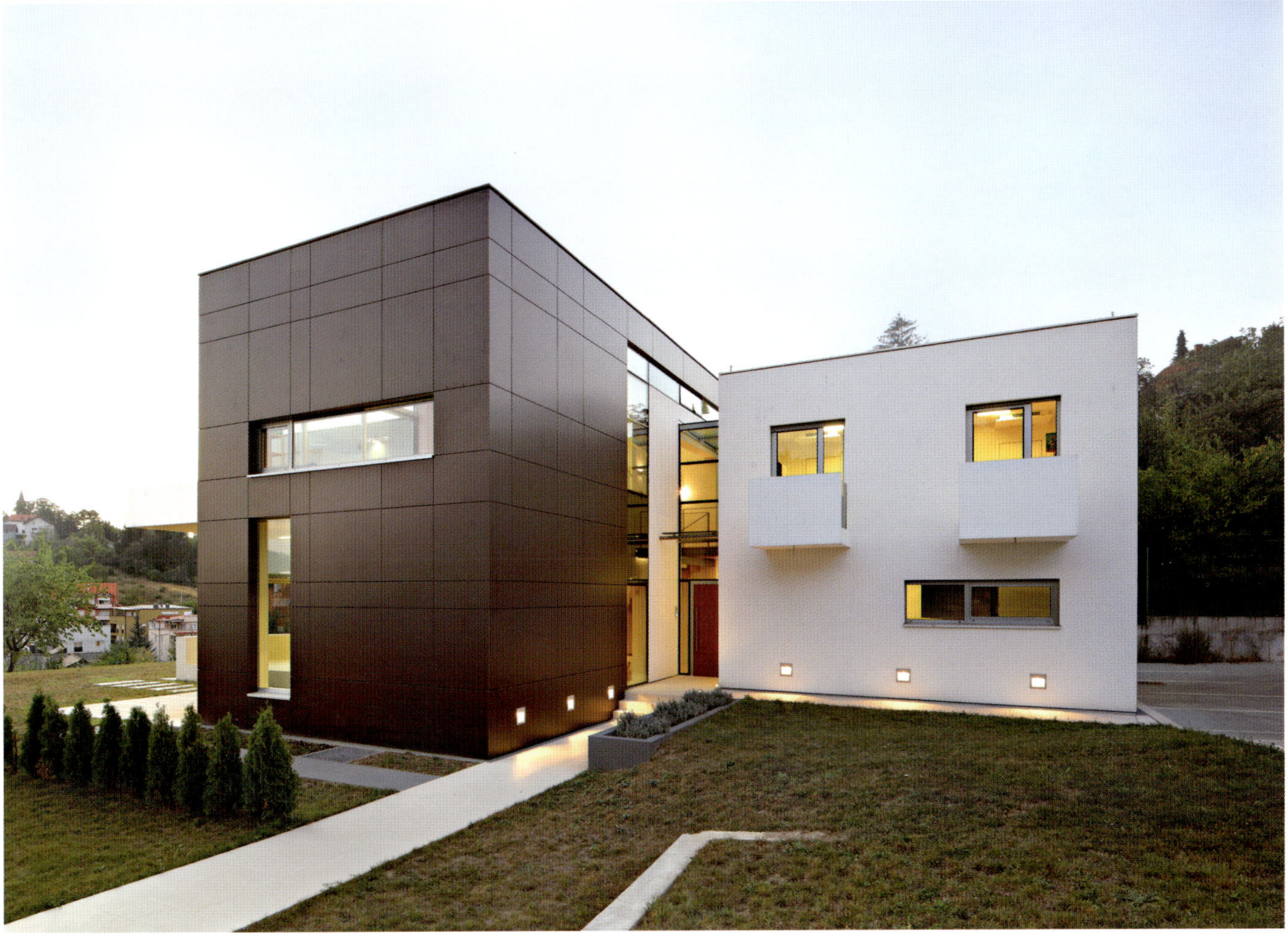

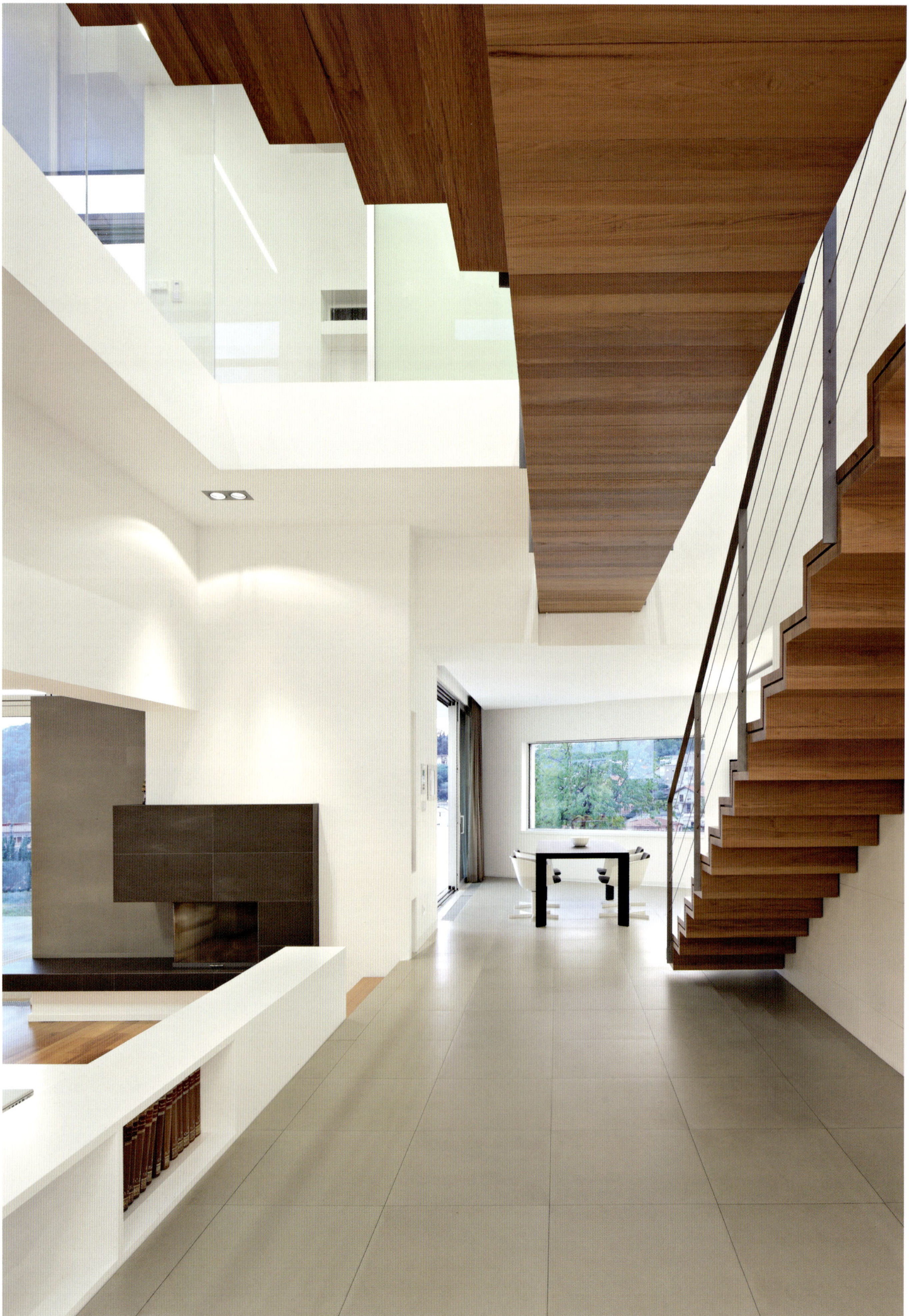

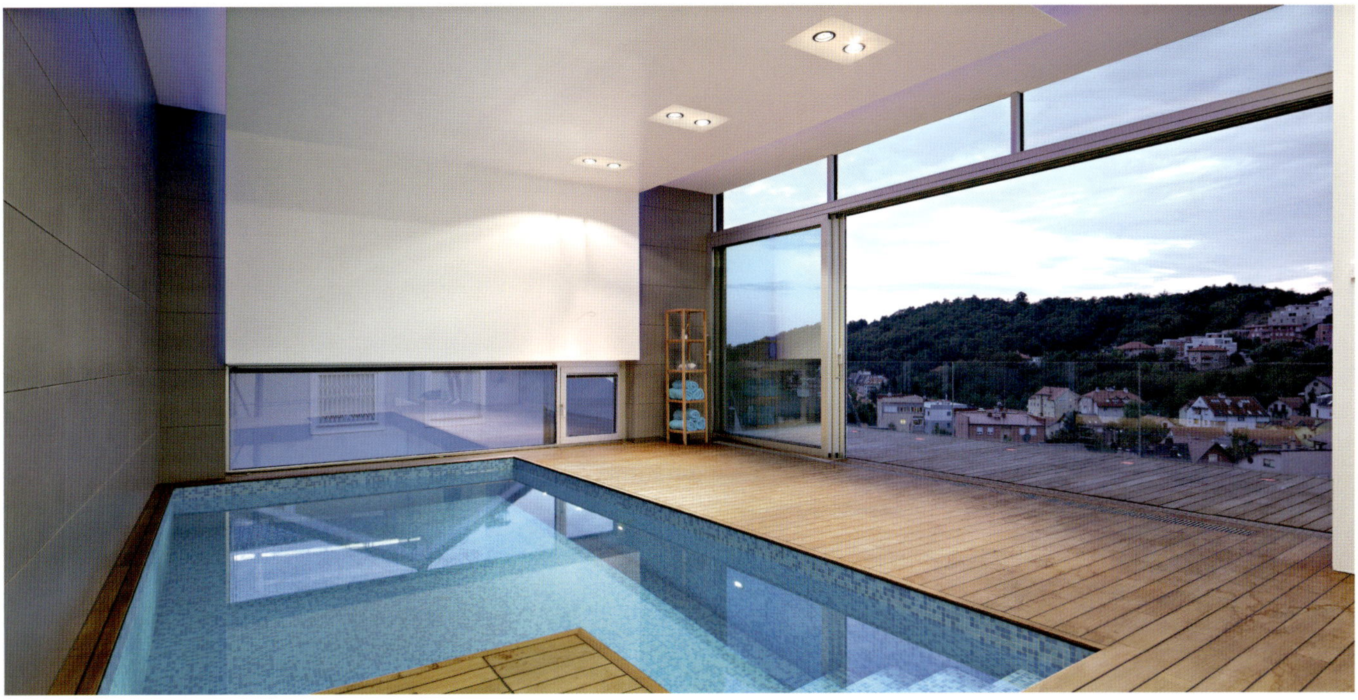

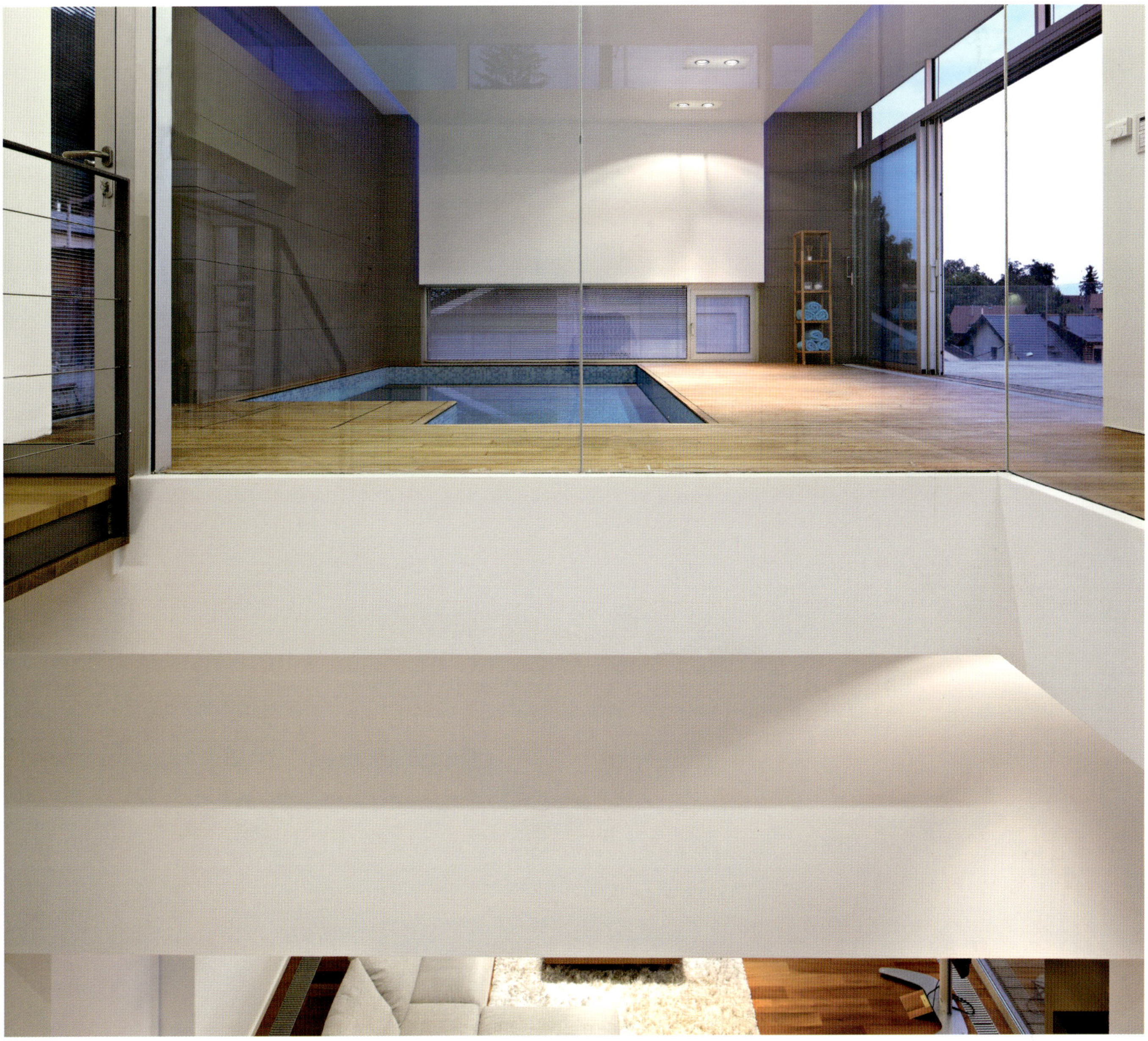

Browne Street House

The cantilevered cottage **Browne Street House** is a deliberate subversion of the Queenslander paradigm and aims to recalibrate the perception of the house.

Shaun Lockyer Architects
Brisbane, Australia
330sqm

The house is split into indoor and outdoor living on the ground floor with the bedrooms on the upper level. This arrangement offers the benefits of zone separation within a small area. A series of voids punctuate the floor plan and give much needed access to light and views in all areas. Large sliding doors and screens afford control and flexibility of the environment, maximizing the indoor/outdoor relationships and the ways in which spaces can be used. The mezzanine space can also be controlled with a series of doors and shutters to open and close the space as required.

The completed work sits comfortably amongst its neighbours while equally re-calibrating itself to address 21st century needs in a subtropical environment. To this end, while the cottage is sympathetic in its presentation to the street, it is overtly contemporary in its application of materials and details within the development guidelines. The result is one of a considered and relevant approach to the interaction between new and old in established neighbourhoods, concealing the more contemporary elements at the rear.

The design has been optimized to take full advantage of the north sun, local breezes, and light in order to reduce dependence on artificial light and heating and cooling. The more exposed façades of the house have had operable sun screening installed (and integrated into the architecture) to control the temperature without the use of air-conditioning. FSC timber was used to the greatest extent possible for the flooring and wall cladding. A 10,000L water tank was added, which is double the legislated requirement. Low energy lighting has been cleverly integrated and concealed to offer a warm creative light source that costs very little. Ceiling fans have been installed in all living and bedroom areas to reduce dependency on air-conditioning. All the walls and floors (both internal and external) have more than twice the amount of insulation required.

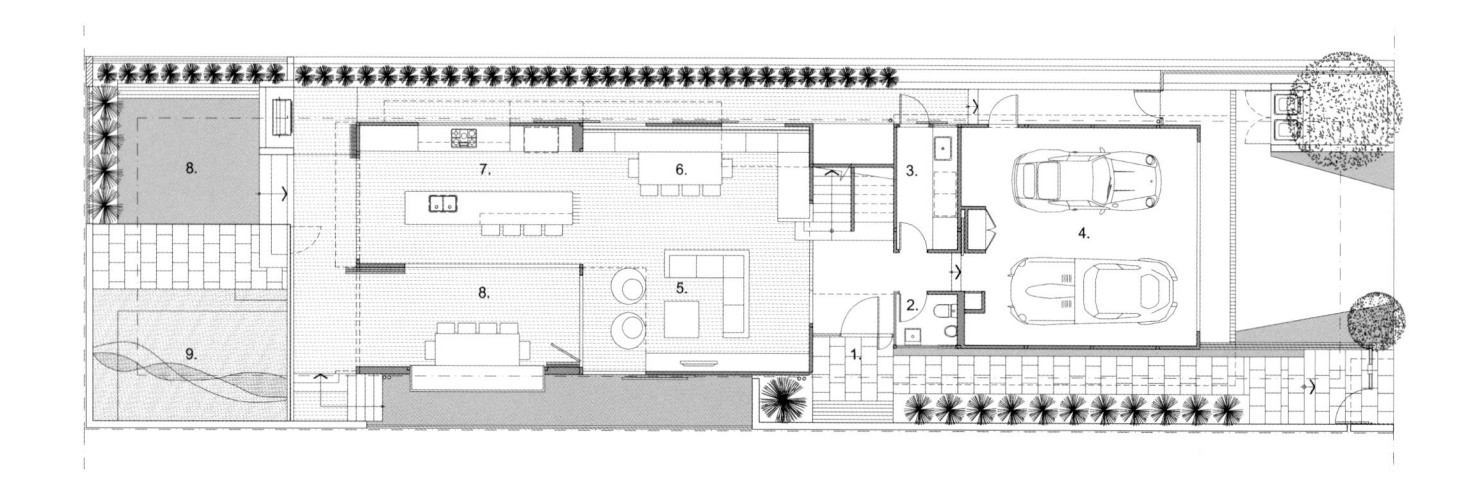

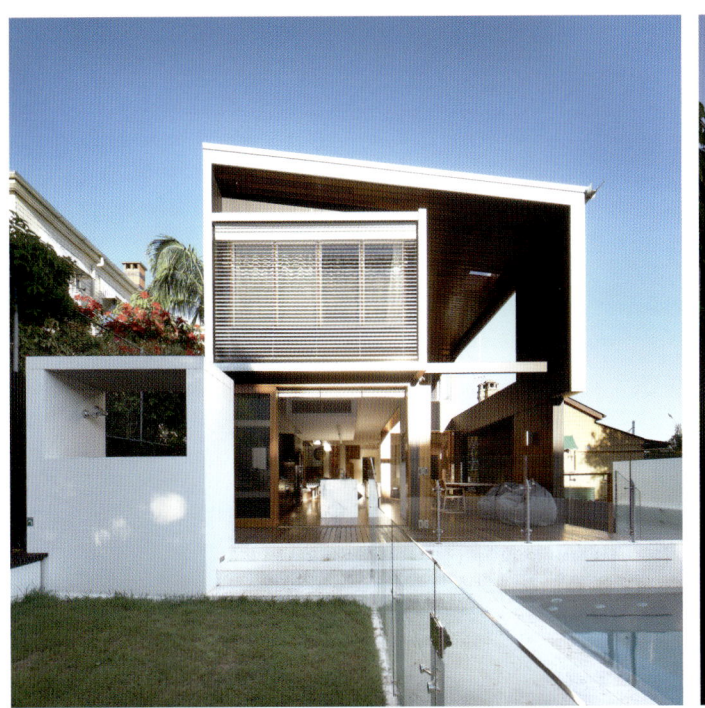

Shaun Lockyer Architects

85

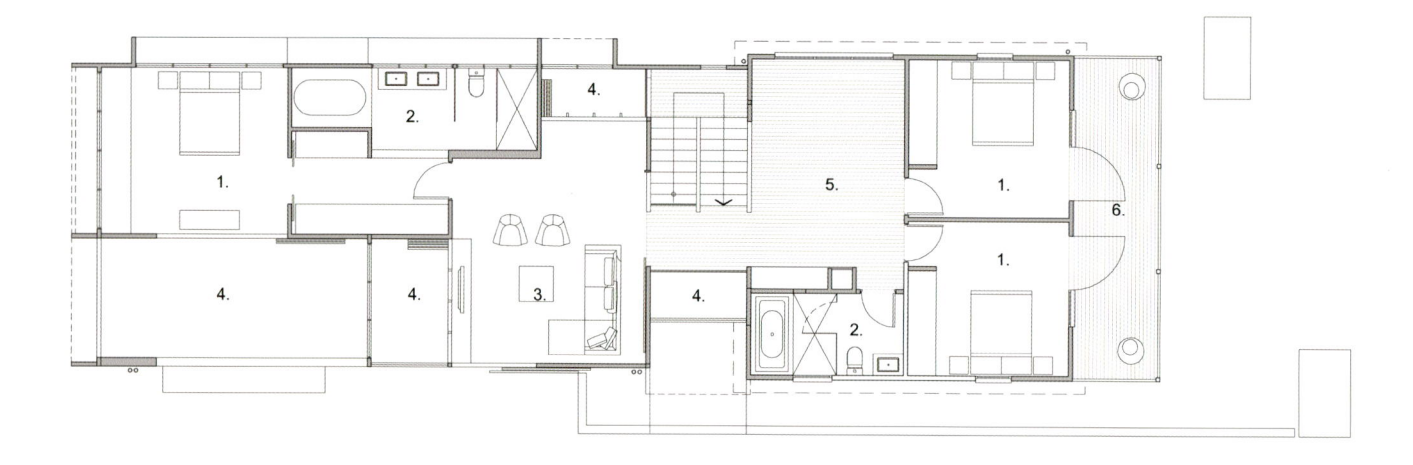

By using the kitchen as a node around which spaces are ordered, integration and balance between the indoor and outdoor domains is achieved. Access to north sun and light always shapes a great deal of the planning, and the manipulation of void and volume facilitate the transformed experience of the space.

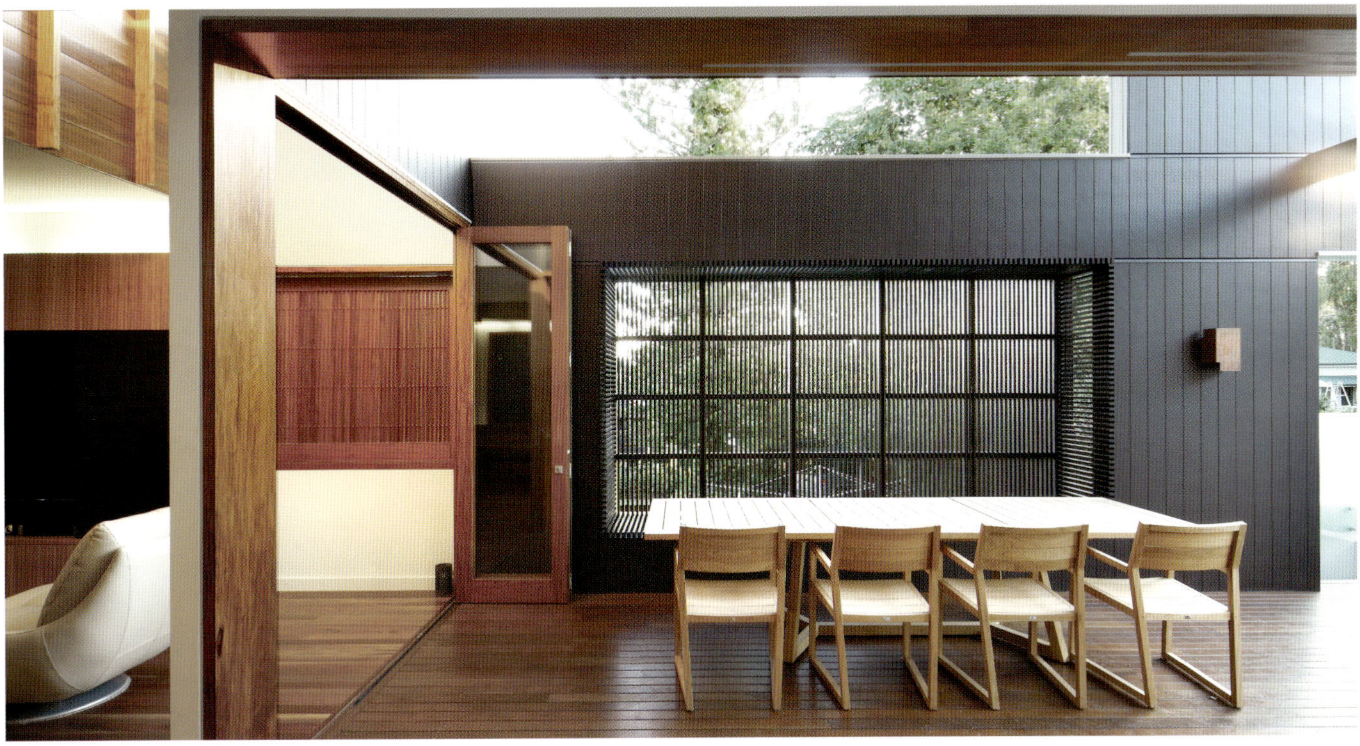

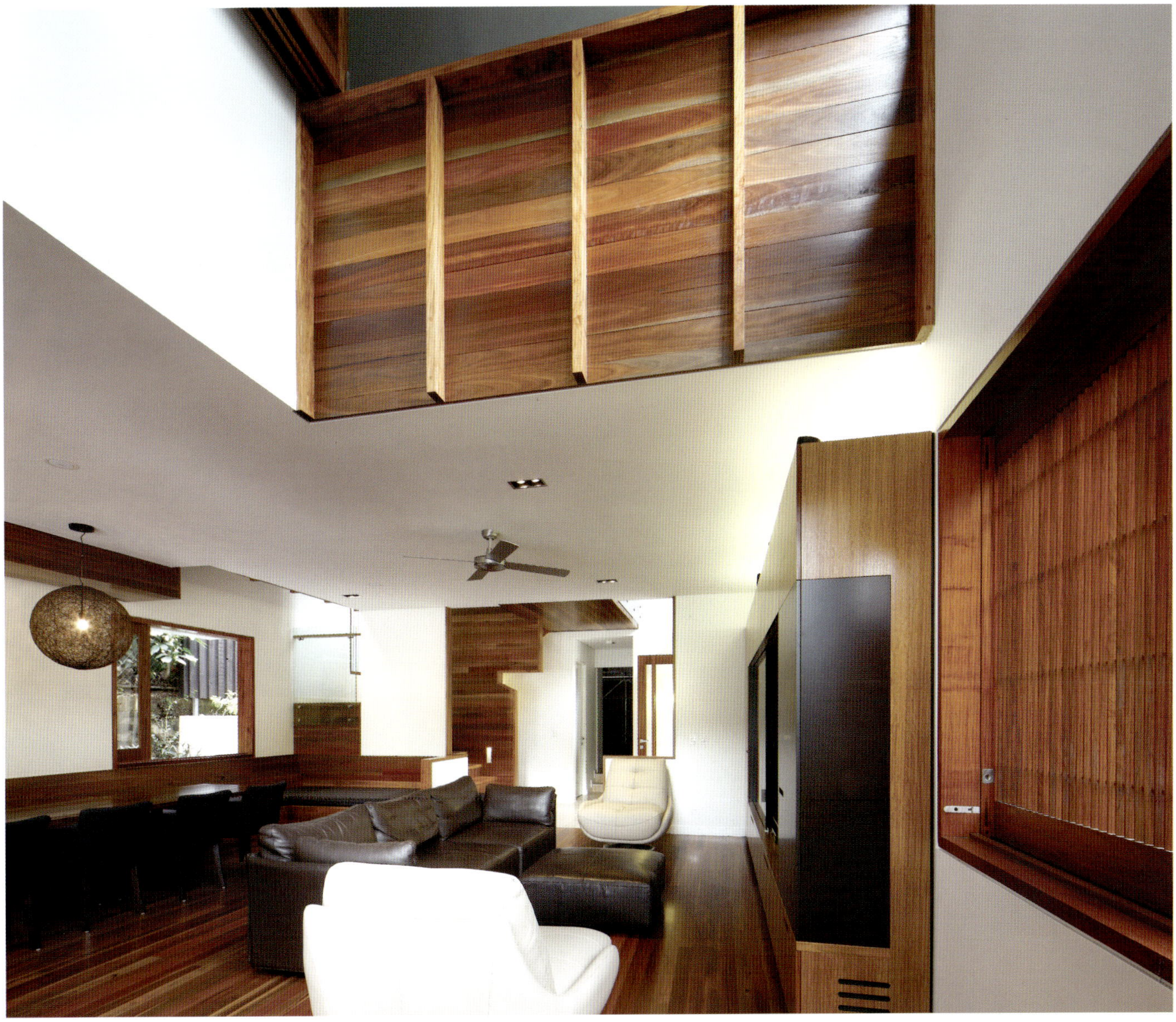

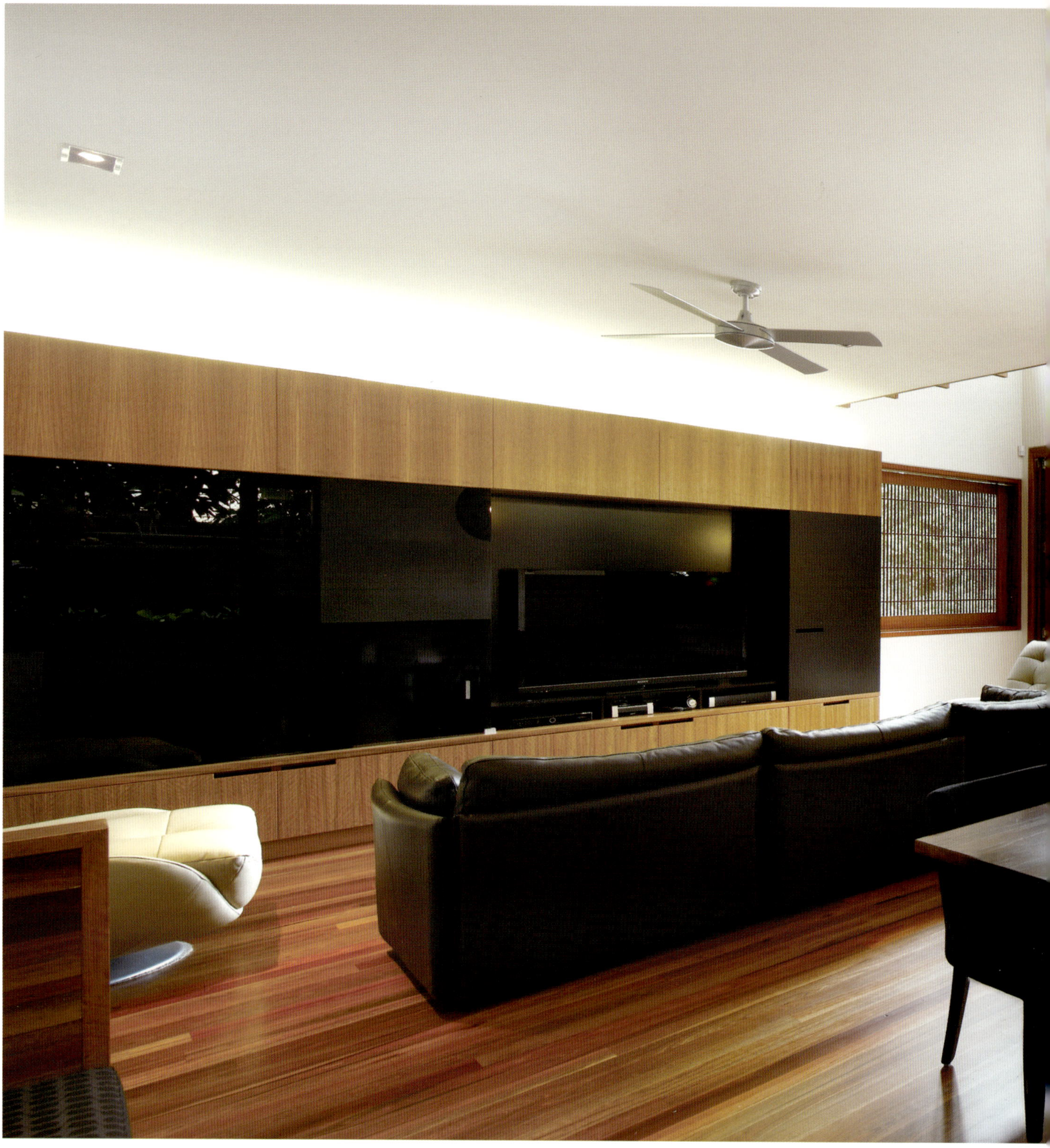

Shaun Lockyer Architects

G1 House

An avocado tree was the starting point for the design of G1 House.

**Arch. Gabriel Rivera +
Arch. Cristina Vargas
Guayllabamba, Ecuador
353sqm**

Located in Guayllabamba, a place of warm weather and fertile land, G1 House is a composition of architecture and nature. An avocado tree (12m in height) is the central node that helped determine the location for this project. Consequently, the tree became the starting point for the design.

The lot has a triangular shape and an area of 5,054sqm. It is composed of multiple gardens and contains many fruit trees. No tree was cut down. The house was positioned such that all the vegetation could be preserved. The avocado tree is located at the highest point in the lot. Due to its shadow, there is less vegetation surrounding it. This made the spot a good location for the project and allowed us to pay tribute to the magnificent tree.

The house is characterized by its clear architectural language. In its longitudinal direction, a circulation that works as a backbone runs throughout the house, dividing it in two, and separates the served spaces (bedroom, living room, kitchen), from the service spaces (bathrooms, closets, pantry, machine's room). In a transverse direction an axis that starts from the avocado tree passes through the entrance hall and ends at the inner garden, separating the private areas from the social areas.

All served spaces reflect themselves in a clear way in the front façade. This façade opens onto the garden and thus integrates the garden and the house. A wooden deck runs along the front of the house. Consequently, the architecture opens itself to the site and its vegetation. A structural modulation of 4.20m was used along the whole house.

As a result, the house itself shows the viewer clear volumes that are easy to understand. The functionality of the spaces can be read in the house's façades.

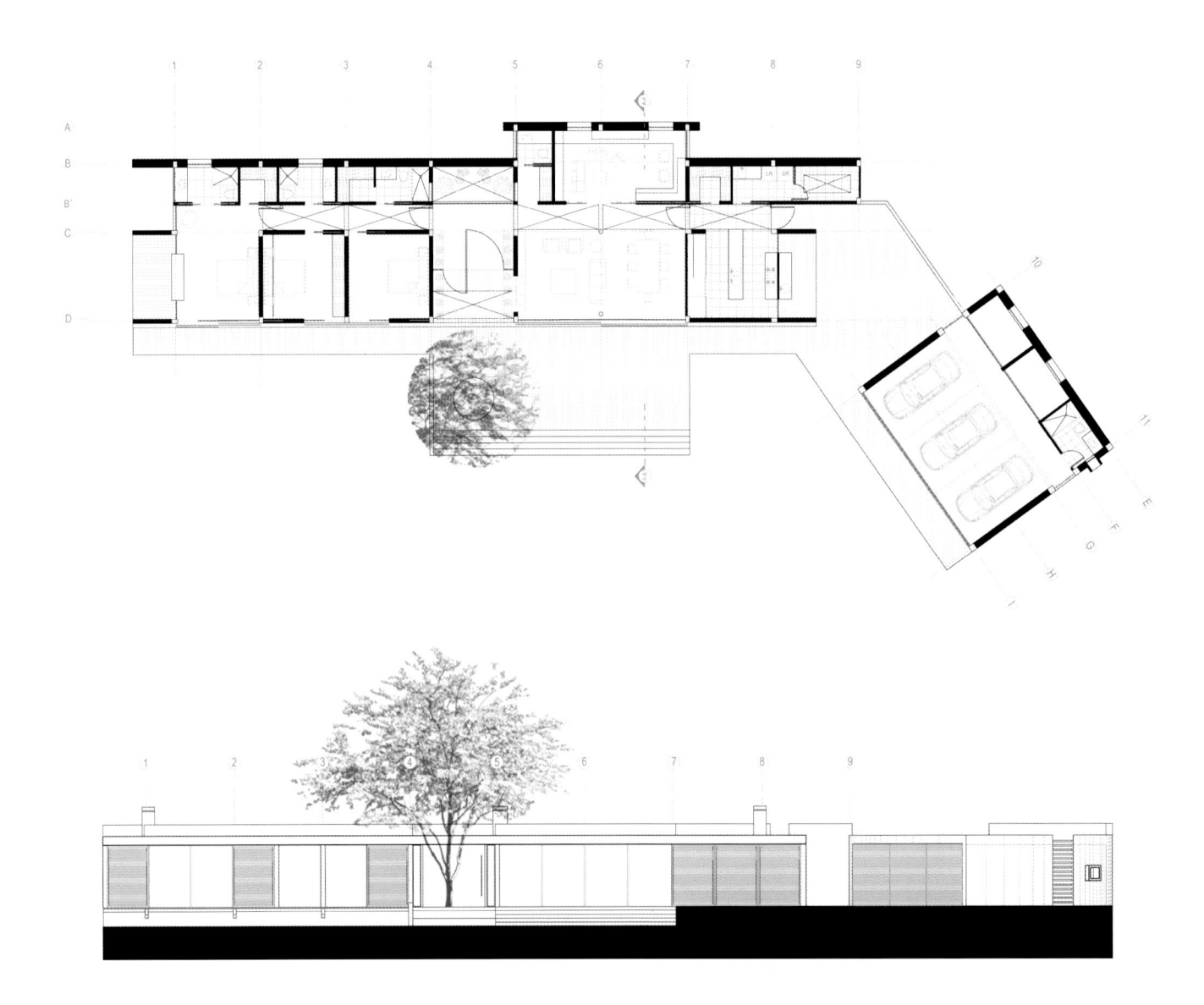

Arch. Gabriel Rivera + Arch. Cristina Vargas

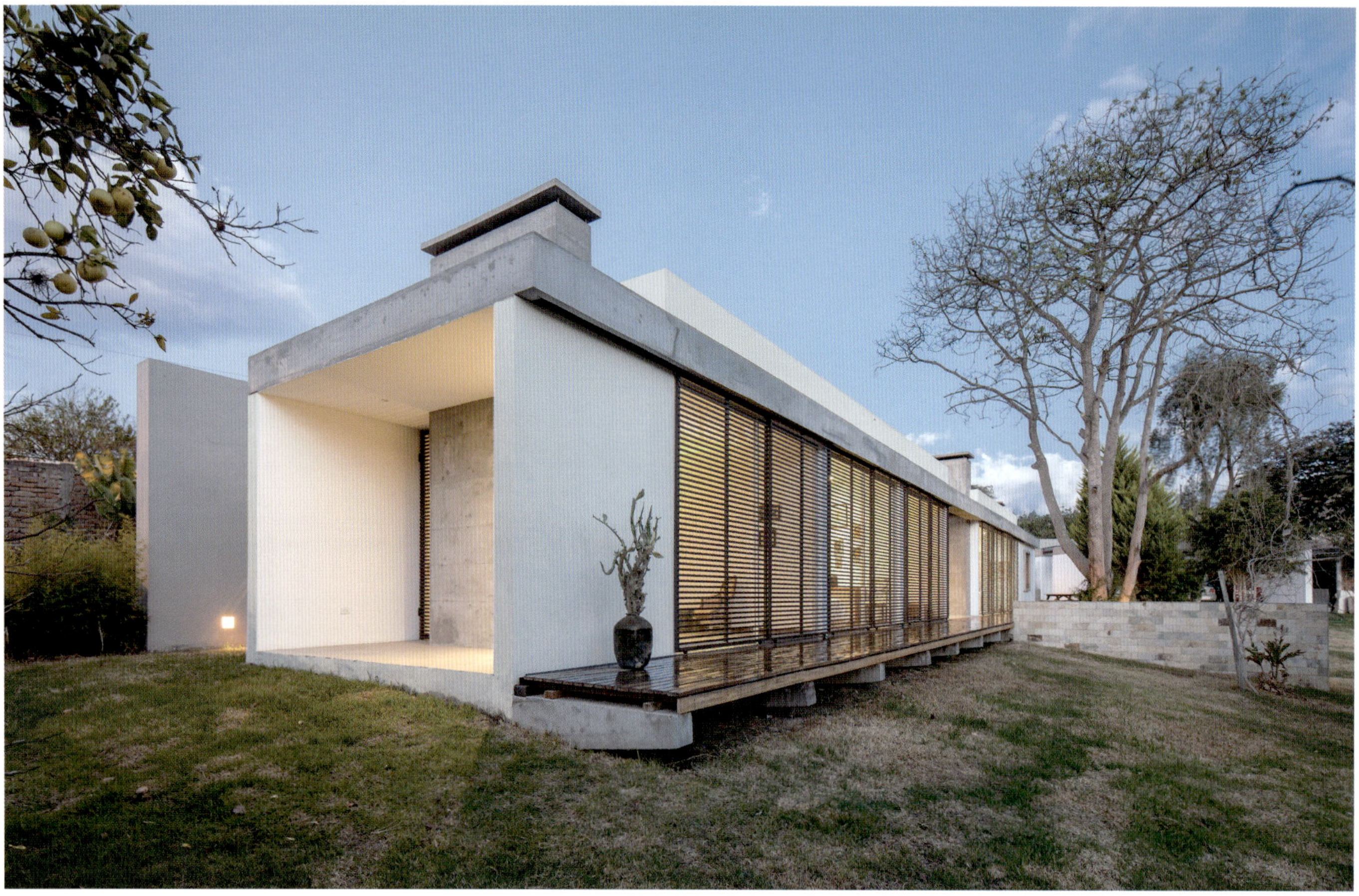

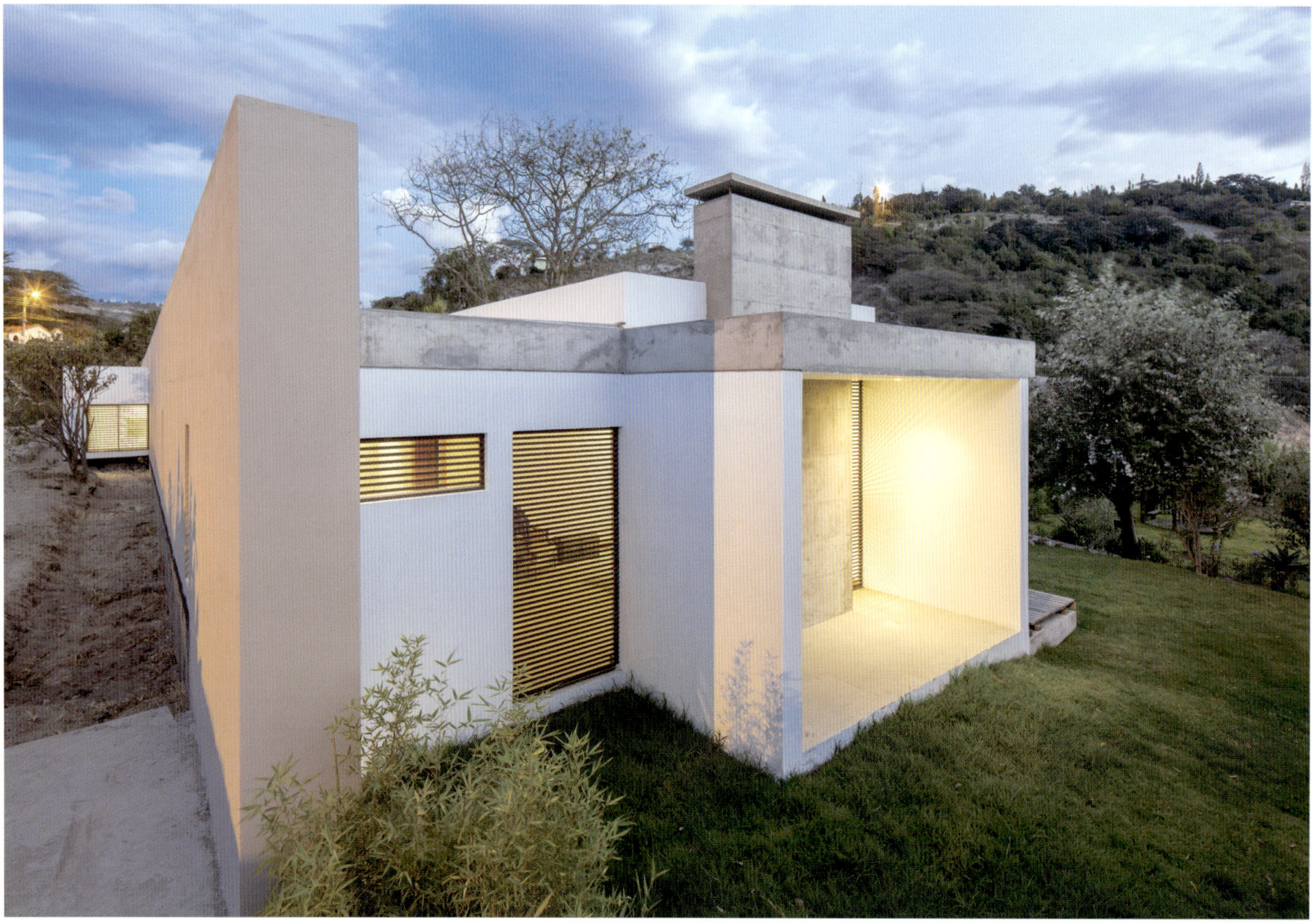

Arch. Gabriel Rivera + Arch. Cristina Vargas

W House

In **W House**, the function areas on the lower level support the private quarters of the house on the second floor, just as a river supports a boat.

IDIN Architects
Nakornratchasima, Thailand
202sqm

The design concept was derived from the client's favorite activities, traveling and kayaking. The designer was inspired by a picture of a boat on a river. The river supports the boat. This relationship became the model for this house. The function areas support the private quarters on the second floor.

The orientation of the building was determined by wind and sun. The house is oriented in a north-south direction, which enables sunlight to come in through the west side of the house. Kayaking is a challenging and adventurous sport. The cantilever design was developed in order to represent those aspects of the sport. The design creates spaces that float like boats and has the added benefit of providing shade to the void space below. There is a deck on the roof hidden above the south bedroom that provides an area for rest and recreational activities. Wooden shutters provide shade and privacy when needed.

The context helped determine the materials and tones. Because the soil at the location is a brown-red, the designer chose to use only three major colors, grey, black-grey, and brown-red. The first floor is a black-grey to separate it from the second floor. The contrast echoes that formed by the river and the boat.

IDIN Architects

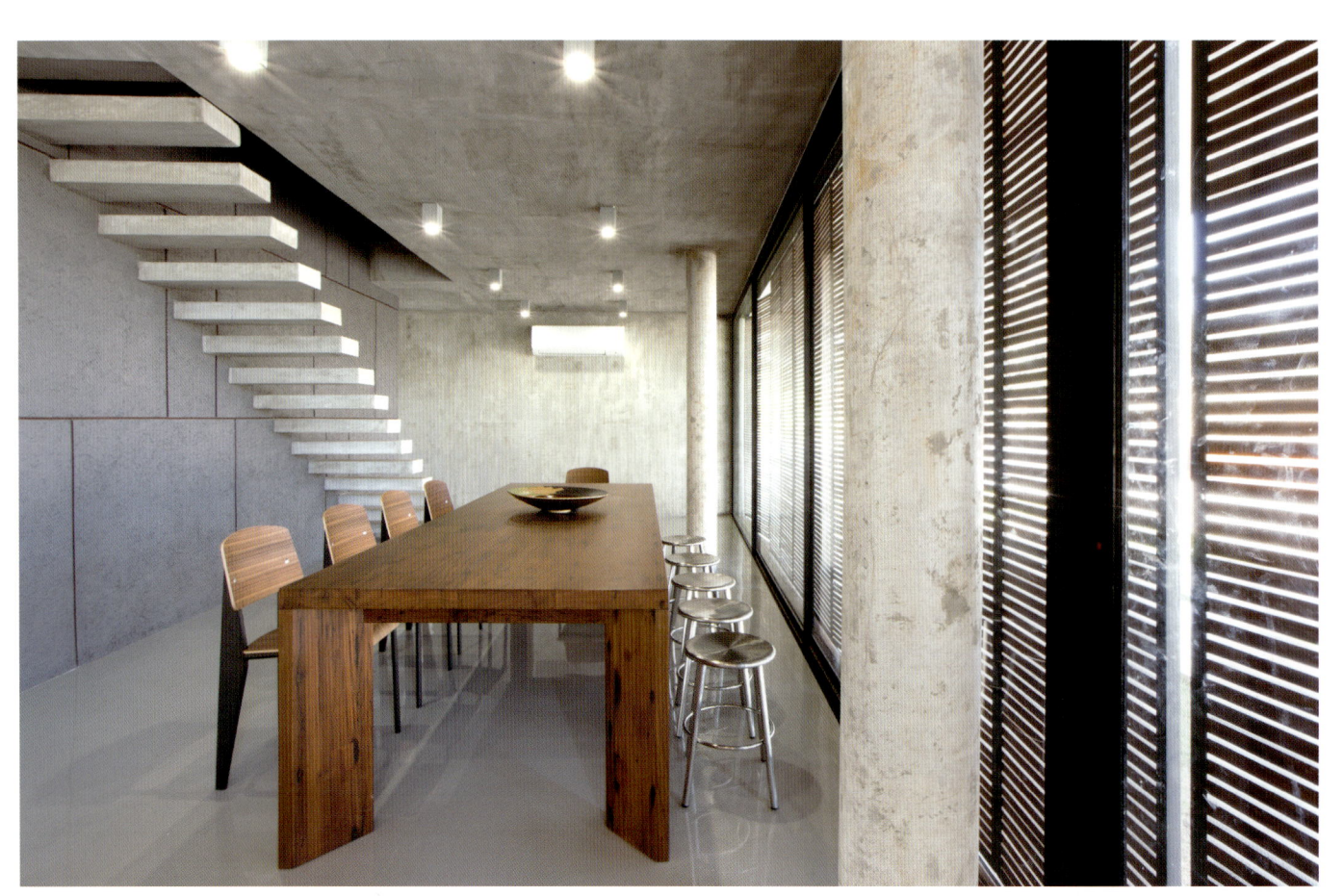

W House

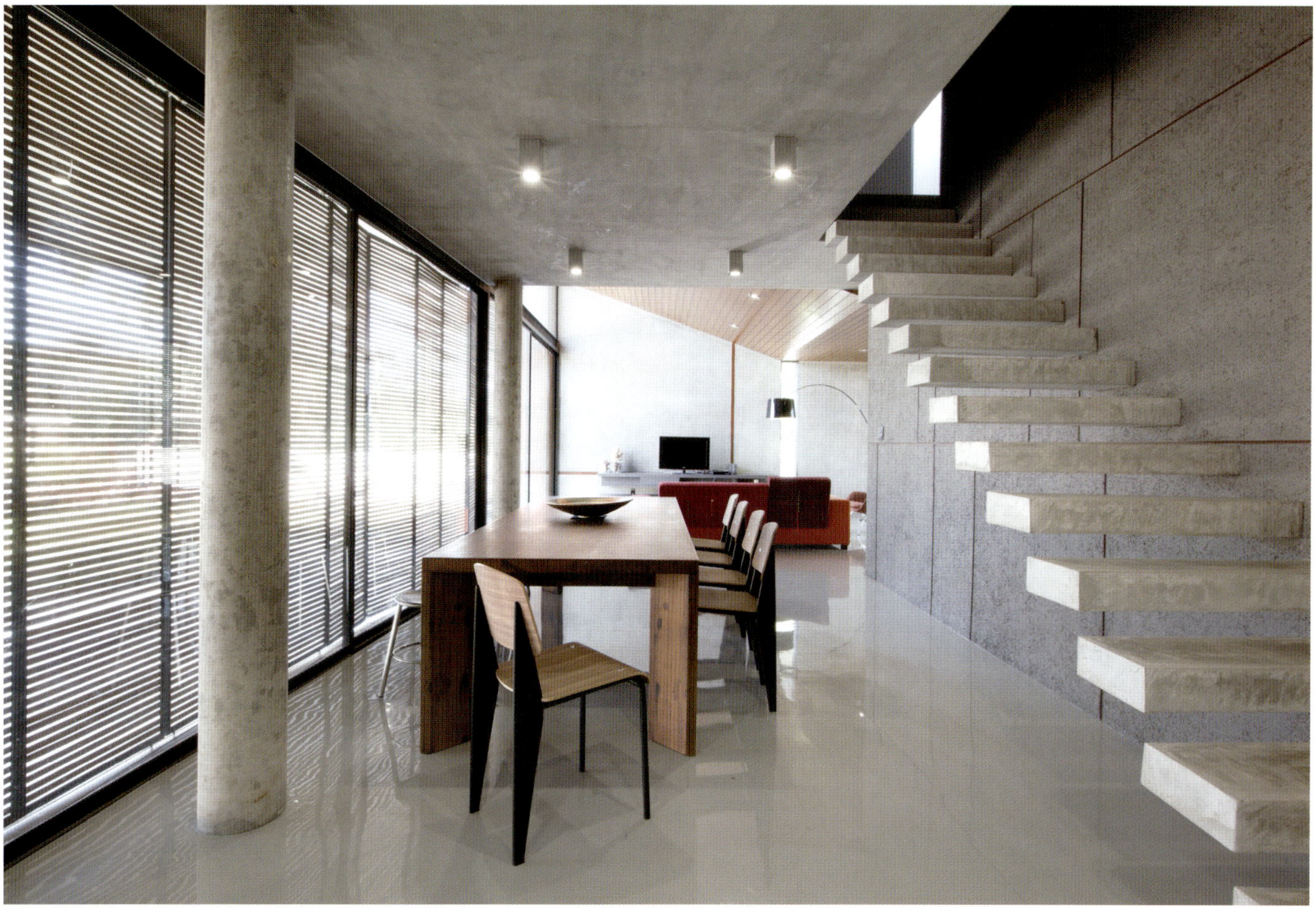

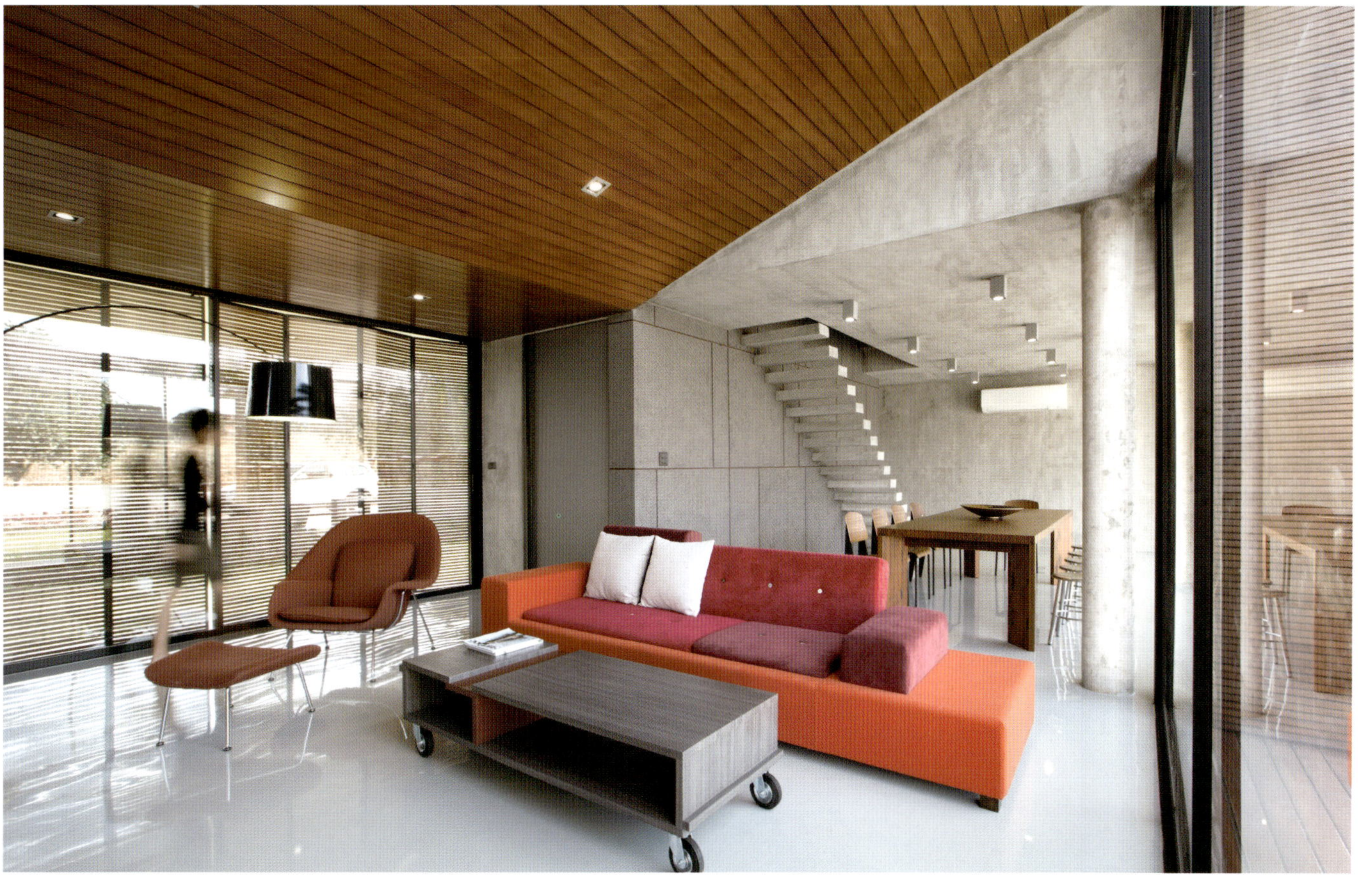

Azuris

The design of **Azuris** responds to three key elements of the location: light, air, and water.

Renato D'Ettorre Architects
Coral Sea, Australia
320sqm

Azuris is a three-bedroom holiday home nestled on a hillside overlooking the Coral Sea with a command of its surroundings.

The design is primarily concerned with creating an ambiguity between the interior and the exterior as well as the public and private areas. This aim is assisted by the climate. In order to facilitate outdoor living, the design features cool, shaded, well ventilated spaces that provide relief from the intense sun.

The design is strictly modern and takes the form of a pavilion with stackable sliding glass doors. An expansive pool wraps around the pavilion, creating a dramatic design element that introduces water's cooling and visual delight to the interior. The pool blends visually with the sea. Two lateral thick walls shield the views from the adjoining properties and enable one to swim above the sea in total privacy. The walls and shading devices are easily opened and adjusted to optimise air flow and moderate sunlight to create a comfortable environment in order to reduce the need for air-conditioning or artificial lighting.

The upper level's living area is close to the pool and has a view of the ocean to the west. The entry courtyard is shielded by high stone walls and has a reflection pond and a fountain that fills the upper level with the soothing sound of water. Directly under the swimming pool are two guest bedrooms with framed views thanks to the deep terraces that provide shade from the westerly sun.

There is also a generously proportioned open living area that remains shaded throughout the day. It is ideal for escaping the heat and sunset viewing.

Renato D'Ettorre Architects

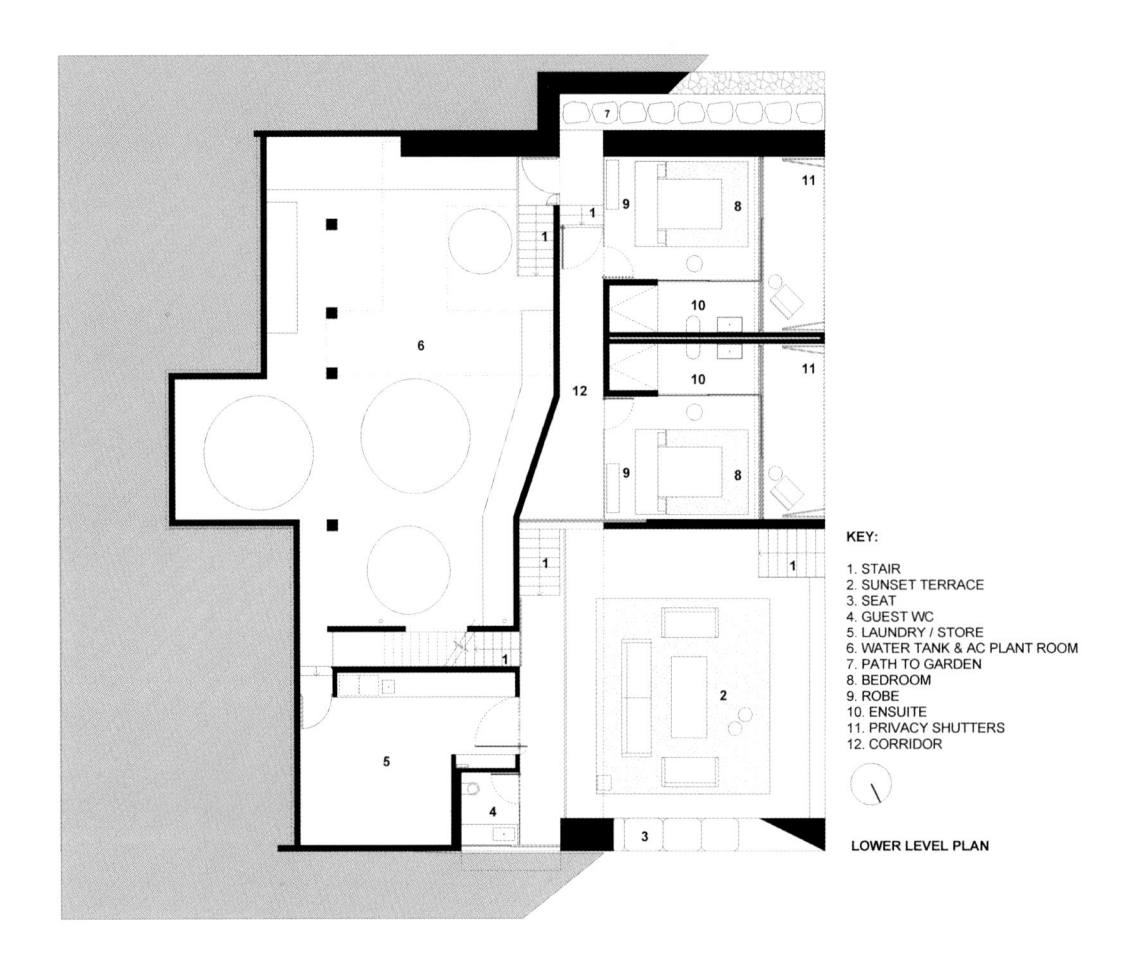

KEY:

1. STAIR
2. SUNSET TERRACE
3. SEAT
4. GUEST WC
5. LAUNDRY / STORE
6. WATER TANK & AC PLANT ROOM
7. PATH TO GARDEN
8. BEDROOM
9. ROBE
10. ENSUITE
11. PRIVACY SHUTTERS
12. CORRIDOR

LOWER LEVEL PLAN

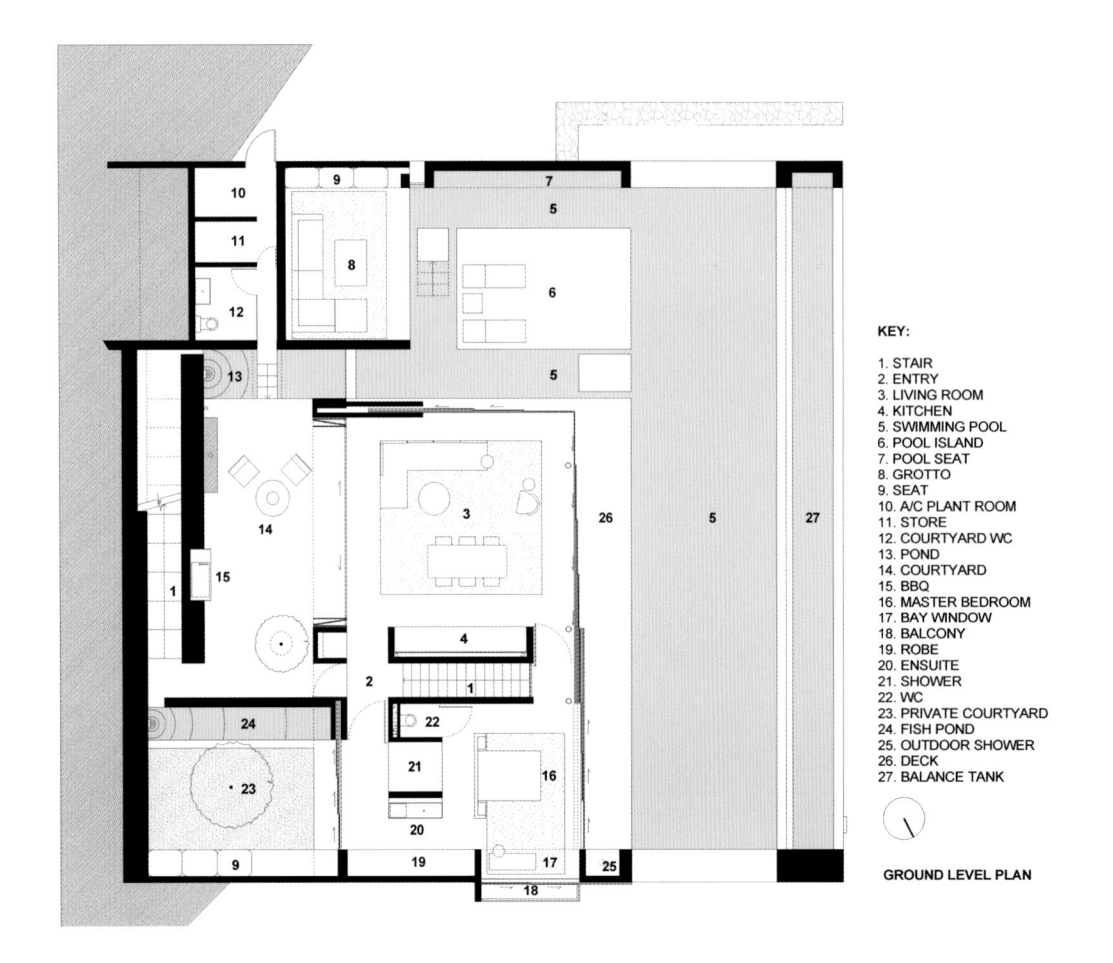

KEY:

1. STAIR
2. ENTRY
3. LIVING ROOM
4. KITCHEN
5. SWIMMING POOL
6. POOL ISLAND
7. POOL SEAT
8. GROTTO
9. SEAT
10. A/C PLANT ROOM
11. STORE
12. COURTYARD WC
13. POND
14. COURTYARD
15. BBQ
16. MASTER BEDROOM
17. BAY WINDOW
18. BALCONY
19. ROBE
20. ENSUITE
21. SHOWER
22. WC
23. PRIVATE COURTYARD
24. FISH POND
25. OUTDOOR SHOWER
26. DECK
27. BALANCE TANK

GROUND LEVEL PLAN

Azuris

Renato D'Ettorre Architects

Photographer's Weekend House
The client wanted **Photographer's Weekend House** to be a space where light and shadow could interplay.

General Design Co., Ltd.
Chiba, Japan
441sqm

The desolate landscape of the 1500sqm site near Kujyukuri Beach made it challenging to find a starting point for this project. After studying the site from a tower overlooking the Pacific Ocean, we decided on a single storey house with four courtyards. The strength and simplicity of the structure suited the expanse of open space. The volume of rough concrete blends in with the desolate landscape as if it had always been there.

In contrast to the simple external volume, the internal space enclosed by the walls is designed to show the depth of space and showcase the interplay of light and shadows. The cross-shaped space formed by the arrangement of the four courtyards in the four corners of the building provides continuity despite the necessary structural walls. The walls are placed to loosely divide the space and allow light and space to play with our visual perceptions to create illusions of distance. There are horizontal spaces connected to the courtyards, dark spaces enclosed within the walls, and vertical spaces that stretch out to the sky. These spaces create and display a continuous play between the inside and outside and between light and shadow.

The client, who is a photographer, wanted the designers to create a space where light and shadow could interplay. Natural light shines into the building through the courtyards throughout the day. Sometimes the light reflects off the walls, creating a mirror-like effect. At other times it casts interesting shadows in the courtyards. The house is in a state of constant change due to the continual play of light and shadow.

General Design Co., Ltd.

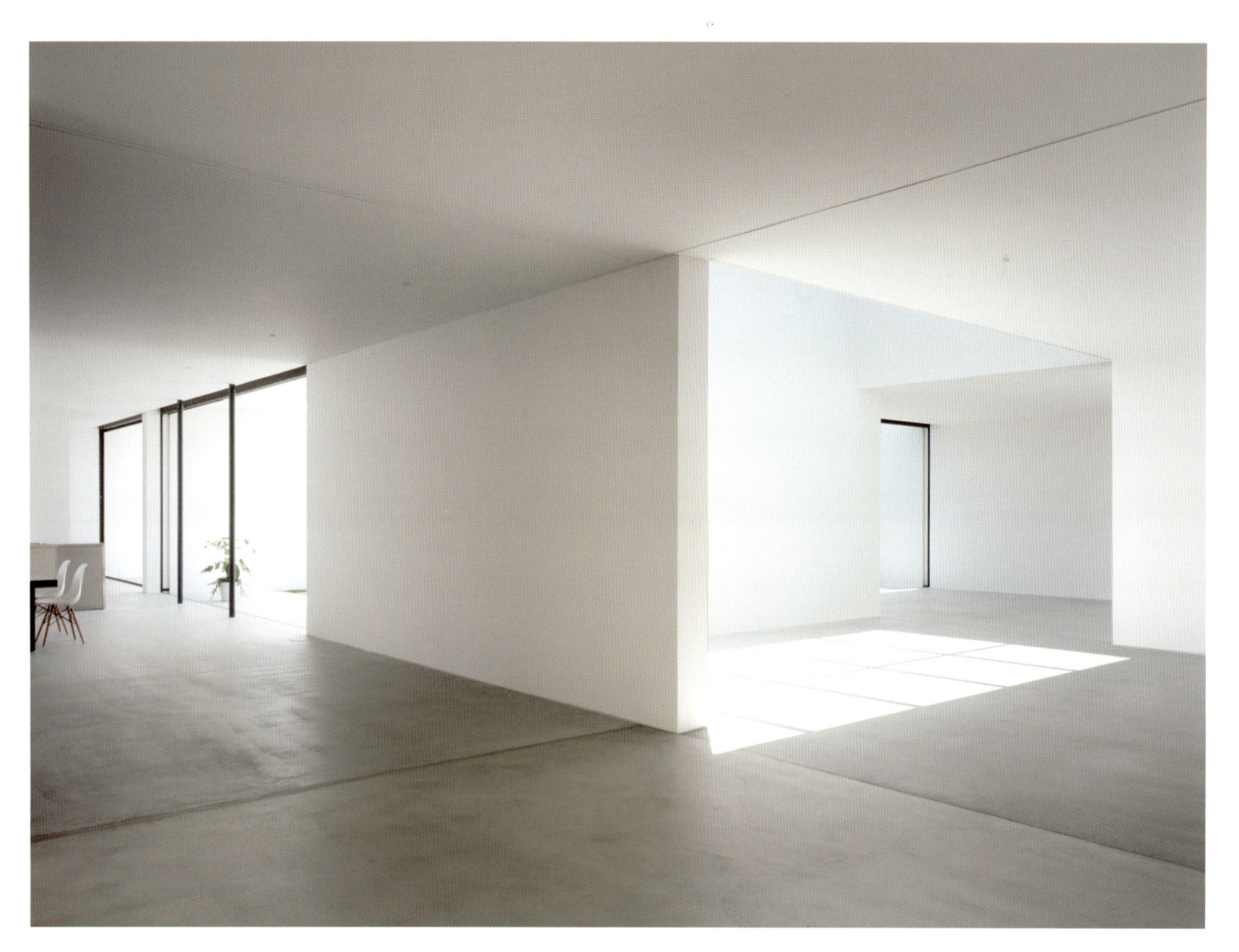

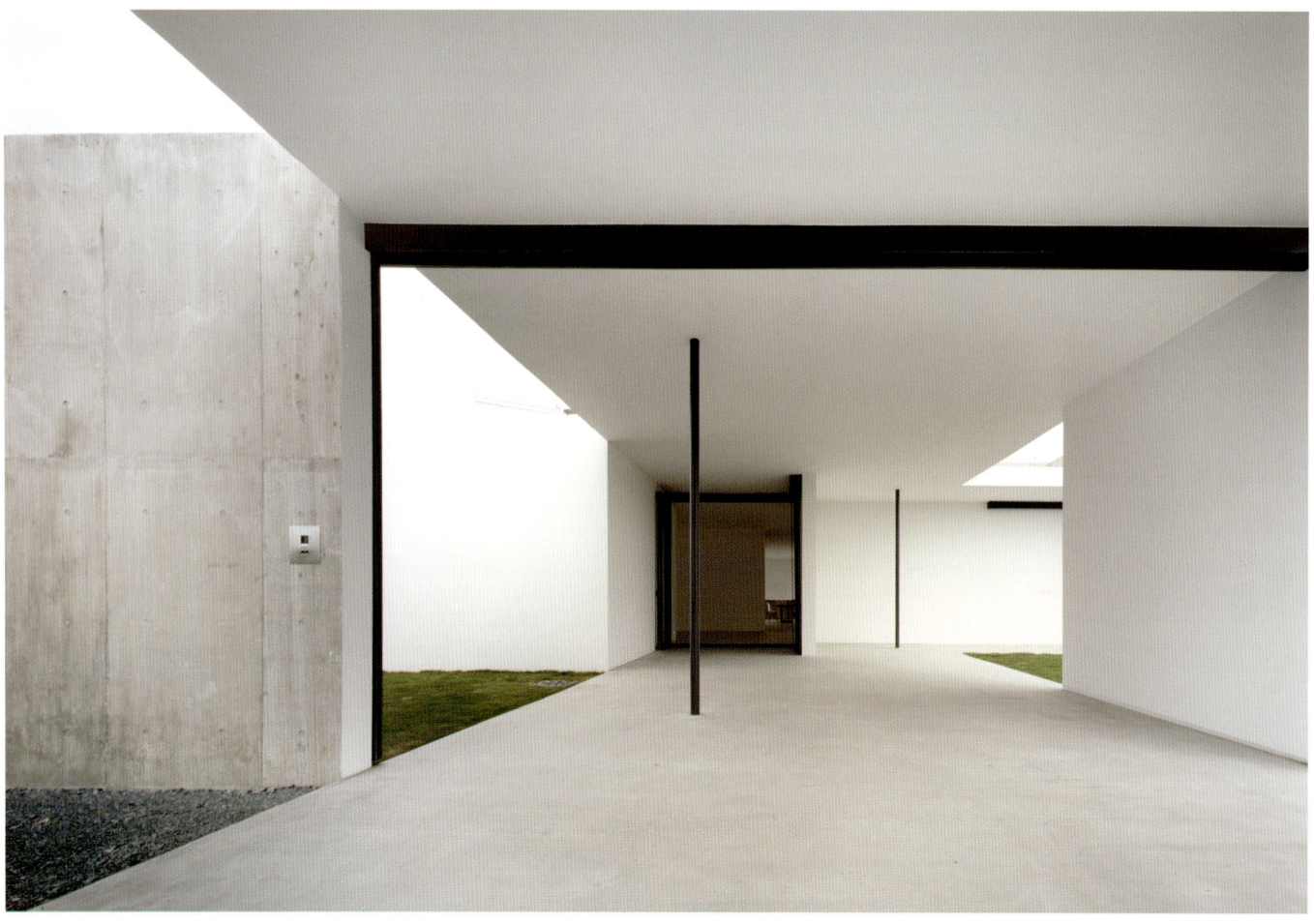

Photographer's Weekend House

General Design Co., Ltd.

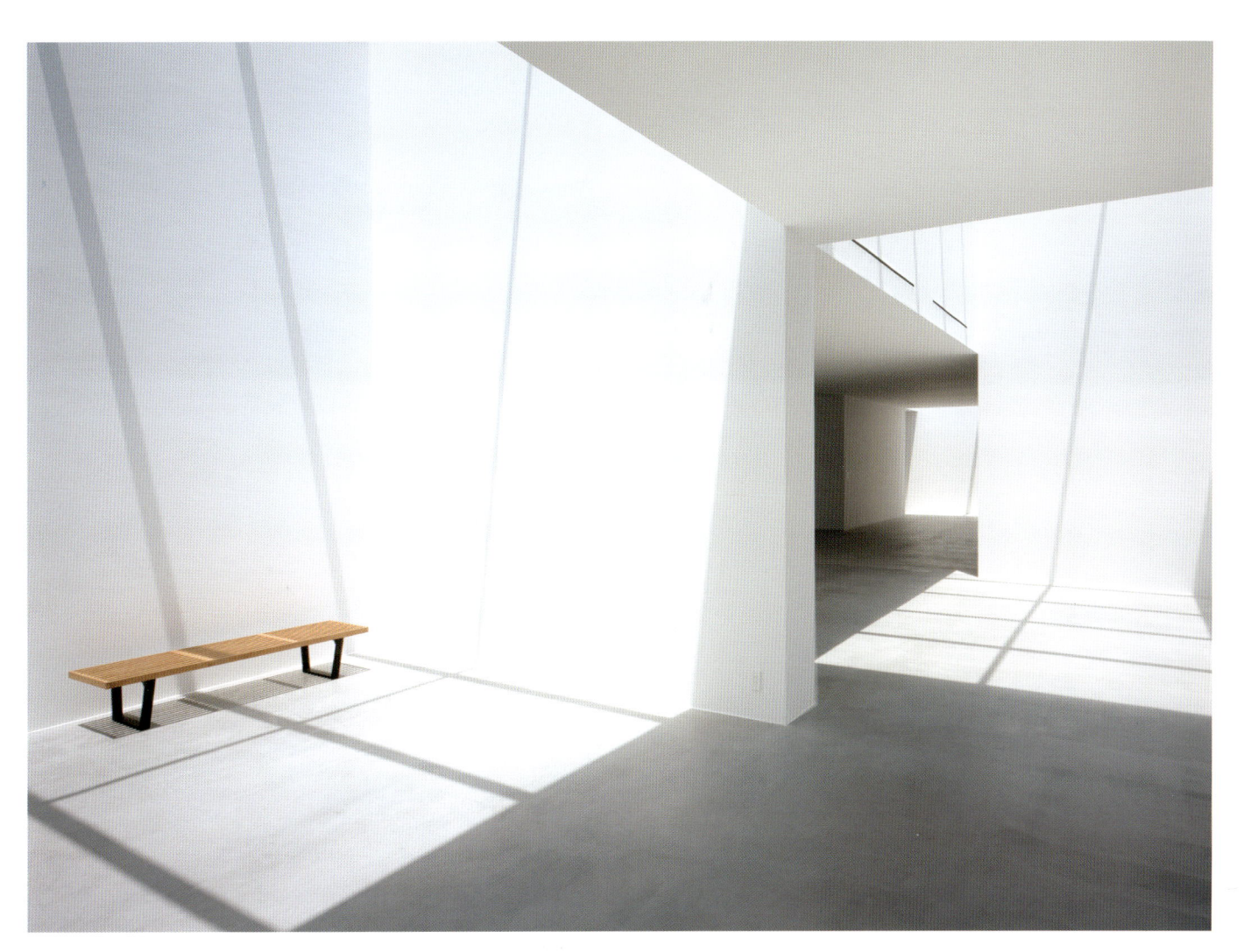

105

Garden Tree House
A Zelkova tree and a Camphor tree have been standing on the site of **Garden Tree House** for 35 years.

Hironaka Ogawa & Associates
Kagawa, Japan
50.9sqm

The two-storey extension branches out into the garden of the 35-year-old family house to provide a residence for the client's daughter and her husband.

Two trees stood in the way of construction and had to be removed beforehand, but the architect was concerned about the connection they had to the family's history. "These trees looked over the family for 35 years," he explained.

The designer decided to keep the trees intact, dry them out, and insert them into a double-height living and dining room. The floor was placed just below ground level in order to accommodate the trees' height.

Utilising these trees and creating a new place for the client became the main theme for the design. The family asked a Shinto priest to perform an exorcism on the trees as they were cut down.

The residence contains a mezzanine loft that squeezes in alongside the trees. The bathrooms are tucked away below it.

The walls and ceilings are painted white, allowing the yellow and brown shades of the trees to stand out.

Hironaka Ogawa & Associates

Garden Tree House

Hironaka Ogawa & Associates

Garden Tree House

Hironaka Ogawa & Associates

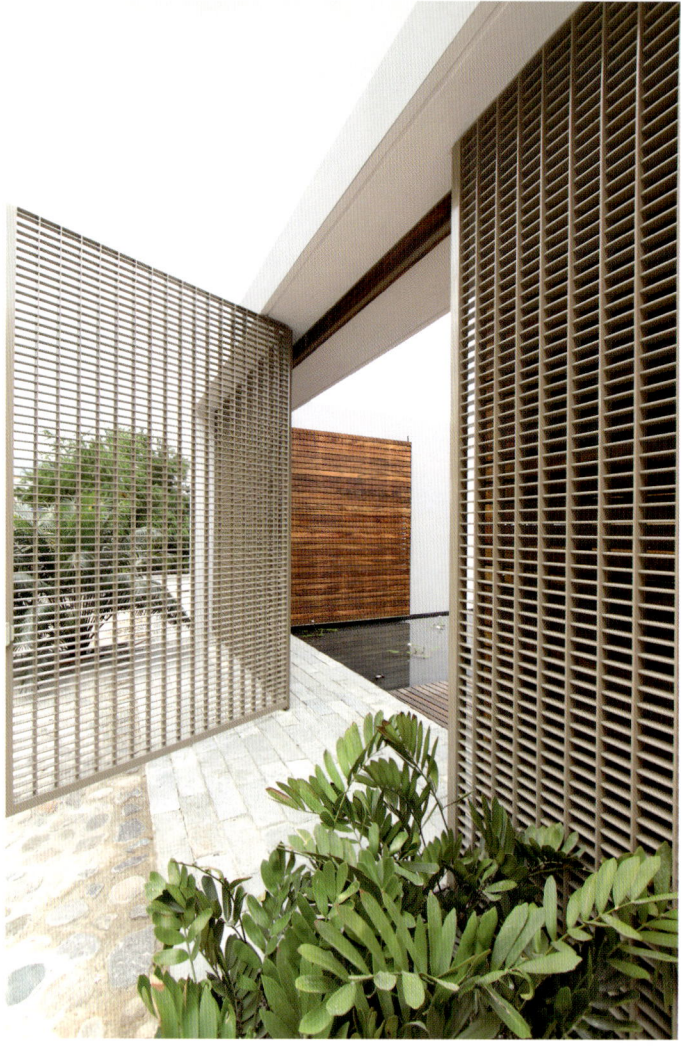

Casa Almare

Casa Almare develops through four floors that take advantage of the breathtaking views of the bay.

Elías Rizo Arquitectos
Puerto Vallarta, México
837sqm

The house is situated on a cliff overlooking Bahía de Banderas. The extraordinary beauty of the location provided the inspiration for the project's contemporary architecture.

The two driving motifs of the project were the verticality of the site and its direct contact with the ocean. The project develops through four floors that take advantage of the breathtaking views of the bay. The main entrance has a direct and uninterrupted view of the ocean and the horizon, hinting at what one will find throughout the whole of the project. The street façade conceals the size of the house with its discreet appearance, but it displays the clean lines and careful aesthetic of the whole project.

The top floor, which is at street level, is comprised of two blocks that are divided by a central patio and connected by a bridge. The first block contains the main entrance, parking, storage areas, engine room, and staff quarters. The second block houses a terrace area, a bathroom, bar, and laundry room.

Each floor opens onto a patio that acts as a buffer between the house and the cliff. This design allows light to enter the rooms off the patios and keeps the house well-ventilated. The two floors below contain four suites – two per floor – each with its own bathroom, dressing room, and terrace with a private pool.

The first floor houses the living and dining areas, the kitchen, a storage area, the laundry room, the master suite, a guest bedroom, and the main terrace, which is surrounded by an infinity pool.

Elías Rizo Arquitectos

Casa Almare

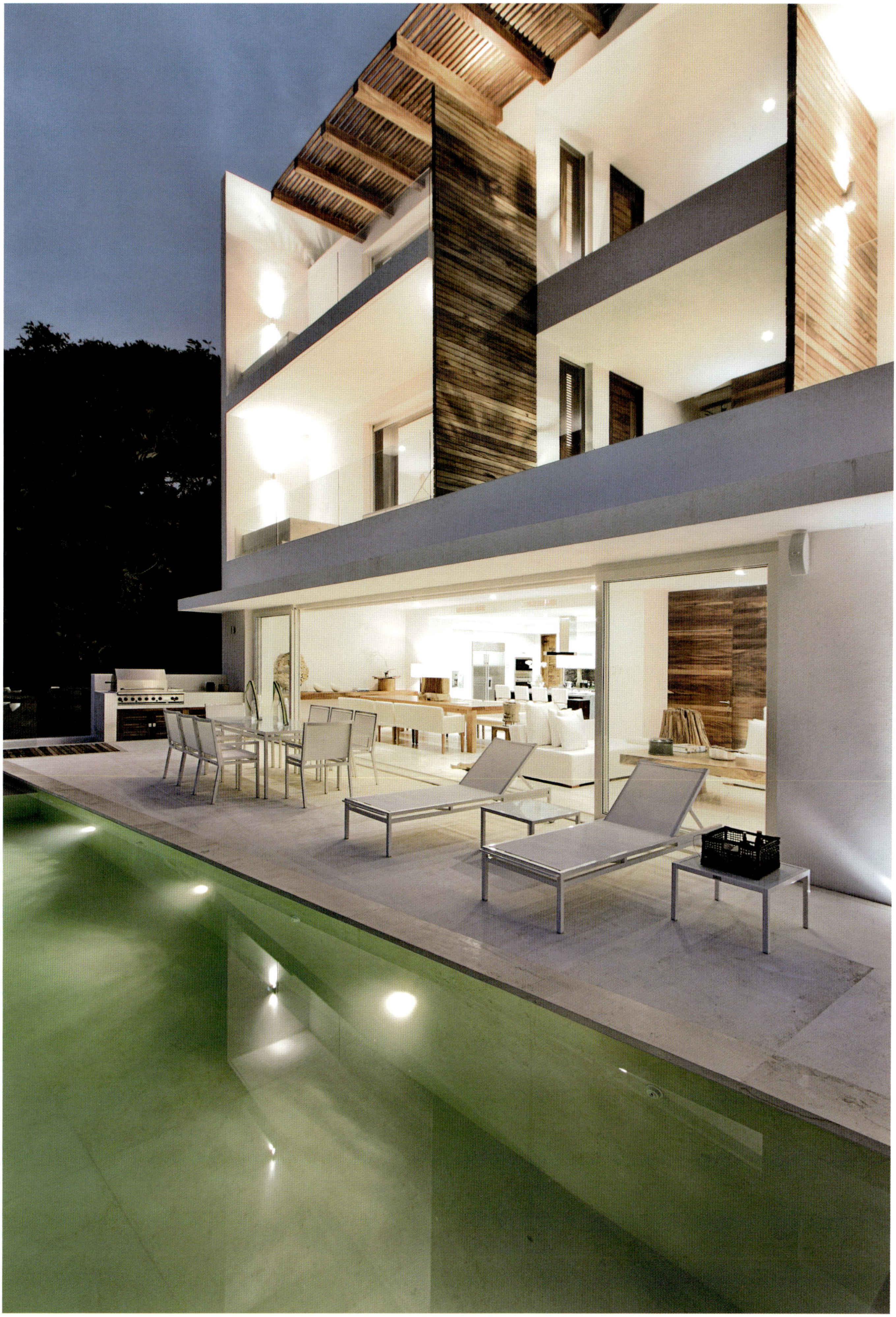

Casa Almare

Elías Rizo Arquitectos

House in Hiyoshi
The simple design of **House in Hiyoshi** accommodates the client's plans for the future.

EANA
Yokohama, Japan
91.1sqm

This house designed for a married couple is located off the south side of a city park on a hill. The house provides views of the neighboring residential district as well as the greenery of the park on its north side.

The simple design accommodates the client's finances and plans for the future. A bedroom for a future child was included in the plan. This bedroom, along with the couple's bedroom, a bathroom, and storage space are located on the first floor.

The living room's ceiling is 4 meters high. The height of the ceiling enabled us to include a large window that allows the sky and greenery from the park into the room.

EANA

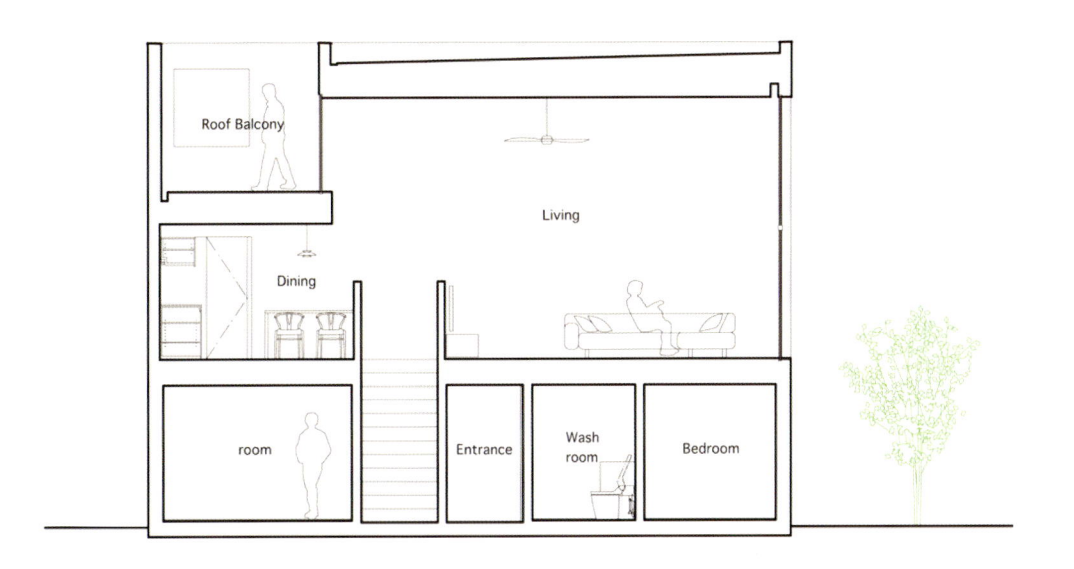

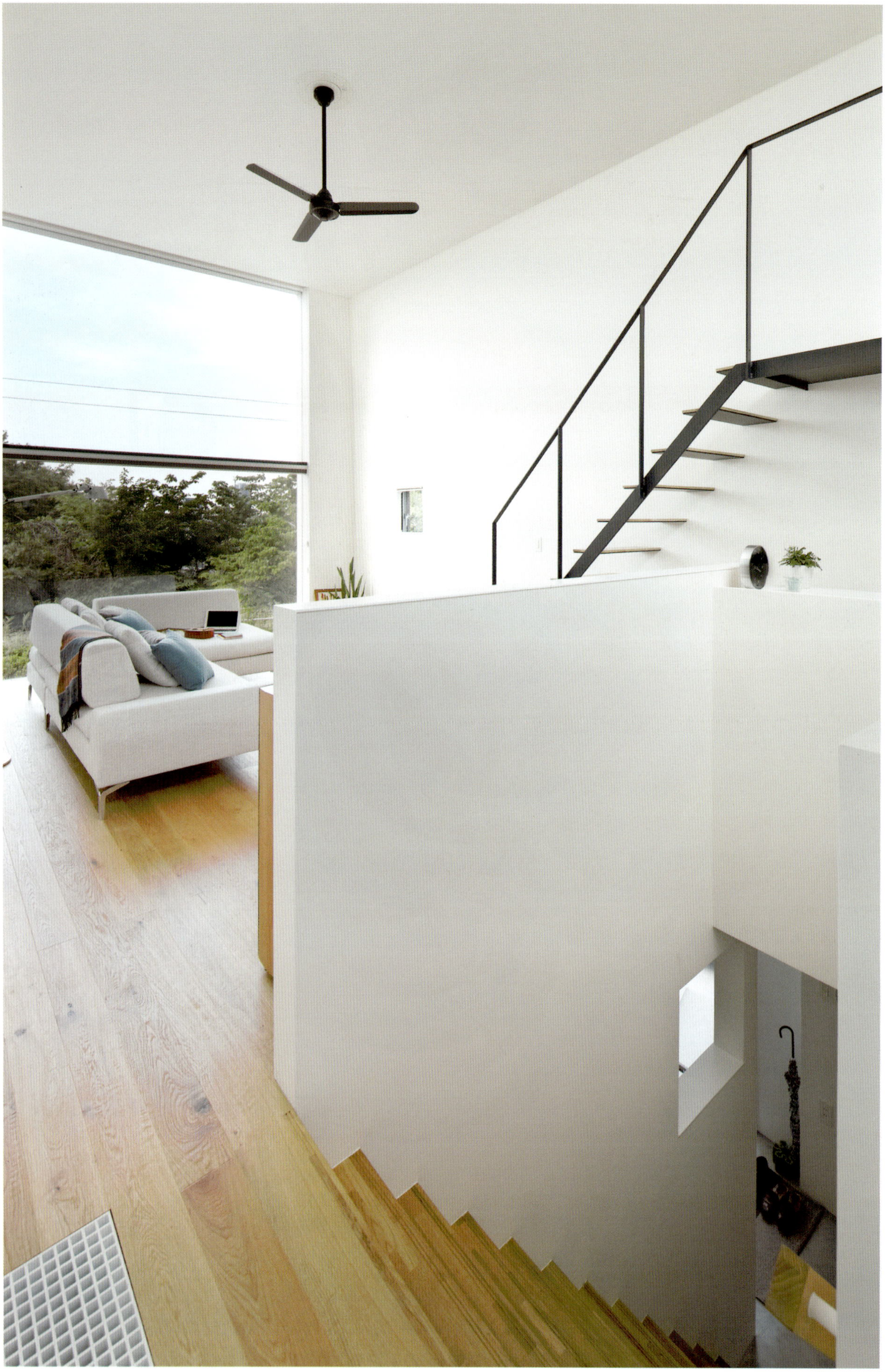

EANA

Toilet
Kitchen
Dining
Living
DN
UP

Roof Balcony
Void
DN

House in Hiyoshi

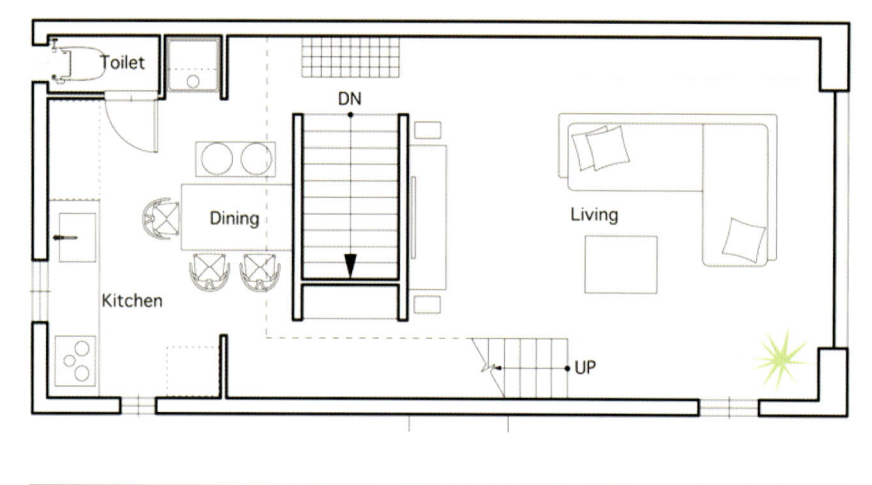

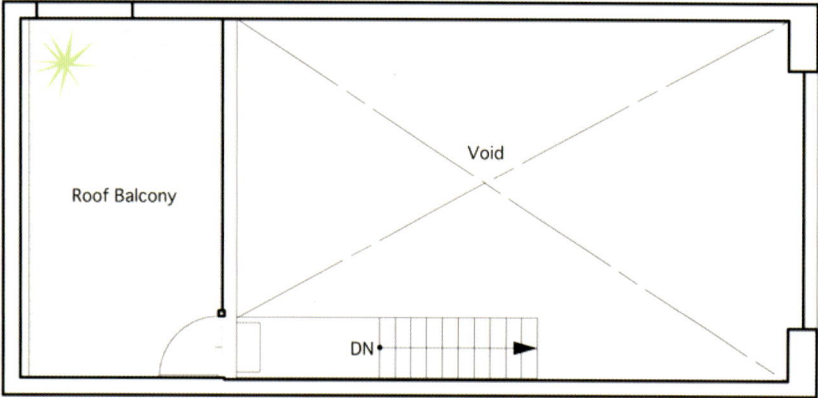

EANA

House in Shimoda

House in Shimoda is defined by three distinct containers and plays with the relationship between the interior and exterior spaces.

EANA
Yokohama, Japan
142.6sqm

House in Shimoda was designed with open and closed spaces in order to suit the client's lifestyle. Because it is located in a densely populated area, it is possible that the residence will some day be more closely surrounded by other houses. The design had to take that possibility into consideration and ensure that, among other things, there was adequate space for turning vehicles. The owner also wanted a large uninterrupted living room to welcome guests.

The client wanted a nesting design composed of three boxes. Another defining aspect of the design is that the entryway penetrates to the center of the house. This feature allows light to enter the living room.

This project explores a new possibility for the relationship between interior and exterior spaces.

EANA 125

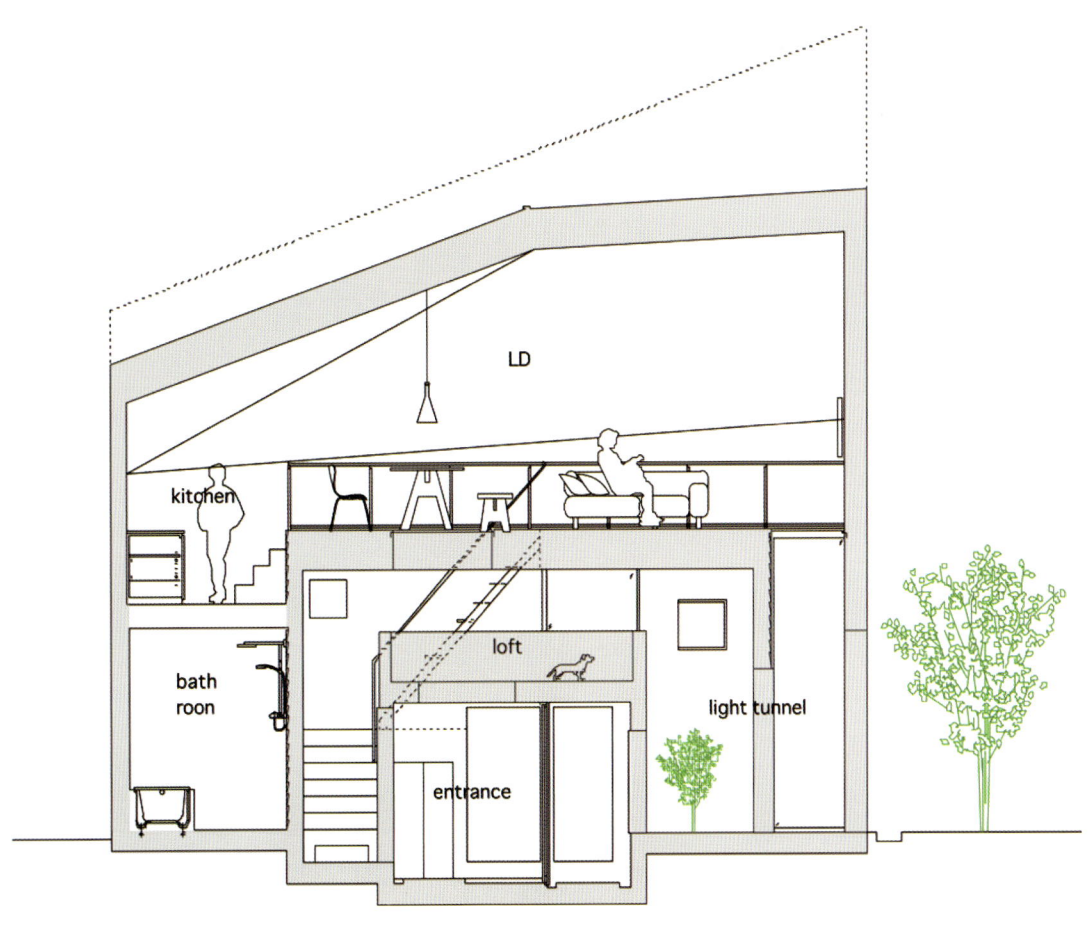

House in Shimoda

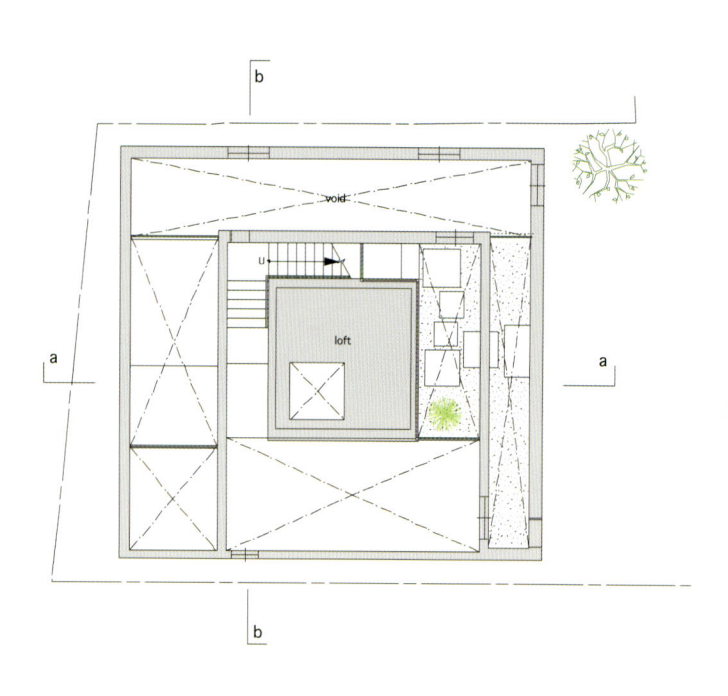

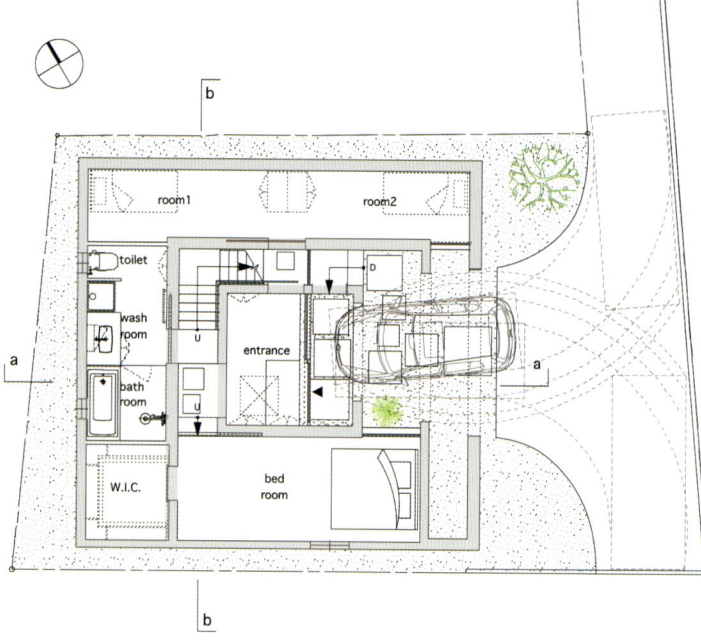

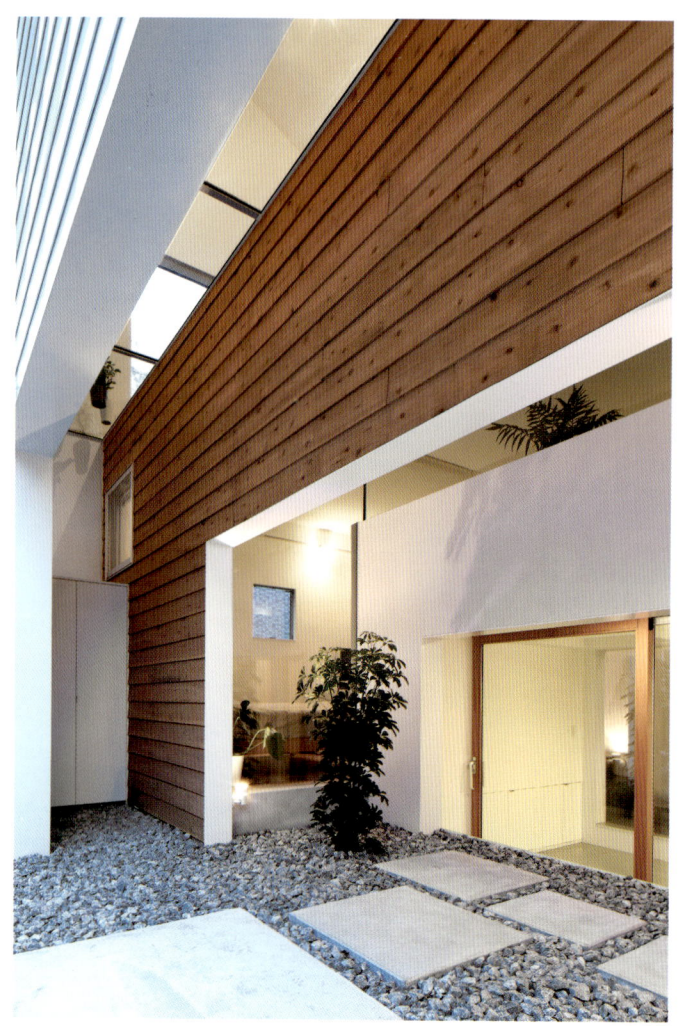

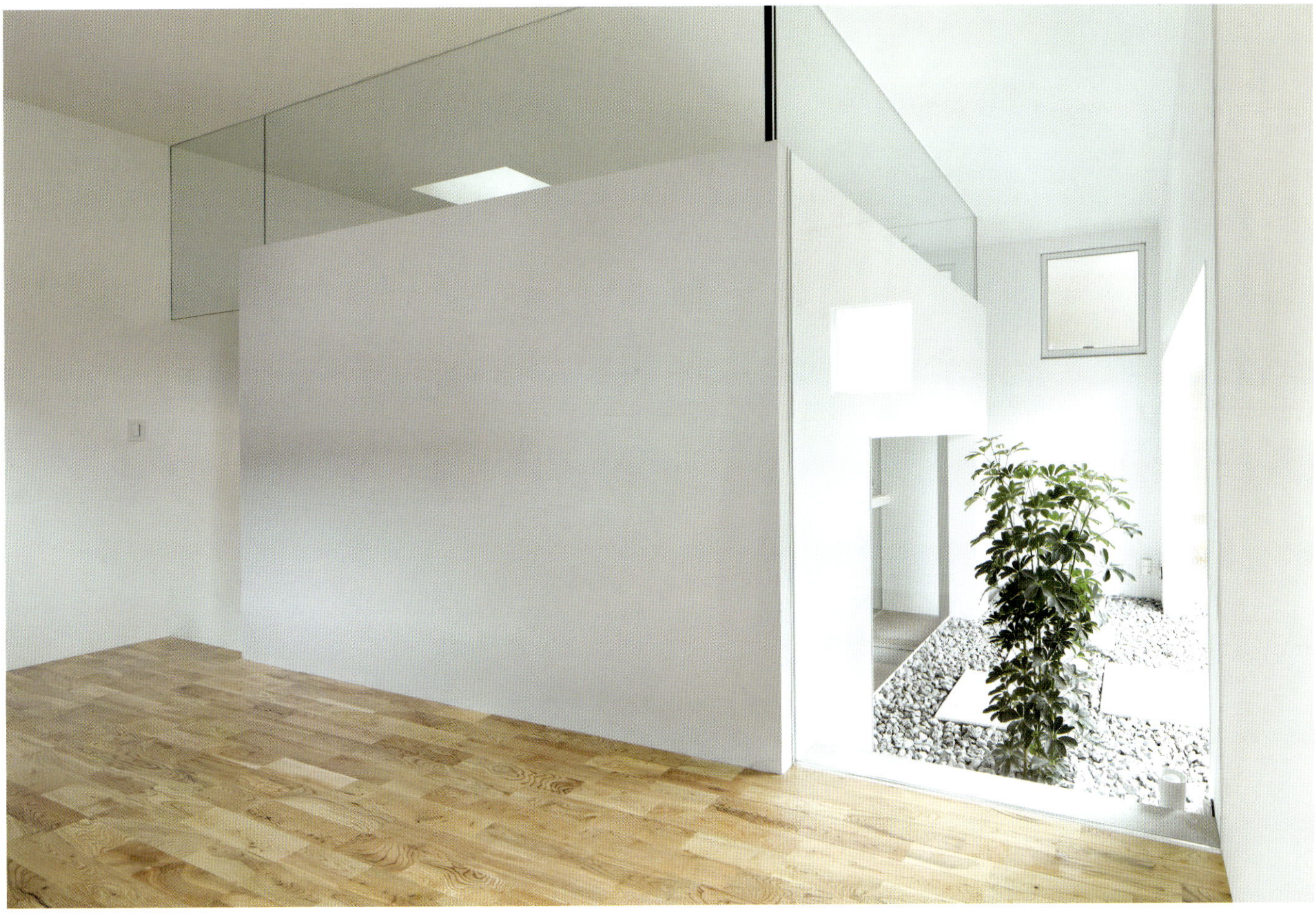

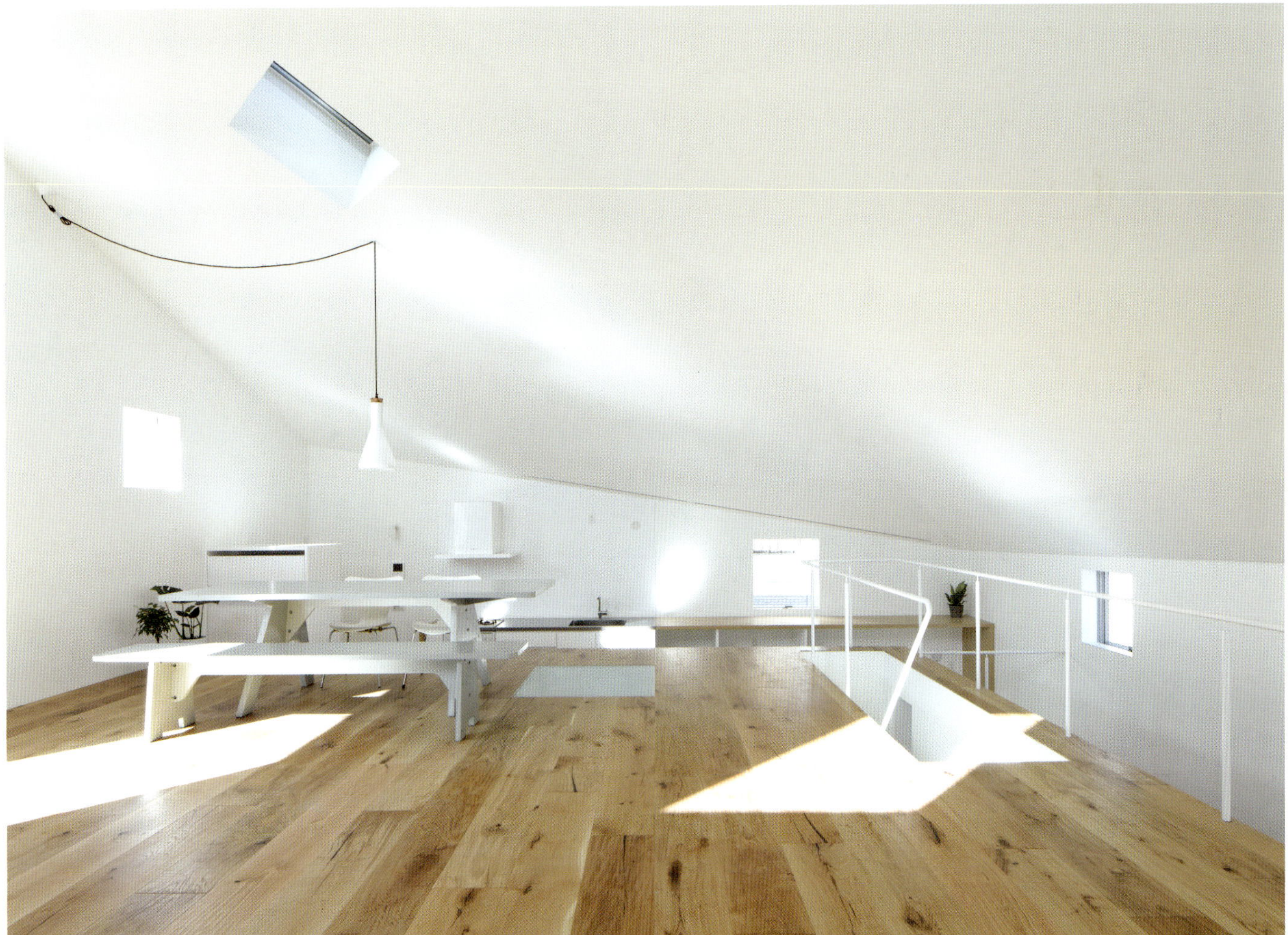

House in Shimoda

EANA 129

Hye Ro Hun

Hye Ro Hun is a dramatic sequence of spaces and features a floating garden.

IROJE KHM Architects
Gwangju, South Korea
168.6sqm

This site is located between a city and mountains. The house has a view of downtown Gwangju as well as one of the mountains on the west side. After passing through a transparent gate, a long walkway leads through an architectural canyon, passes under the upper corridor bridge, and ends at an inner court off the entrance to the house.

Two wooden boxes sit atop a volume that contains the living room and the dining room. One box contains the master bedroom and a study while the other houses two bedrooms and a study for the owner's daughters.

A floating garden sits above the living room. Skylights allow light to shine into the living room. The changing light alters the atmosphere of the room throughout the day.

The house is a dramatic sequence of horizontal, vertical, interior, and exterior spaces.

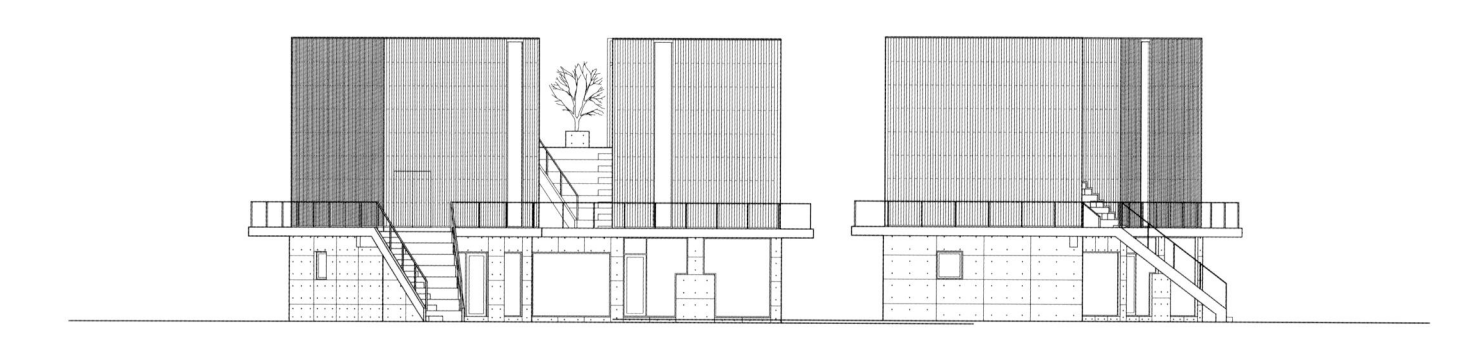

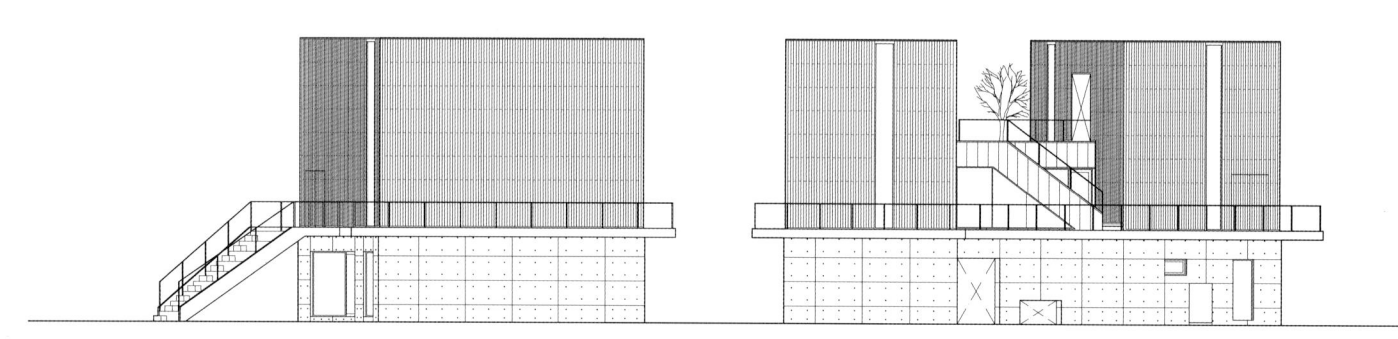

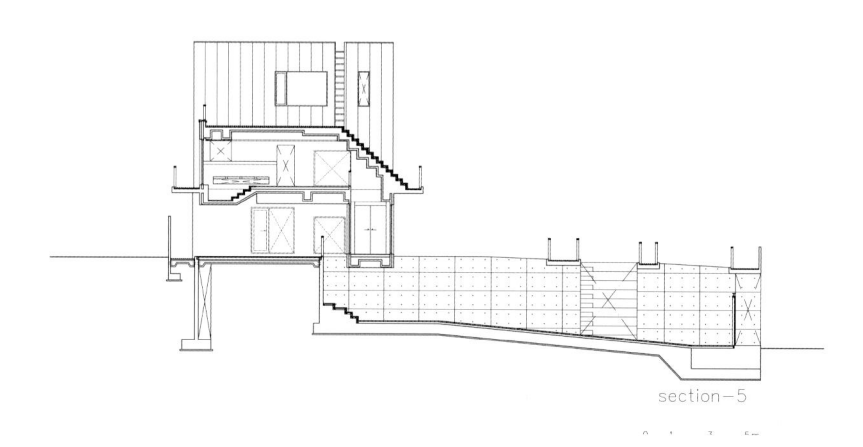

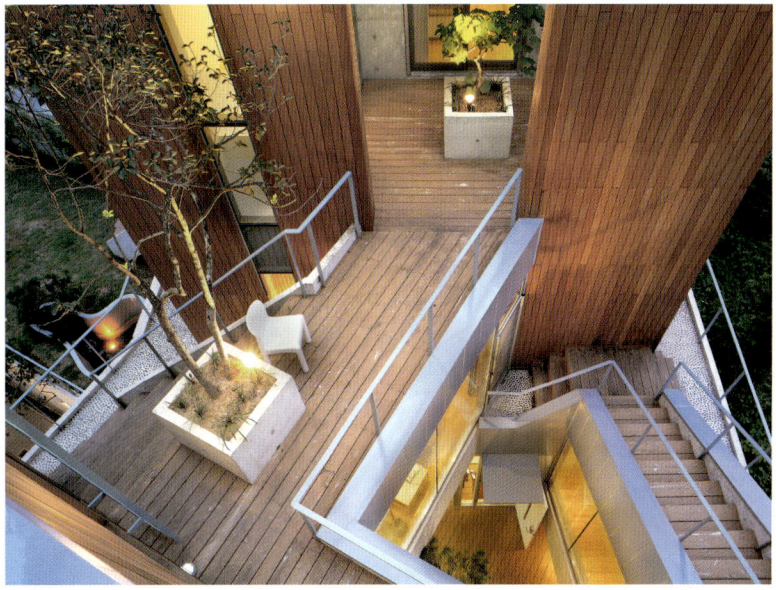

IROJE KHM Architects 131

third floor

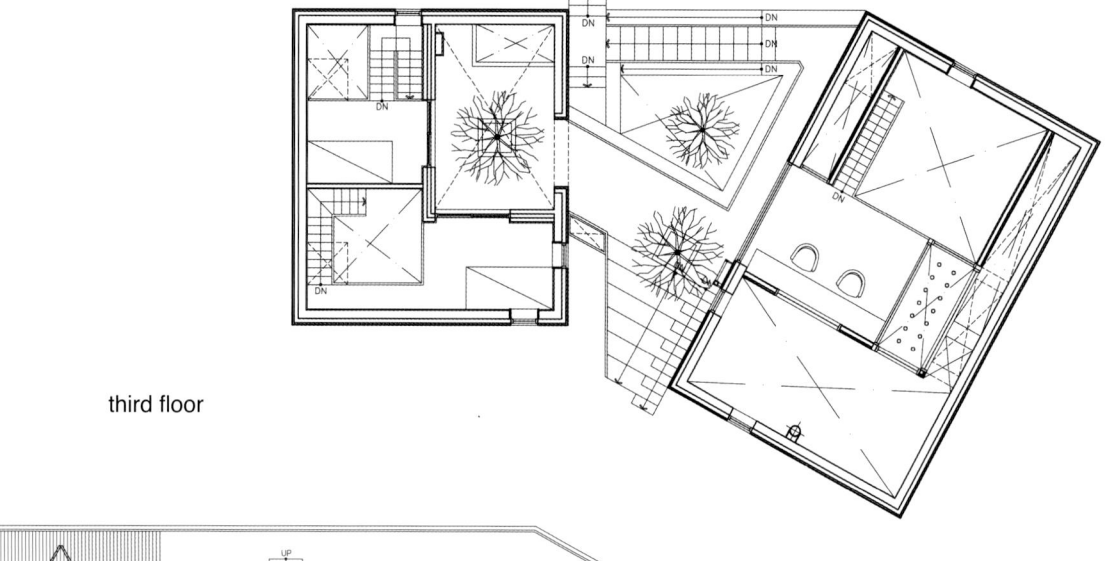

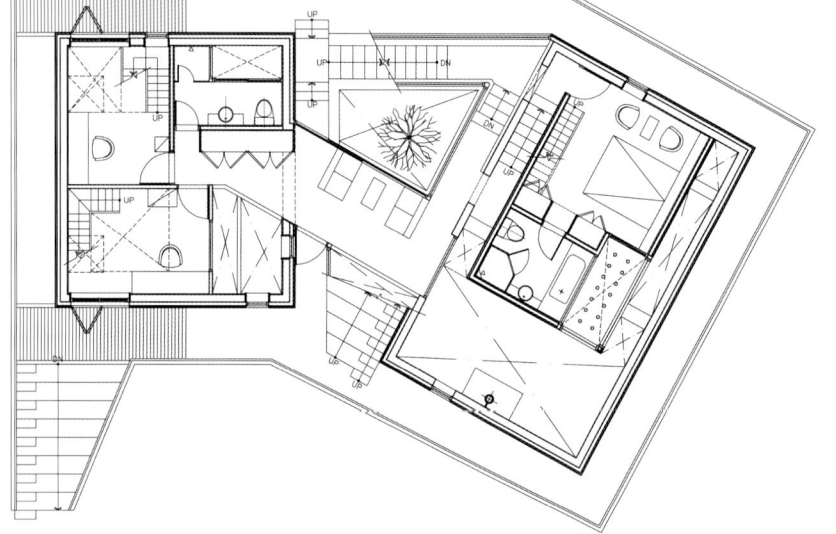

second floor

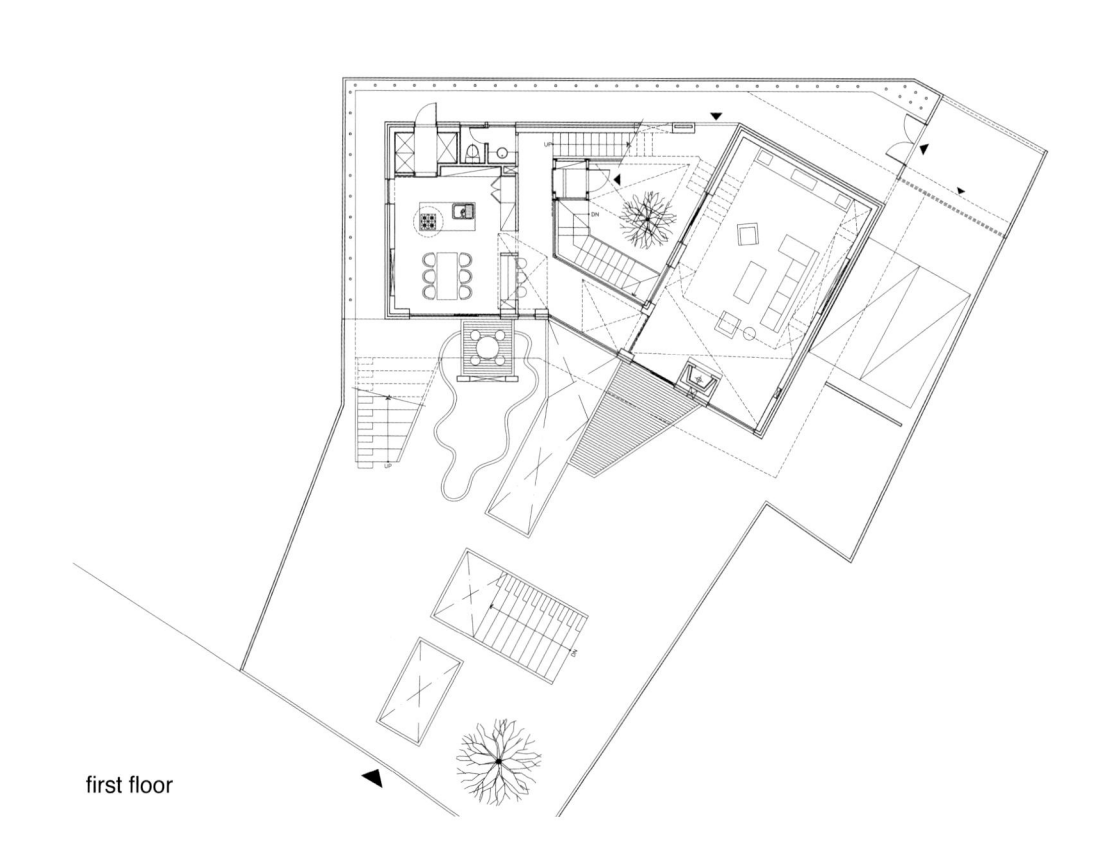

first floor

Hye Ro Hun

IROJE KHM Architects

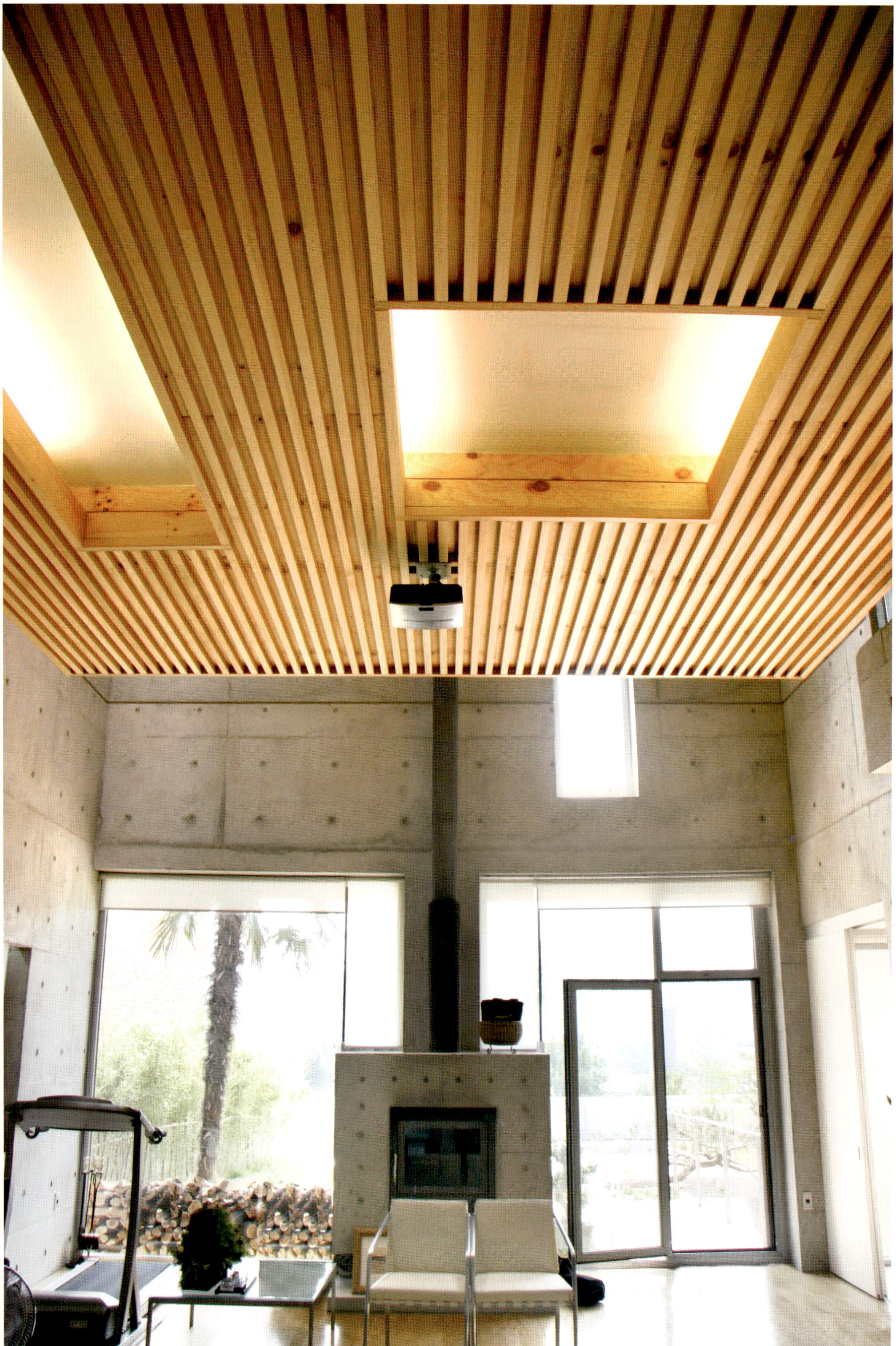

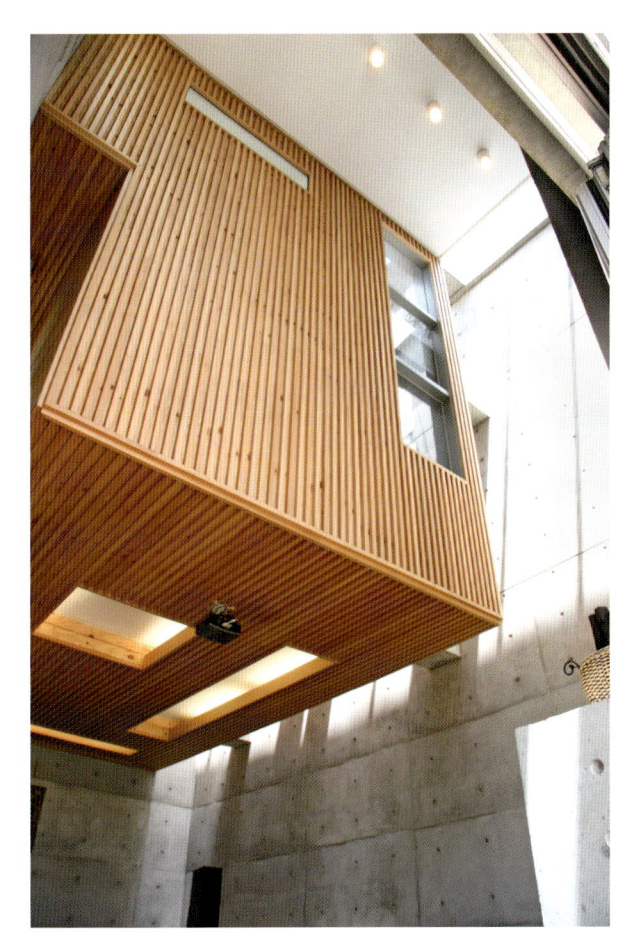

IROJE KHM Architects

Can Manuel d'en Corda

The extension of **Can Manuel d'en Corda** offers views of the island of Es Vedra.

Daniel Redolat + Marià Castelló Architects
Formentera, Spain
595.3sqm

The original house, which reflects the architecture common in Formentera between the late eighteenth and mid nineteenth centuries, and the small forest of pines and junipers on the west side of the estate were preserved during the course of the project. The main volume has a pitched roof and traditional stone walls tying it to its location.

The extension was planned to follow current urban parameters while distorting the original building as little as possible. To accomplish this, fragmented volumes were positioned in a non-orthogonal pattern, attaching to the original structure at the southwest and northeast sides.

This design made it possible to leave the southeast and northwest façades intact. The new structure has the added advantage of making better use of natural light.

Although the original main entrance to the house was maintained, the extension faces the opposite direction and thus enjoys the views overlooking the island of Es Vedra to the northwest.

Daniel Redolat + Marià Castelló Architects

Can Manuel d'en Corda

Daniel Redolat + Marià Castelló Architects

Can Manuel d'en Corda

Daniel Redolat + Marià Castelló Architects

House on the Cliff

House on the Cliff is a monolithic volume that projects out toward the sea.

Fran Silvestre Arquitectos
Alicante, Spain
242sqm

This bright white house features an 18-metre-long balcony that stretches out toward the Balearic Sea. Concrete was used for the entire structure and the walls were coated in stucco to create the clean white aesthetic.

Due to the steepness of the land and in order to contain the living space on a single floor, a three-dimensional structure made of reinforced concrete was designed to fit the topography of the land. The monolithic structure has a horizontal platform at the street level that contains the living area. A staircase climbs through and across an exterior wall to connect the living space to a terrace with an infinity pool. The pool sits close to the sea and a quiet cove. The concrete construction has external thermal insulation with a flexible, smooth, white grout lime coating. The remaining materials, including the walls, flooring, and roof ballasting are all the same color to give the house a homogenous character. The sea views are spectacular and invite you to spend time, relax, and do nothing.

The architects explained that they always try to design houses around the habits of future residents. "Dialogue is always present, since the work becomes part of the identity of those who inhabit it," they explained. "This dialogue seeks comfort and also utility, and examines the conflicts and joys of daily human life."

Fran Silvestre Arquitectos

143

House on the Cliff

Fran Silvestre Arquitectos

145

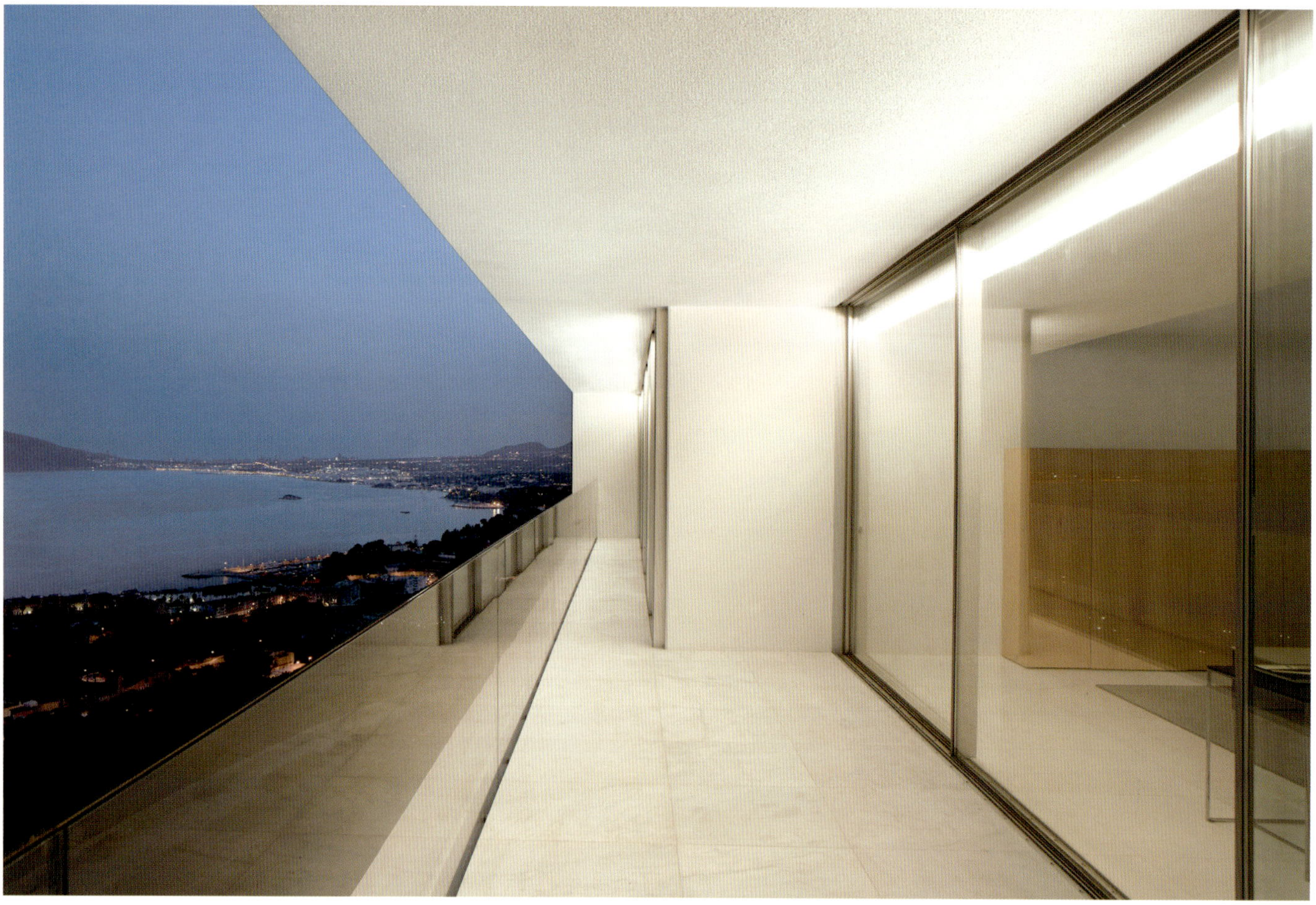

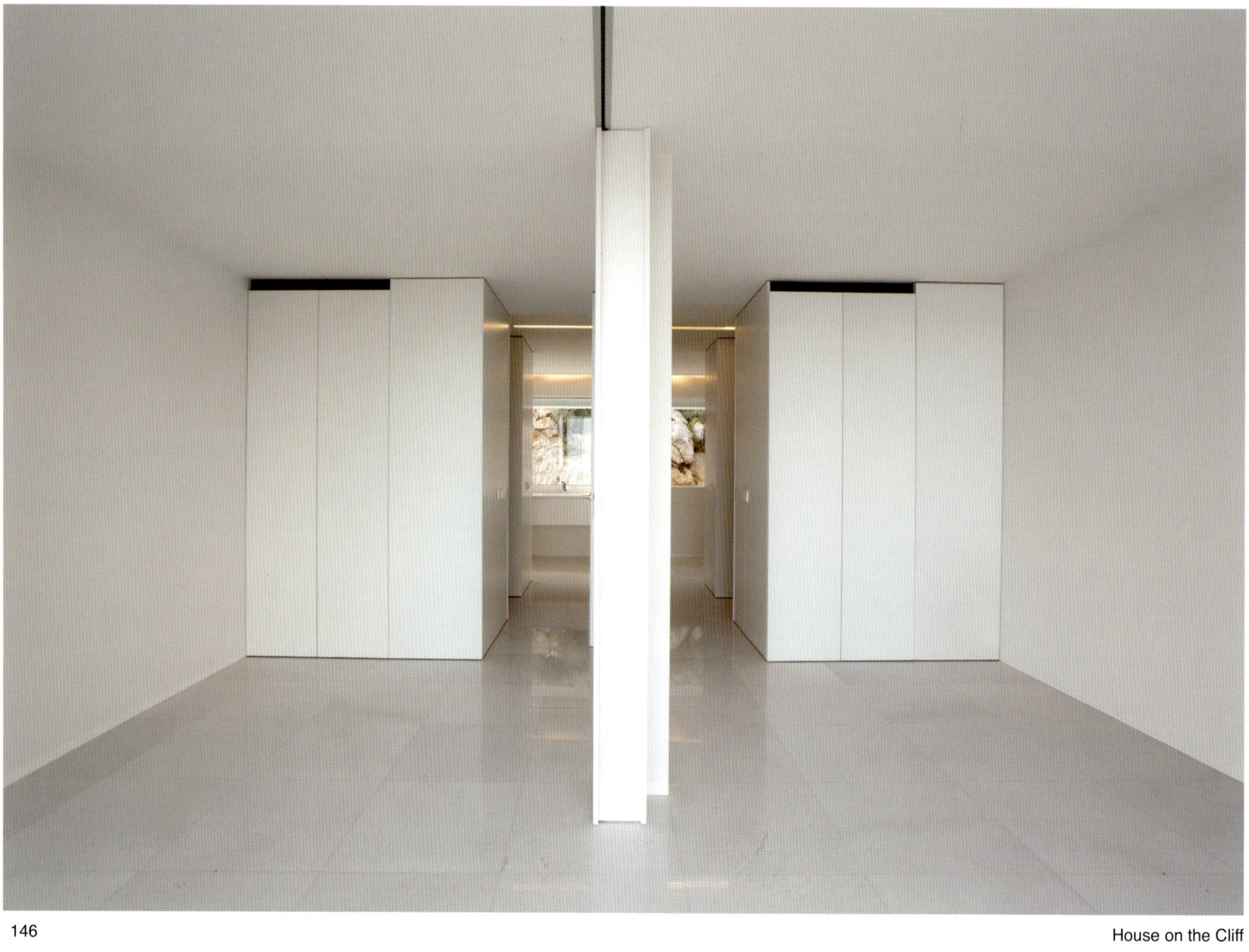

Fran Silvestre Arquitectos

147

Colunata House

Colunata House contrasts with the rocky landscape of the shore and the surrounding water lends it tranquility.

Mário Martins Atelier
Algarve, Portugal
365sqm

When designing this house, the designers wanted to make the most of the location and its panoramic views and create a contemporary architectural element that connected with the surrounding area. In order to make the exterior a pleasant space for living and leisure, it was important to create a gentle transition between the interior and exterior. The designers also wanted to use local materials and building techniques, and ensure effective wind protection. The result was a set of freely and organically grouped white volumes that form a semi-circle to embrace the pool and the view of the sea. The terrace around the pool is the main space of the house. It offers privacy and showcases the spectacular view of the horizon.

The house is structured around the terrace on a single floor. There are five bedrooms with bathrooms and a large living room leads to the kitchen.

The intense light, with its strong and distinct shadows, gives color and variance to the white of the house. The surrounding water and landscape lend tranquility to the house.

Mário Martins Atelier

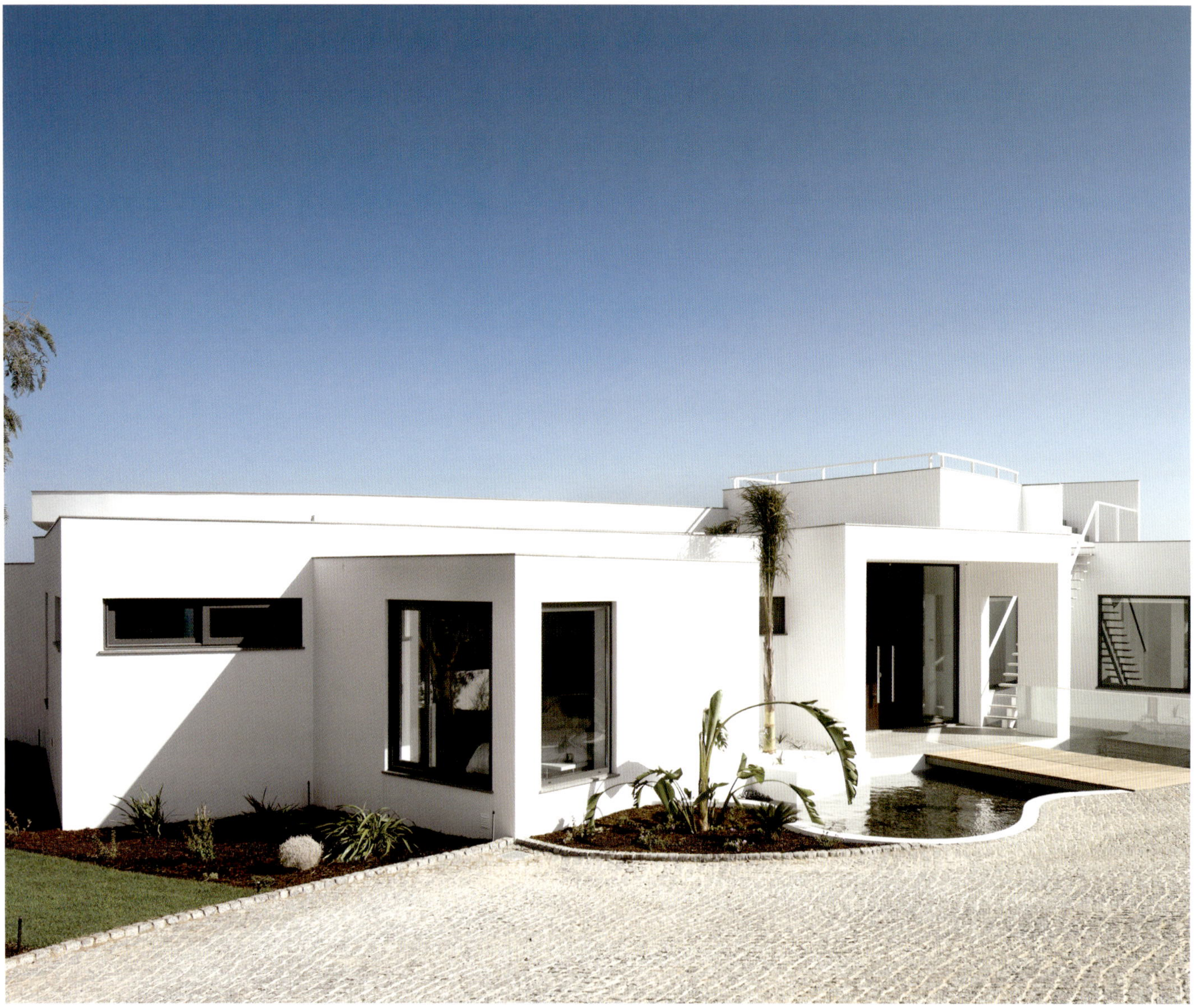

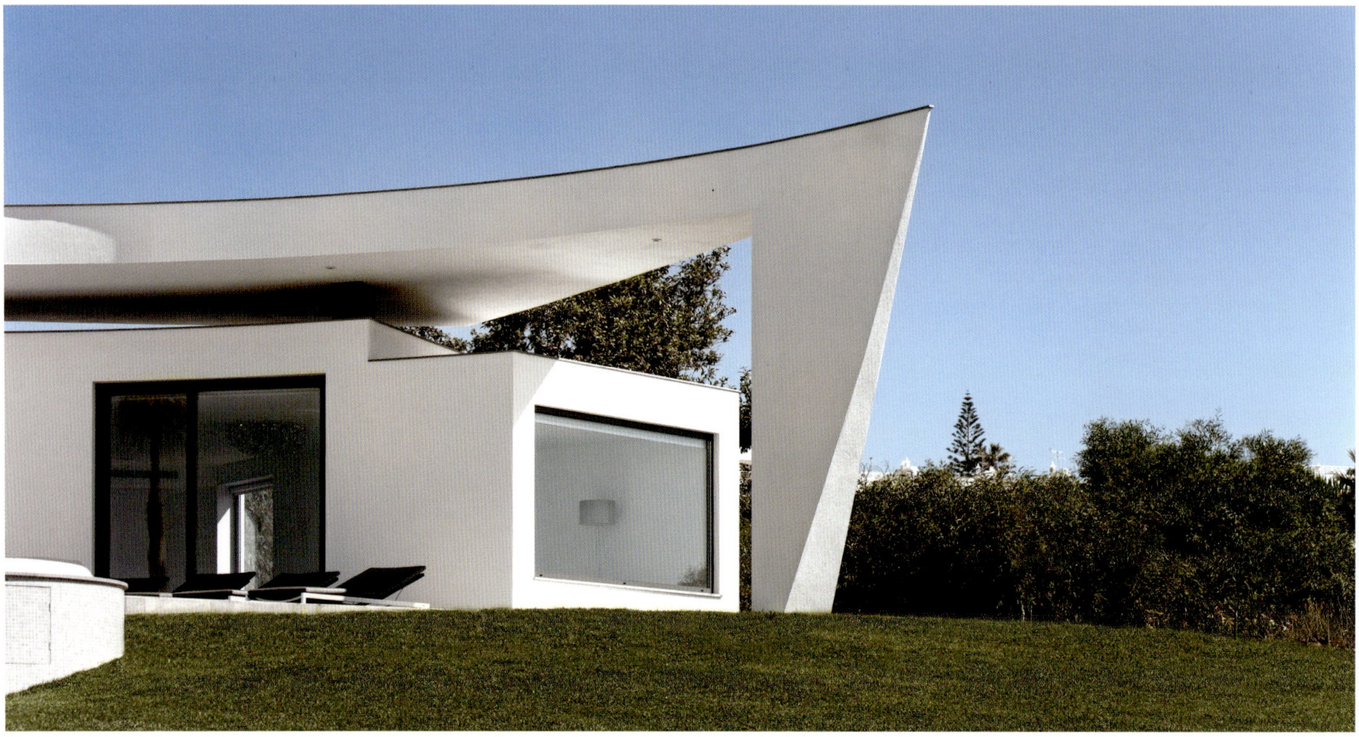

Mário Martins Atelier

151

House in Travanca

Each storey of House in Travanca is treated as a separate volume of meticulously poured and colored concrete, resulting in a pleasing orthogonal composition of layers.

Nelson Resende Arquitecto
Santa Maria da Feira, Portugal
456sqm

This spectacular contemporary house draws its form from its irregular sloped site - the three levels respond directly to the differing elevations. Each storey is treated as a separate volume of meticulously poured and colored concrete, resulting in a pleasing orthogonal composition of layers. The lower floor is partially embanked and opens out onto the garden at the rear of the house. The first floor provides direct access to the street level at the front, while reserving private access to the terraced upper lawn and backyard pool. The upper floor projects towards the horizon, capturing expansive views of the Atlantic Coast.

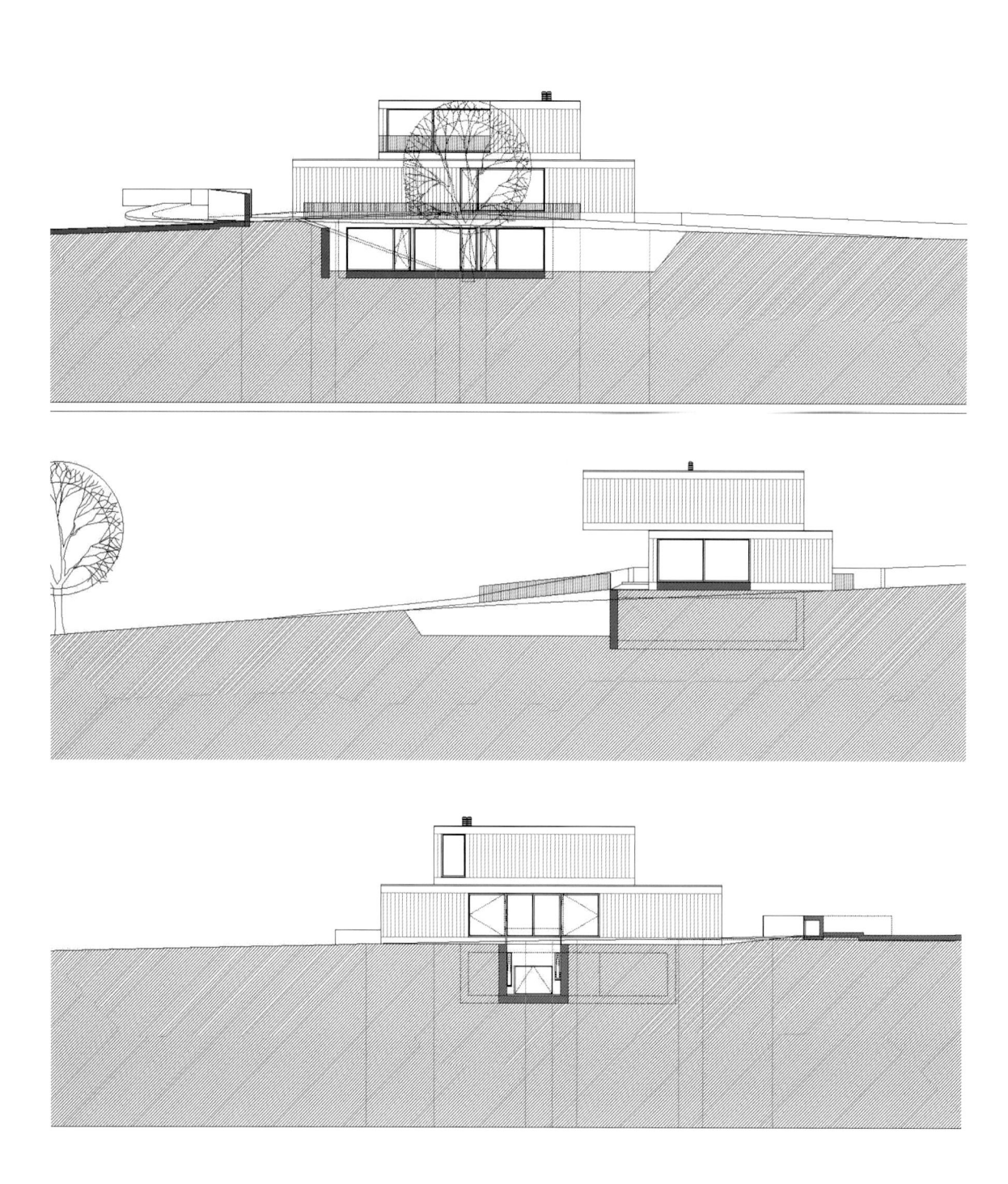

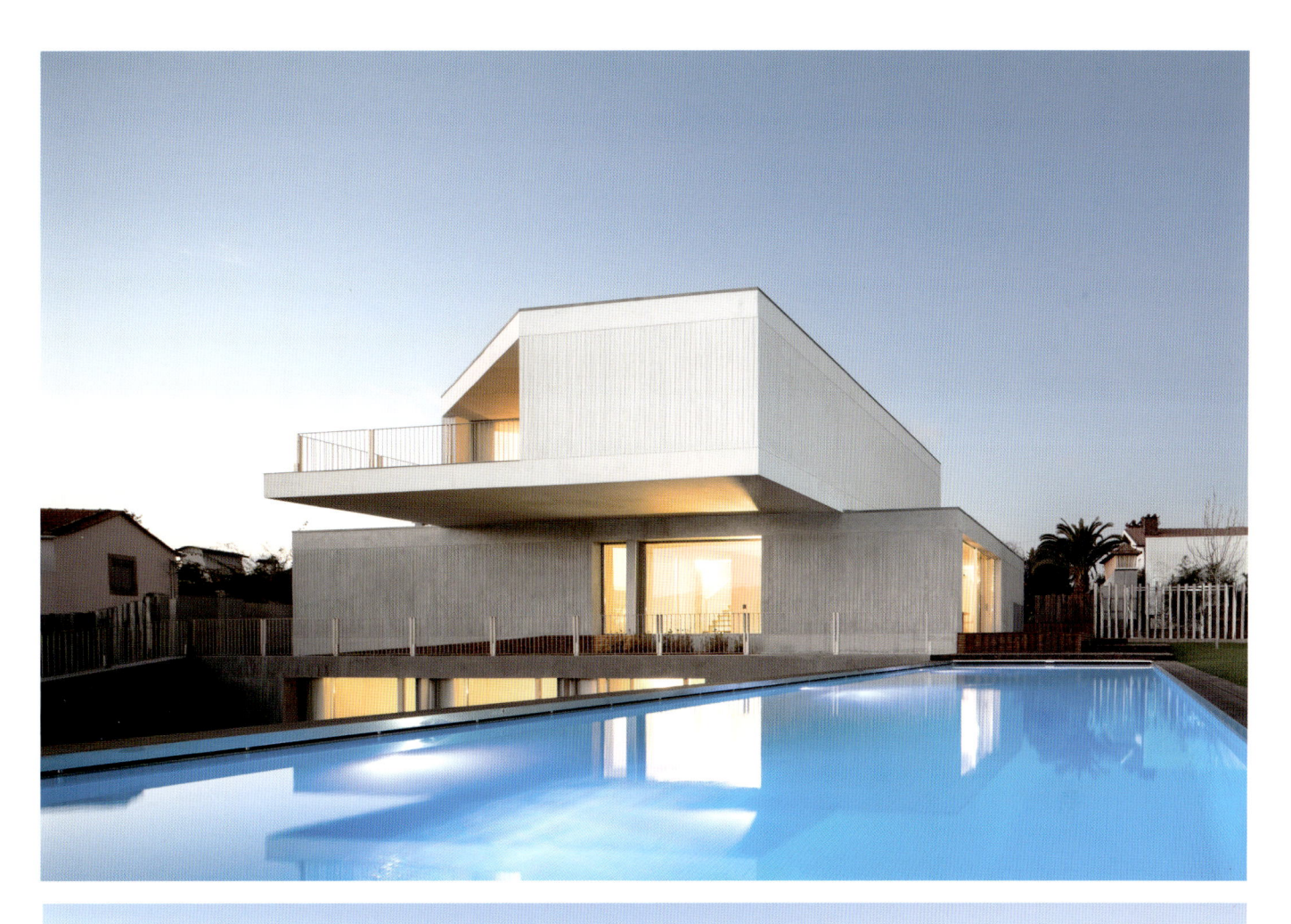

Nelson Resende Arquitecto

House in Travanca

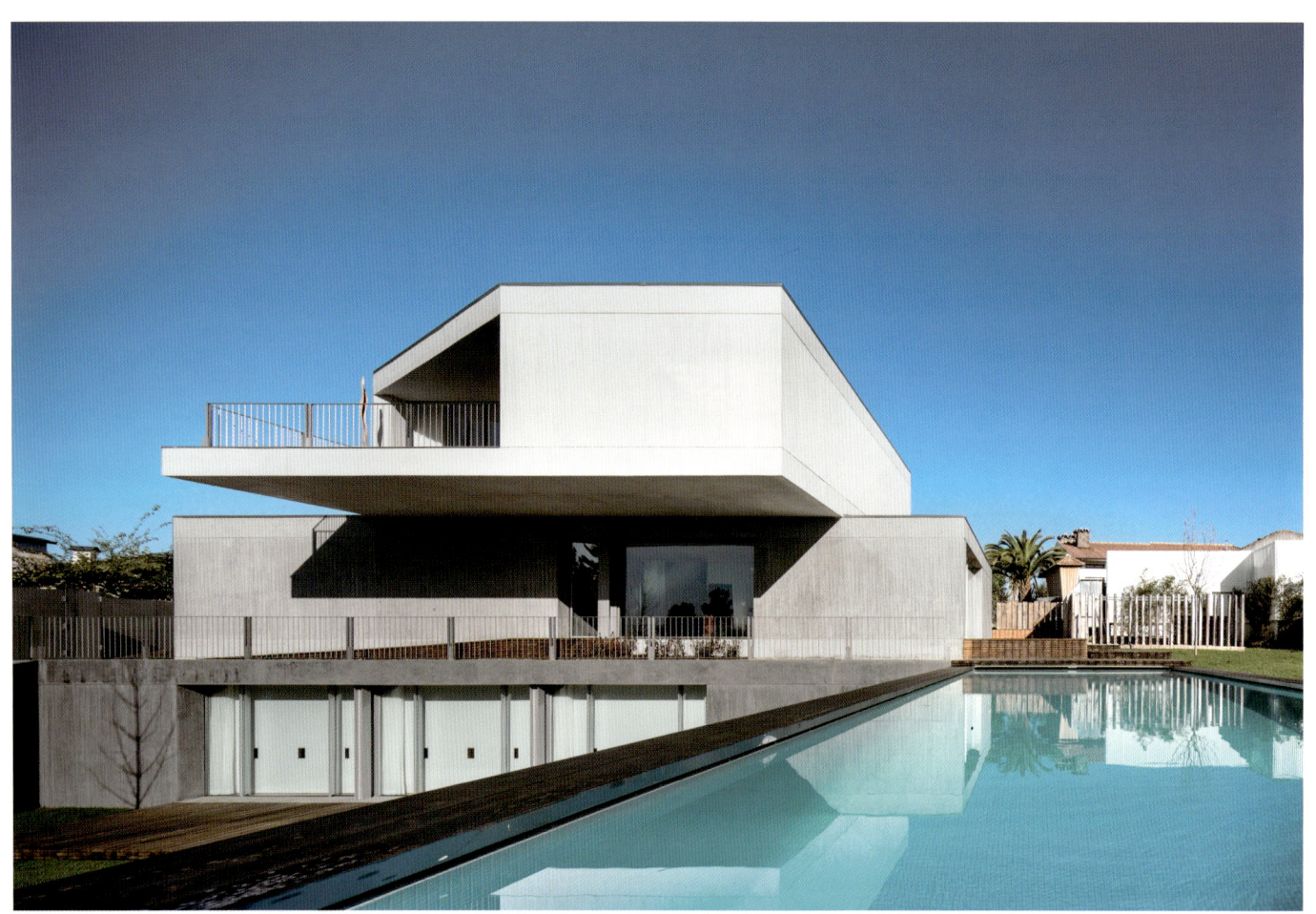

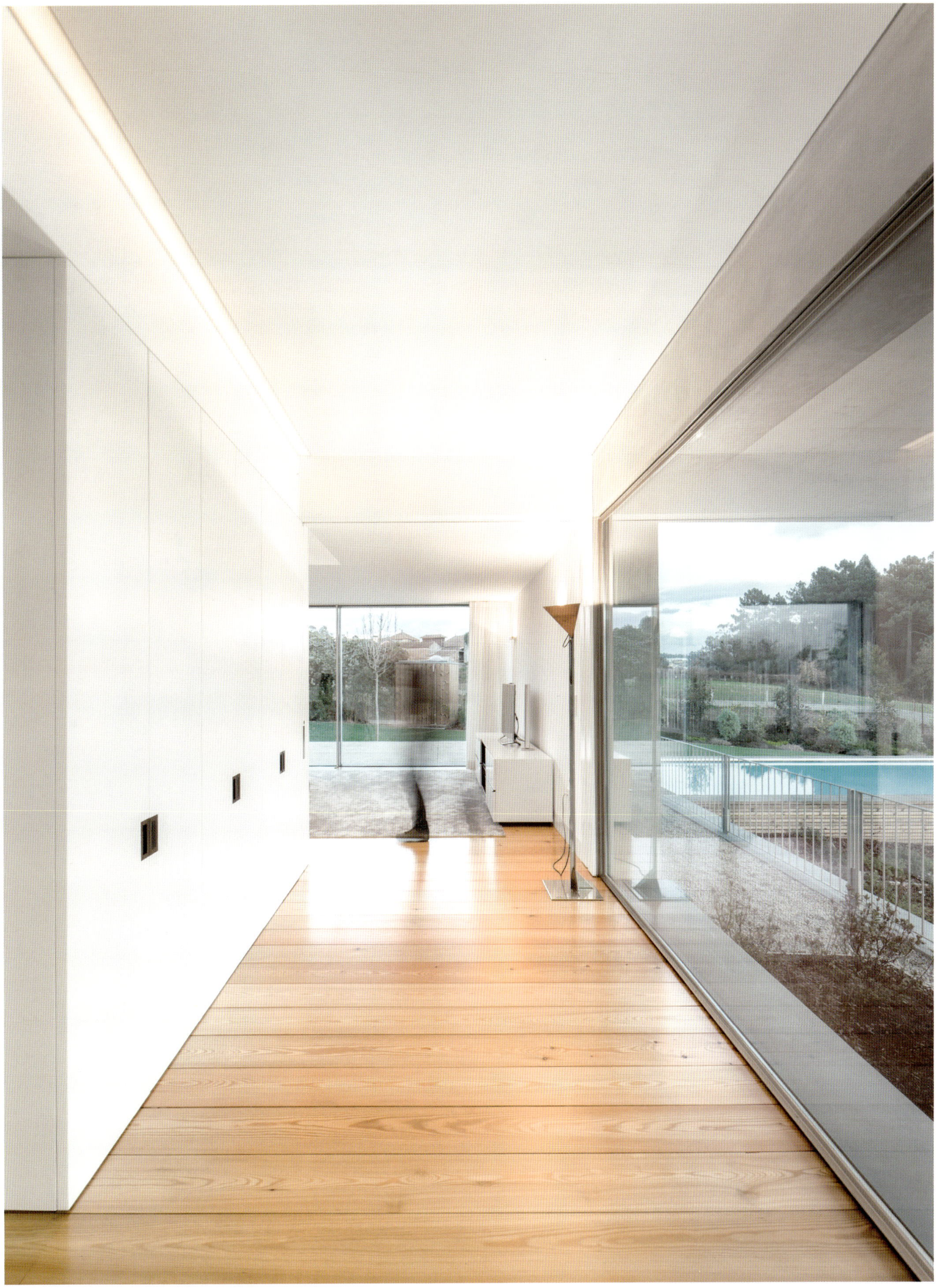

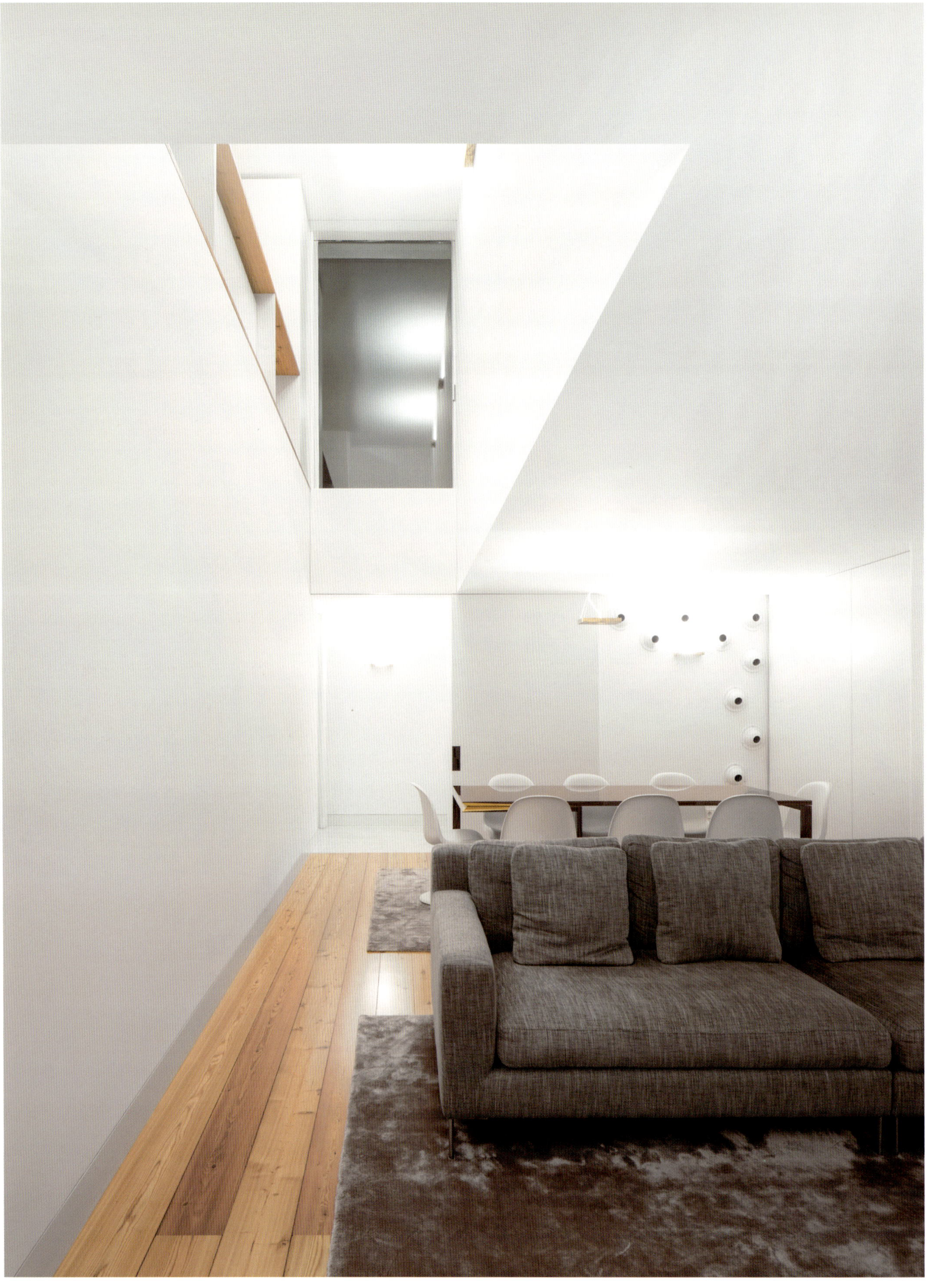

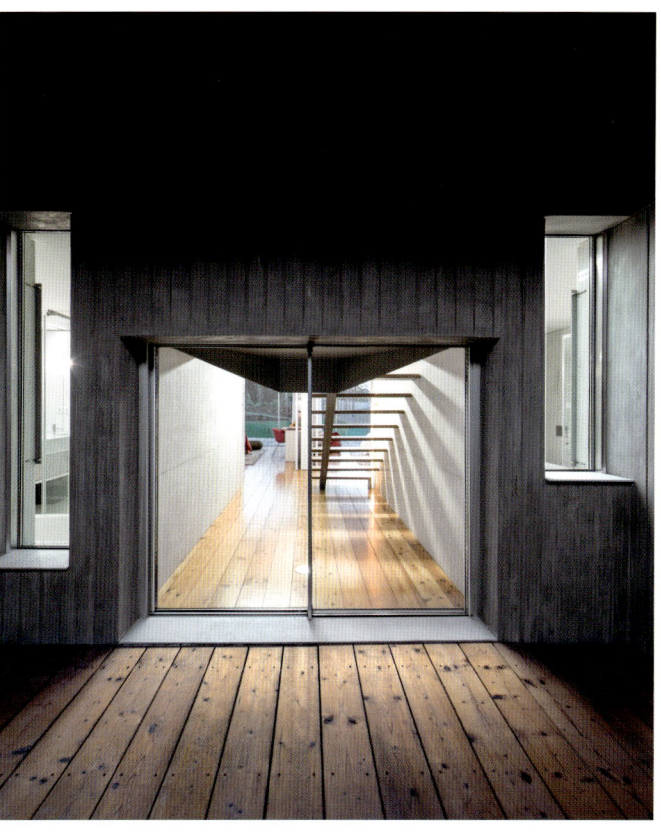

Nelson Resende Arquitecto

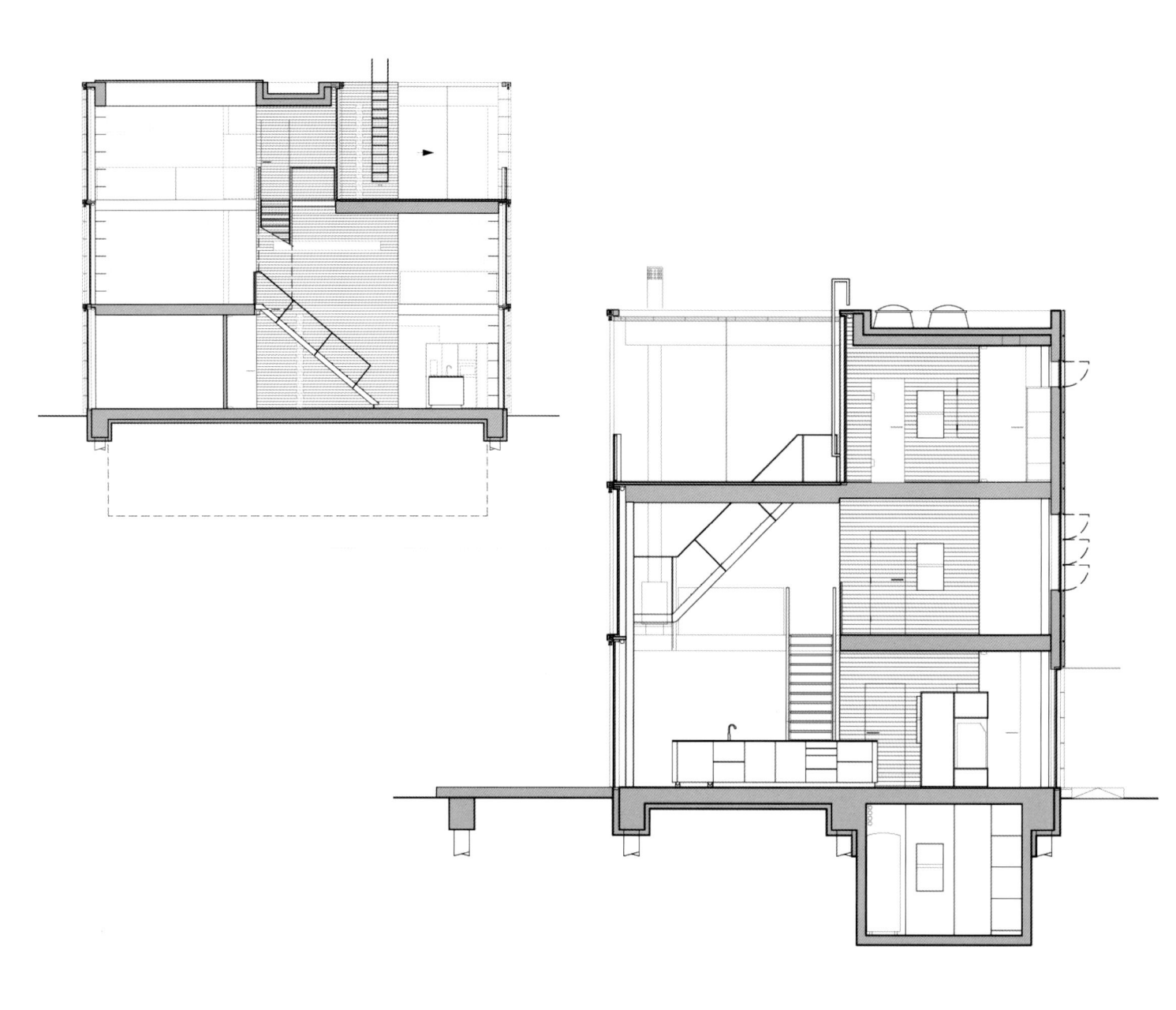

Rieteiland House
The intention with Rieteiland House was to emphasize the relationship with the terrain and create a surprising contrast between the interior and exterior.

Hans van Heeswijk Architects
Amsterdam, the Netherlands
275sqm

Architect Hans van Heeswijk designed Rieteiland House for himself and his family. The attractive plot of land is part of a newly established island at IJburg on the outskirts of Amsterdam in the Netherlands.

The boxlike street façade is completely clad in perforated aluminum panels, some of which can be opened to expose the windows behind them. The aluminum panels are punctuated by perforations that create a wave pattern. The façade on the water side is made entirely of glass panels and sliding doors.

The house is an elongated rectangular block with three floors and a basement. Inside, the aesthetic shifts and the space opens up. Most of the floors have a double height and are open. In this way, the house can be seen as a sort of spatial grandstand. This creates a panoramic view towards the west, the water and the park, on every level.

A roof terrace adjacent to the bathroom on the second floor provides a place to sit unseen. Every night, magnificent sunsets can be watched from the house, thus creating a special holiday atmosphere.

At the core of the house, a three-floor tall service tower contains a toilet on each floor, storage spaces, installation shafts, and a dumbwaiter. The block is clad in small wenge slats for acoustical reasons.

Particular attention was paid to the use of energy. The house uses an underground heating and cooling system, a heat pump, and solar collectors on the roof. Sustainability is addressed by an efficient and compact design, good insulation, the effective use of available energy, the use of natural materials, and assembly techniques.

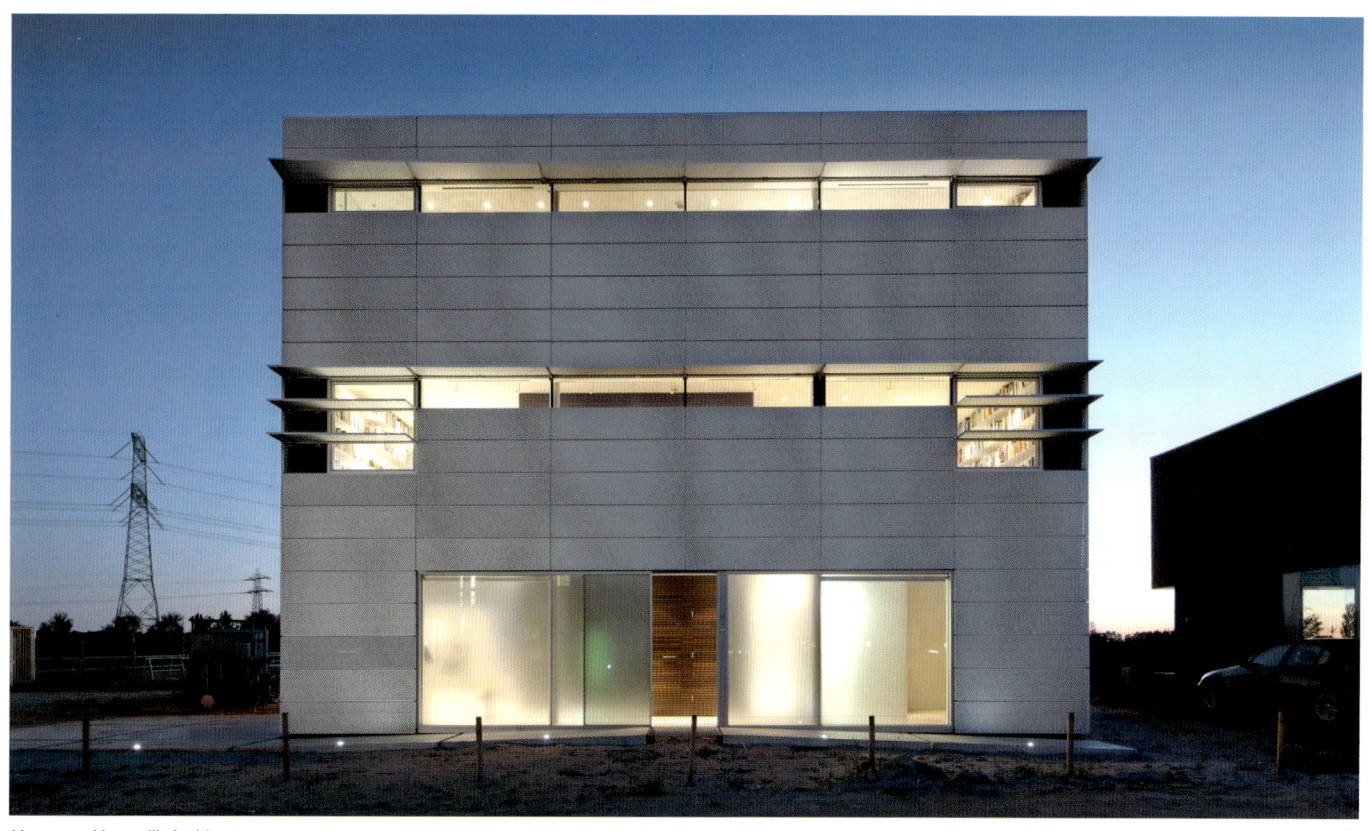

Hans van Heeswijk Architects

Rieteiland House

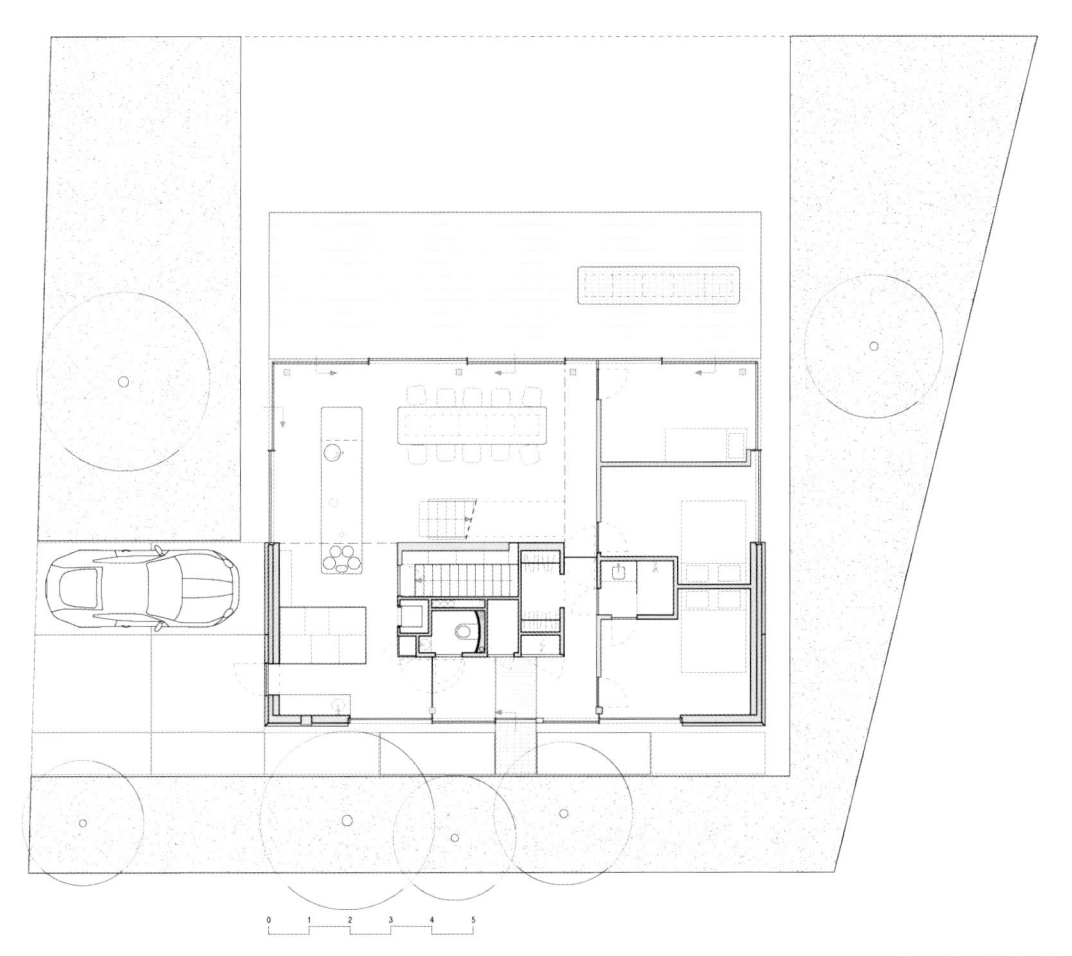

Openings in the floorplates create double height spaces in both a large ground-floor dining room and a first-floor living room. While the face of this waterside house near Amsterdam is cloaked in perforated aluminum, the rear is made entirely of glass so that residents can watch the sun set.

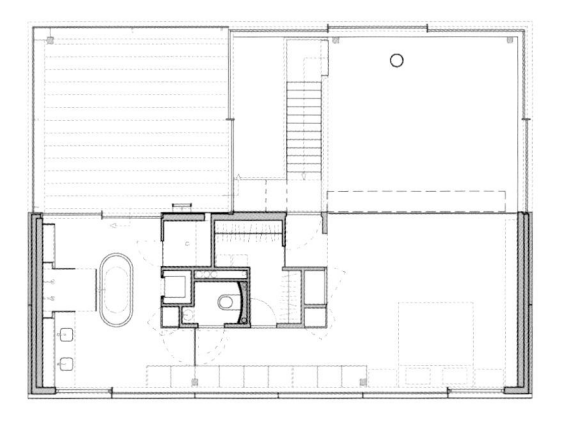

Hans van Heeswijk Architects

Rieteiland House

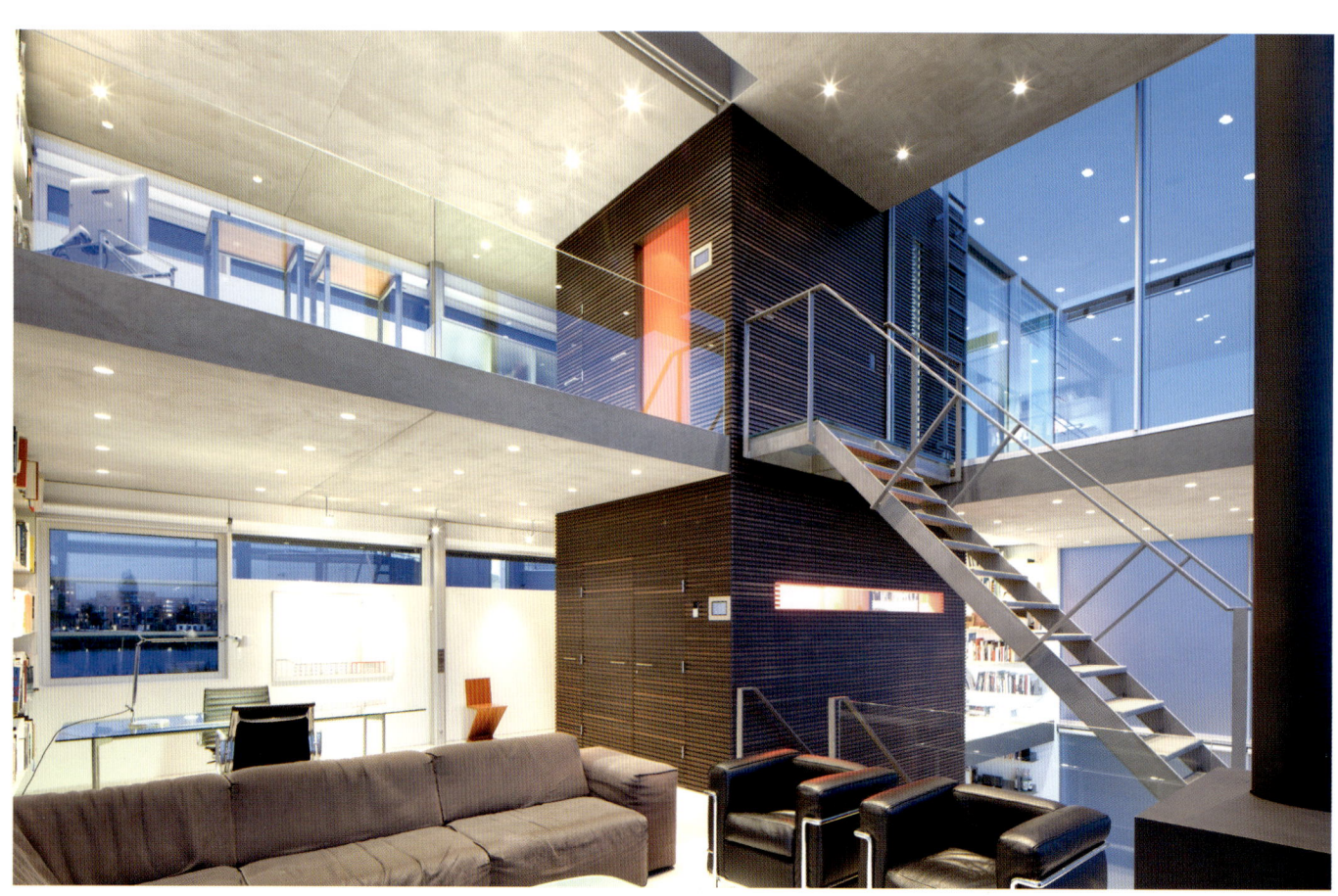

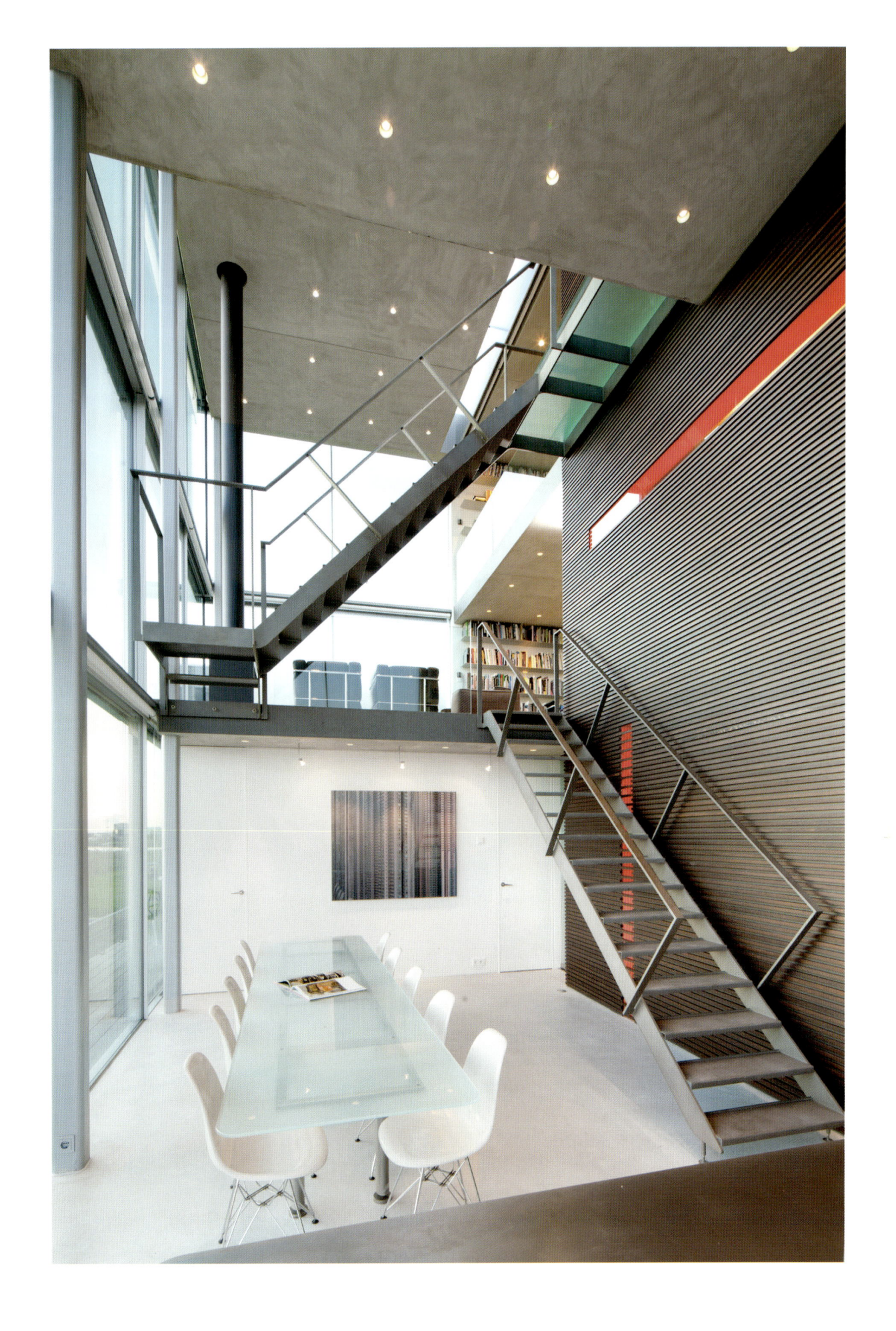

Hans van Heeswijk Architects

YAK01

The architect's main concerns with YAK01 were to keep the building cool during the day and ensure that every room was cross-ventilated.

Ayutt and Associates Design
Bangkok, Thailand
500sqm

YAK01 is situated on 560sqm of private land. The house is L shaped and the bathrooms, service areas, storage, and staircases act as buffers to absorb heat and give the north side of the house more privacy. 50% of the land was reserved for gardens. The pool was placed parallel to the house so that cool air could be drawn inside for natural ventilation.

The first floor is arranged in traditional Thai fashion with a central courtyard that functions as a foyer. A staircase enclosed in a glass box floats over the courtyard. The living space connects with the terrace, the garden, and the swimming pool and features double-height folding windows that fuse the spaces together. The master bedroom cantilevers over the foyer.

Ayutt and Associates Design

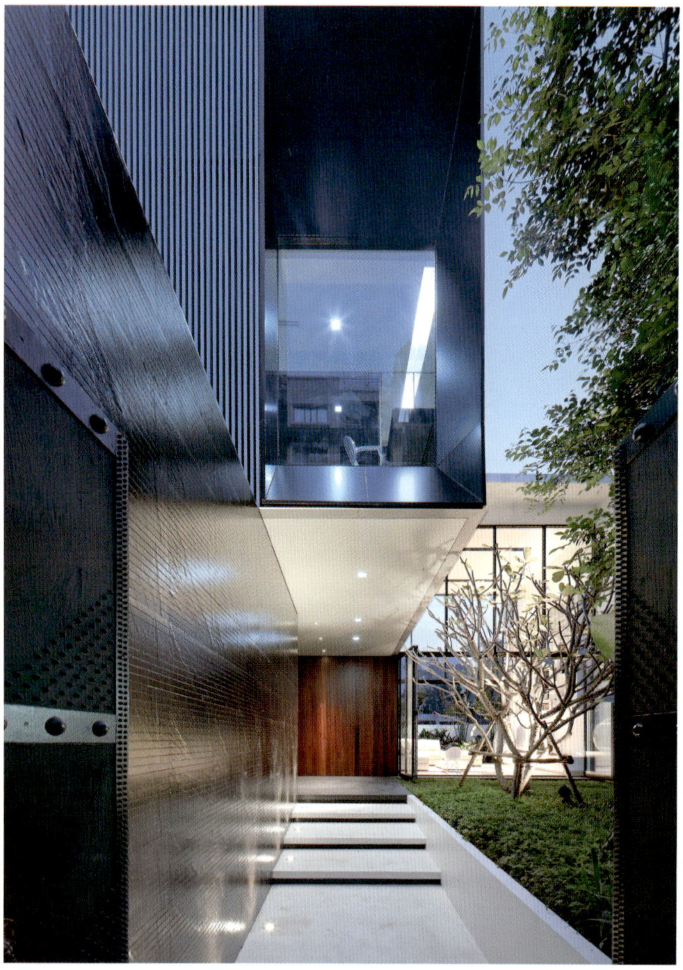

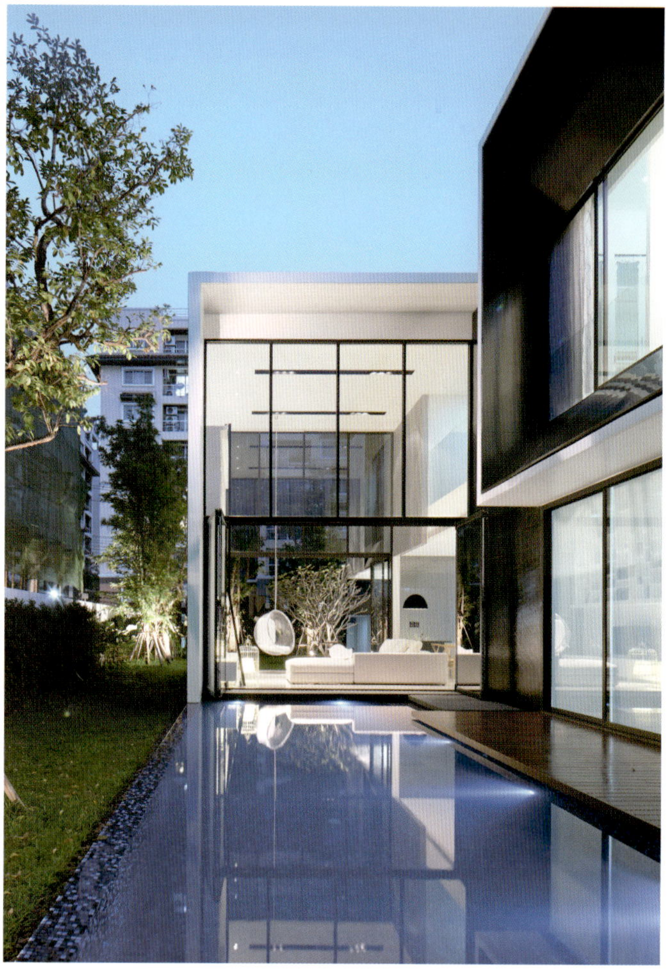

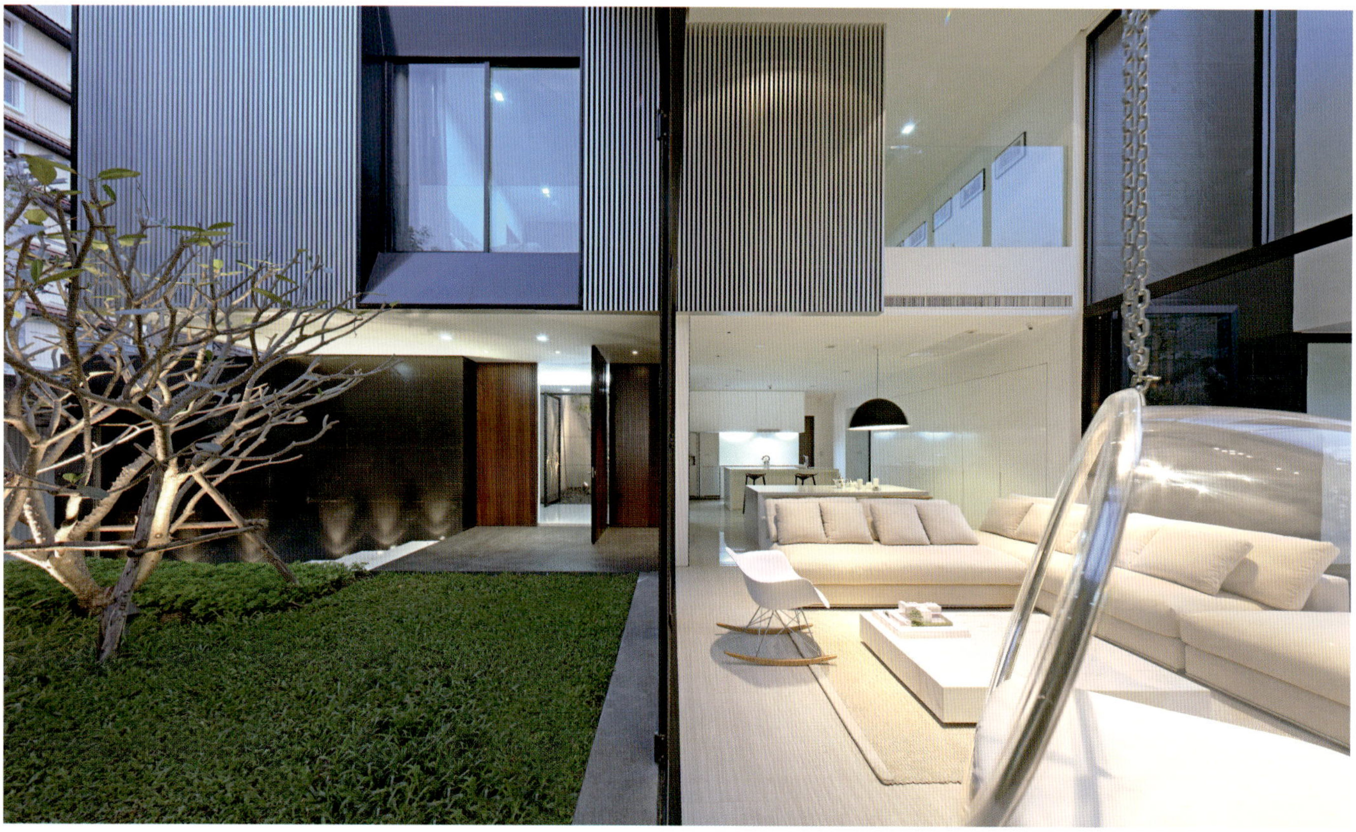

WEST ELEVATION

YAK01
1 ALUMINUM EXTRUSION STRIP
2 ALUMINUM COMPOSITE
3 PLASTER AND PAINT WALL
4 BLACK GRANITE
5 CLEAR GLASS WINDOW
6 TEXTURE PAINT

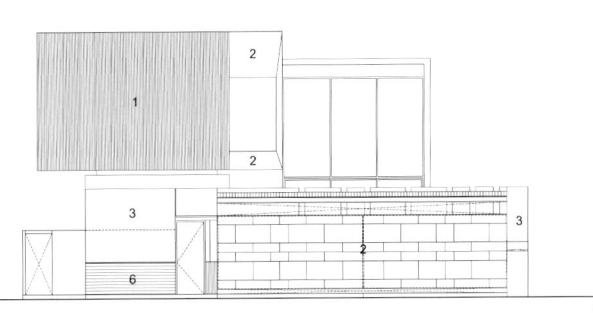

SOUTH ELEVATION

EAST ELEVATION

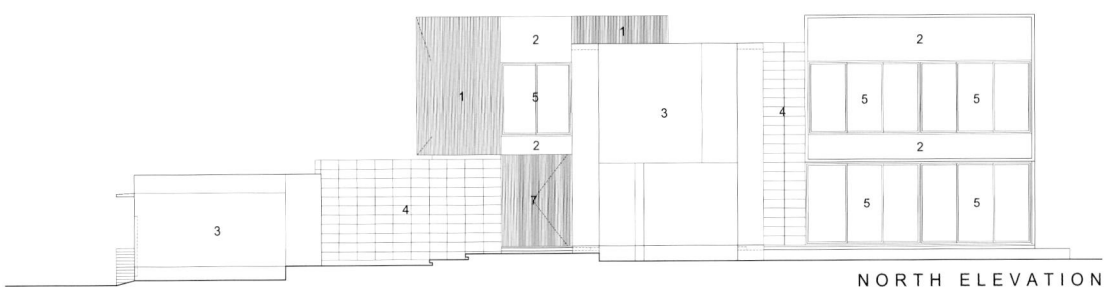

YAK01
1 ALUMINUM EXTRUSION STRIP
2 ALUMINUM COMPOSITE
3 PLASTER AND PAINT WALL
4 BLACK GRANITE
5 CLEAR GLASS WINDOW
6 TEXTURE PAINT
7 SOLID TIMBER STRIP

NORTH ELEVATION

Ayutt and Associates Design

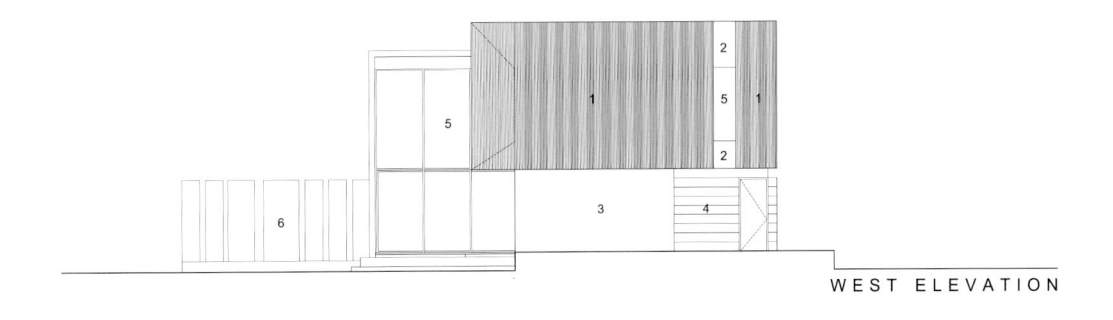

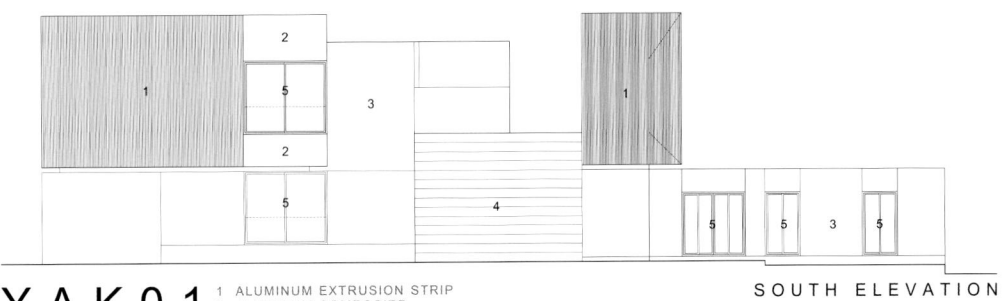

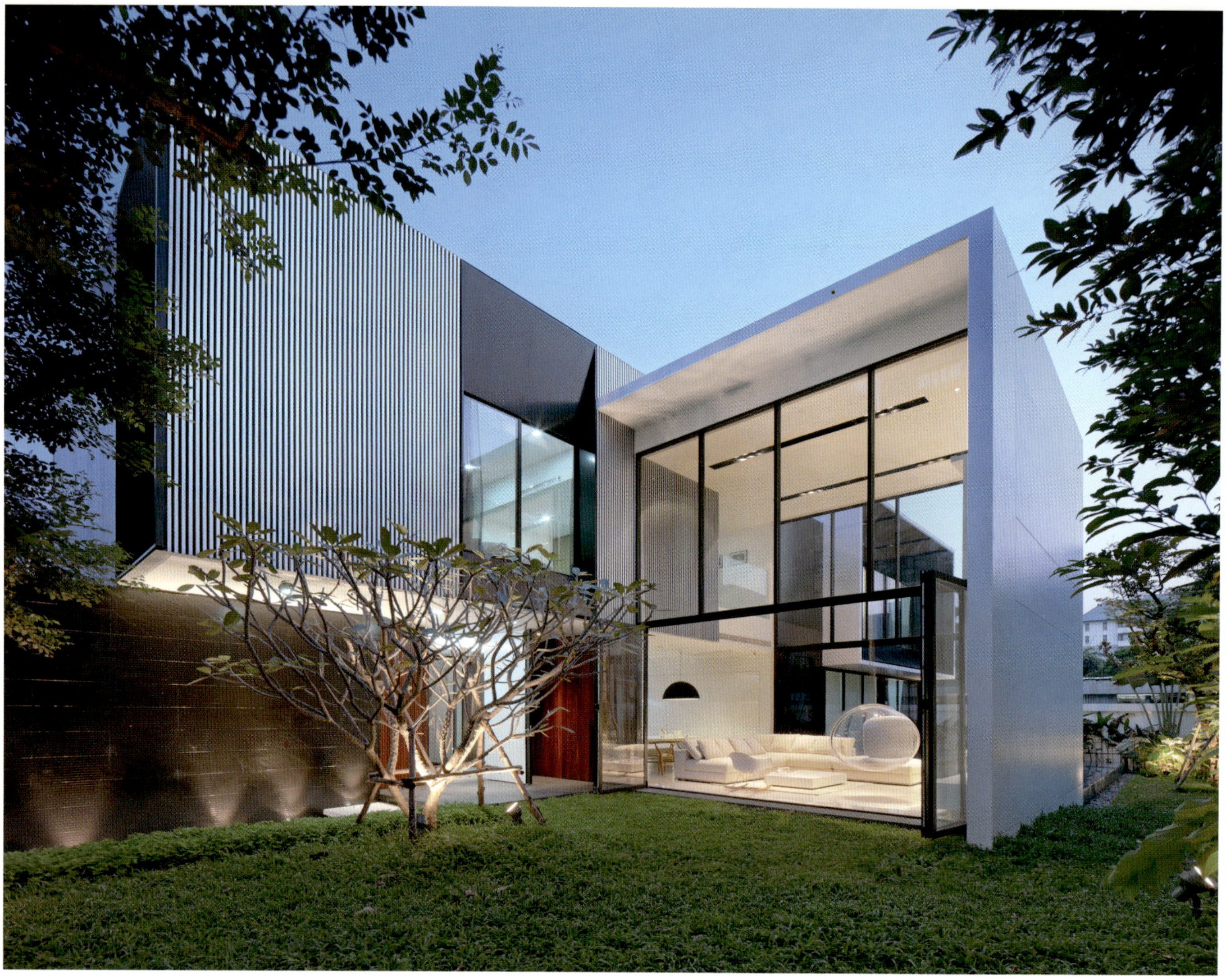

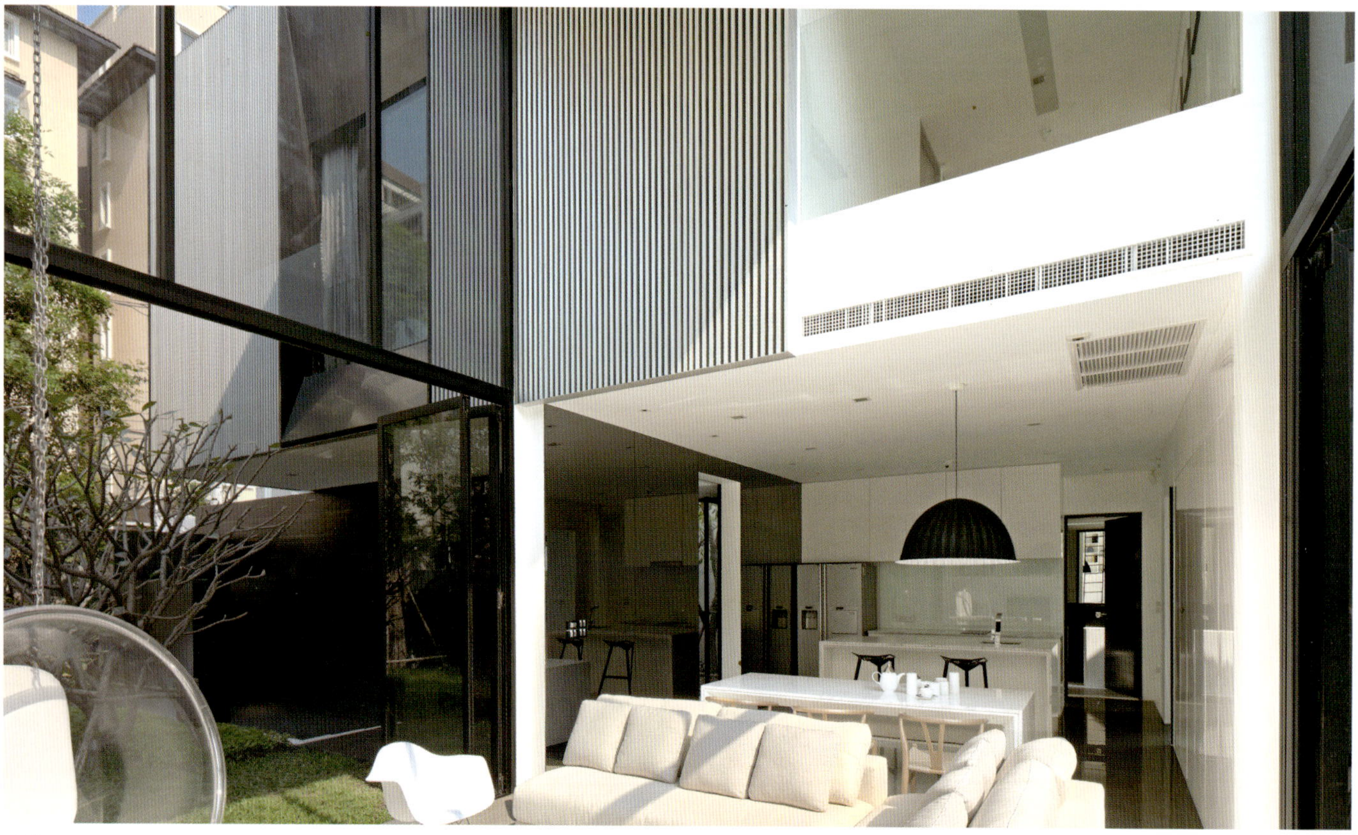

Ayutt and Associates Design

The main living space is located at the center of the house near the garden and swimming pool. The living space directly connects to the garden, and the swimming pool; it features double-height folding windows that serve to fuse the spaces. Placing the swimming pool at the back of the house helped create a space suitable for various activities.

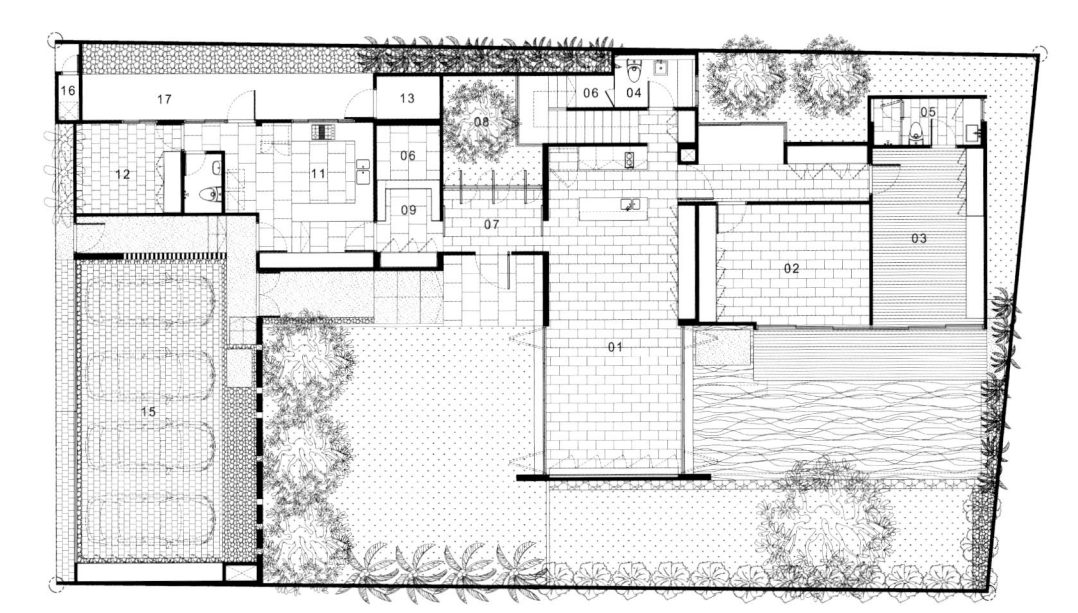

FIRST FLOOR PLAN
MAIN SPACE
01 LIVING SPACE
02 WORKING ROOM
03 GUEST BEDROOM
04 POWDER ROOM
05 GUEST BATHROOM
06 STORAGE
07 FOYER
08 INTERNAL GARDEN
09 SHOE CABINET

SERVICE SPACE
11 ASIAN KITCHEN
12 MAID ROOM
13 PUMP ROOM
14 STORAGE
15 PARKING SPACE
16 GARBAGE ROOM
17 YARD

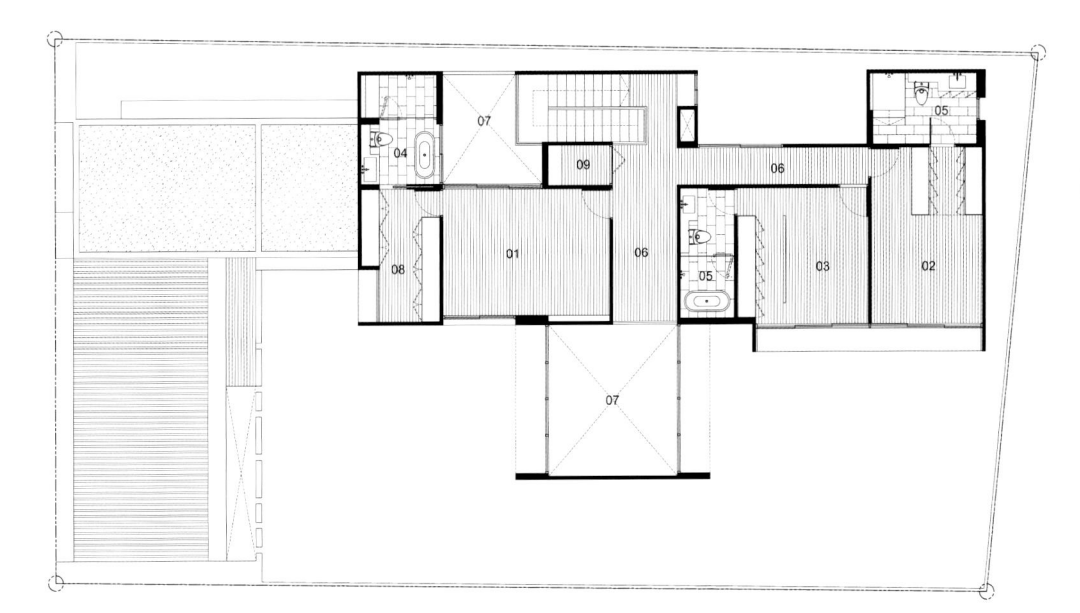

SECOND FLOOR PLAN
MAIN SPACE
01 MASTER BEDROOM
02 SECONDARY BEDROOM
03 THIRD BEDROOM
04 MASTER BATHROOM
05 BATHROOM
06 GALLERY
07 OPEN WELL
08 WALK-IN CLOSET
09 BUDDHA ROOM

Ayutt and Associates Design

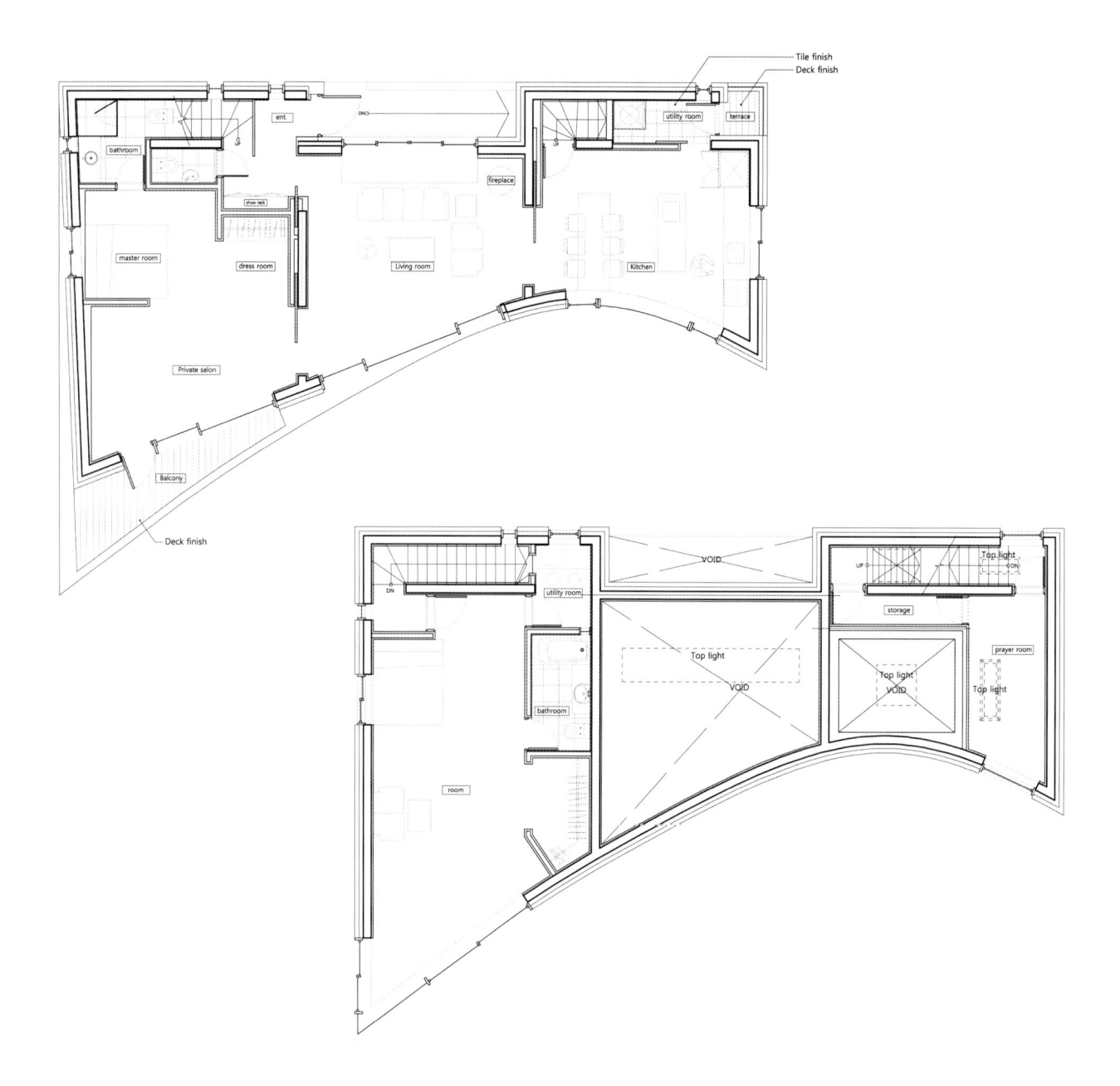

The Curving House
The Curving House's façades are constructed from contrasting materials that ultimately achieve a balance.

**JOHO Architecture
Yongin, South Korea
186.3sqm**

The house was designed to encase the lot by curving around it. The building sits above the ground, supported by pilotis, to create a parking space underneath. The designers stacked bricks coated with a silver colored water-repellent in the shape of a concave lens to form the southern façade. The stainless steel used on the front and sides of the house reflects the surrounding landscape. Although the two materials contrast, they ultimately achieve a balance.

The design was influenced by traditional Korean architecture. Elevating the house increased the surface area exposed to outer air, thereby improving ventilation. This design is similar to the traditional Korean model of open living rooms that help keep houses well ventilated. In the winter, the concrete floor acts as a thermal mass, similar to Ondol floors in traditional Korean architecture, and prevents cold air from entering the house. The second floor has an open living room, bedroom, and kitchen, which can be divided and combined with sliding doors. The house is thus a modern reinterpretation of traditional Korean homes.

JOHO Architecture

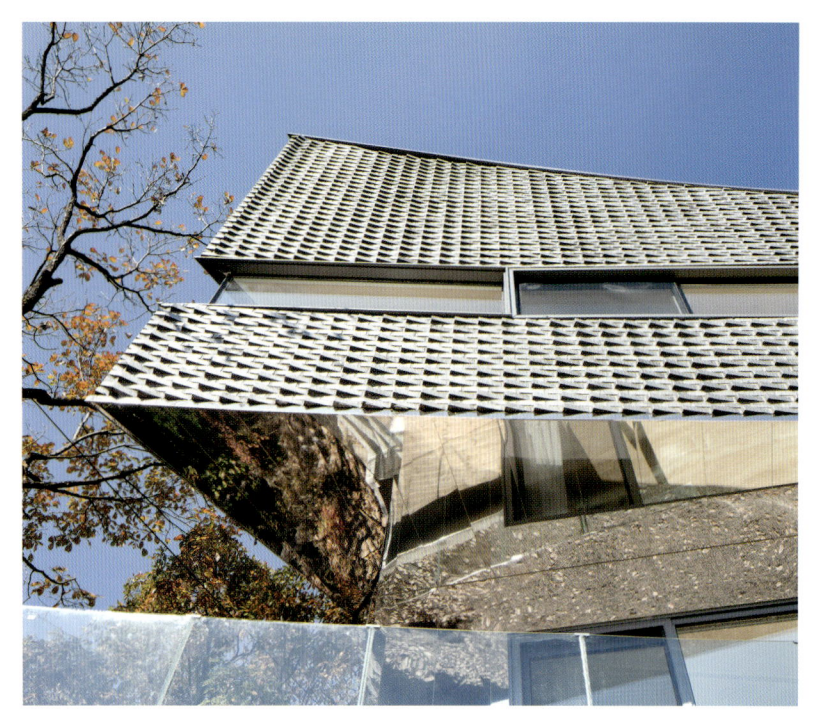

Bricks coated with silver colored water-repellent were arranged in the shape of a concave lens to form a southern façade.

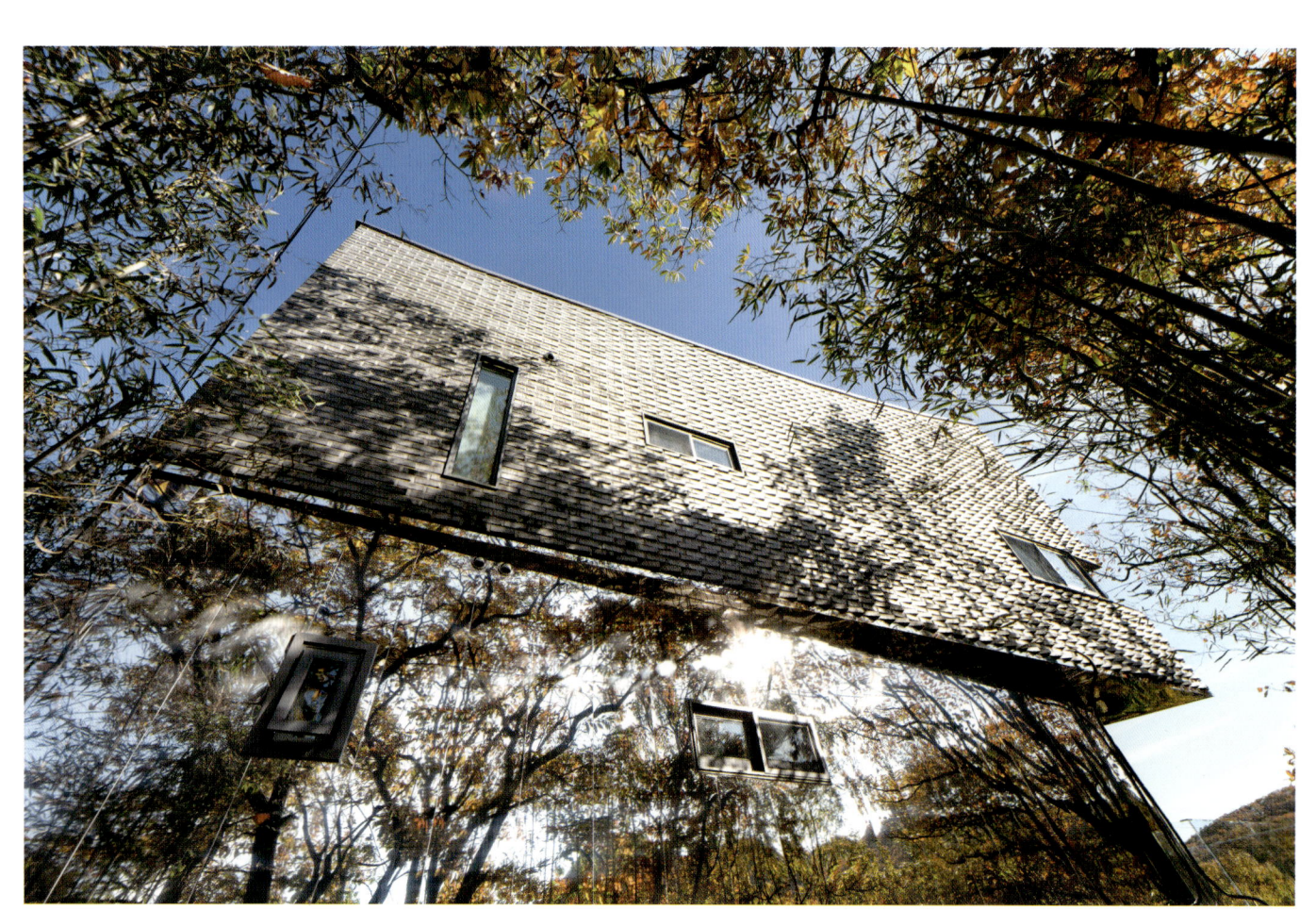

JOHO Architecture

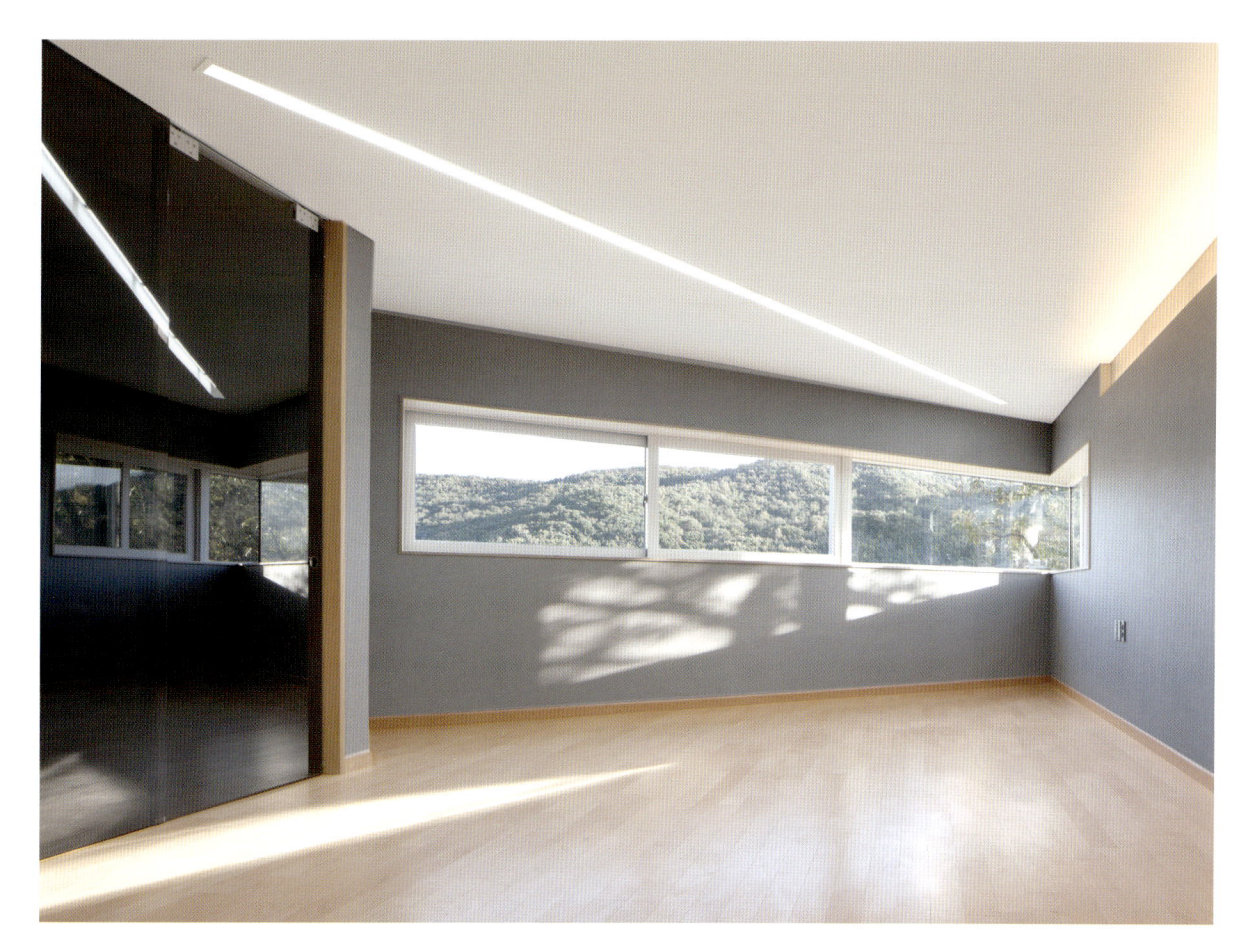

The Curving House

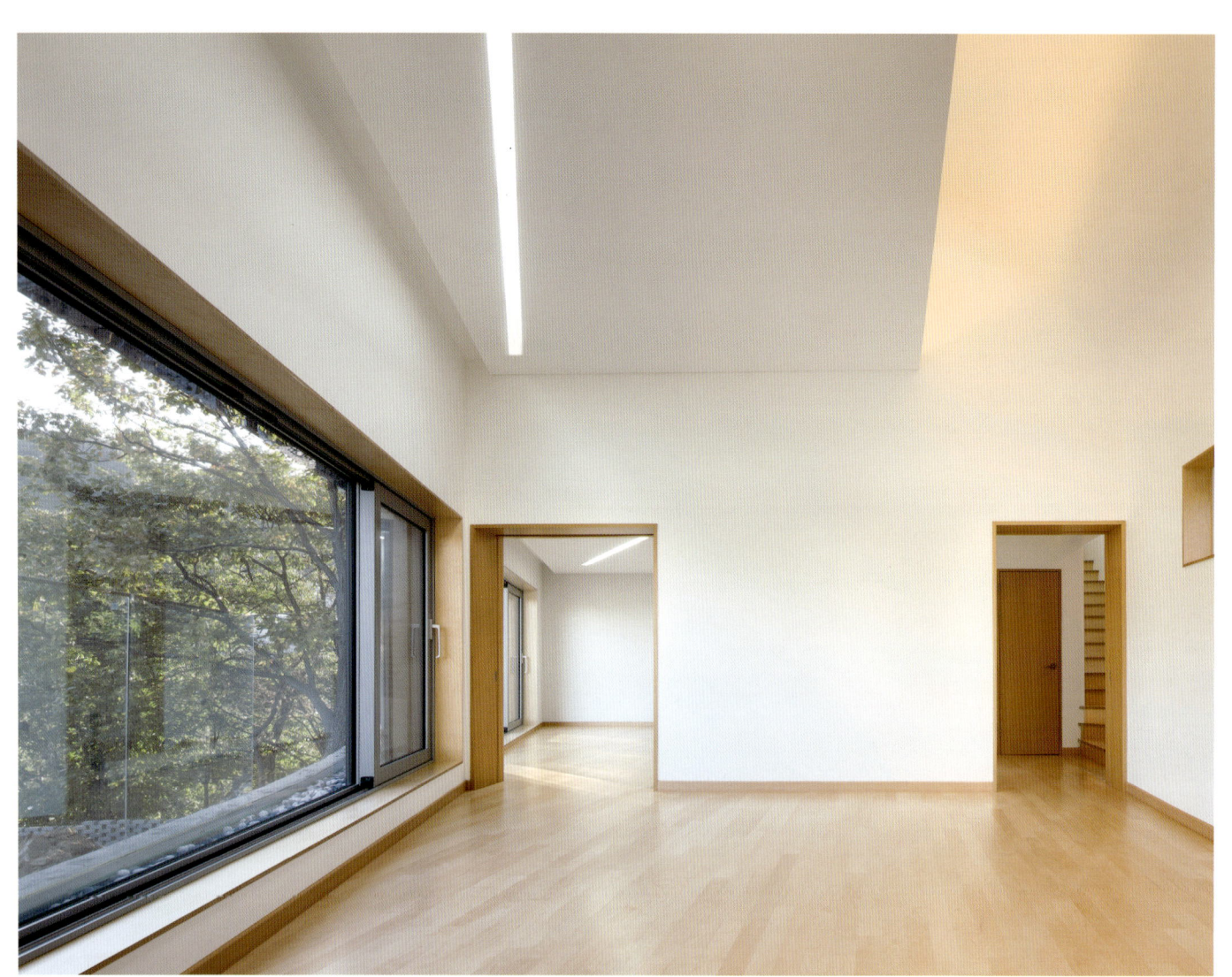

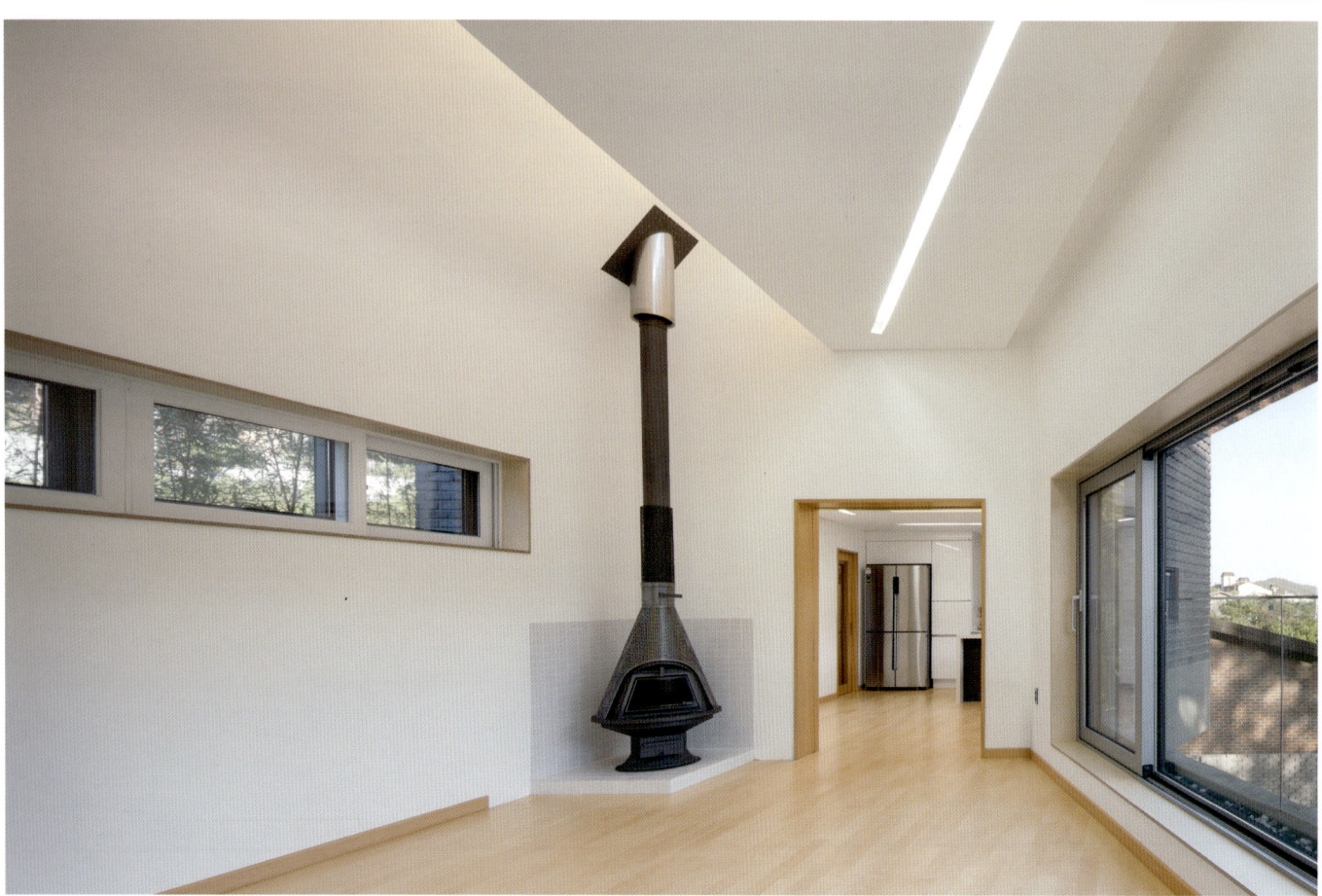

JOHO Architecture

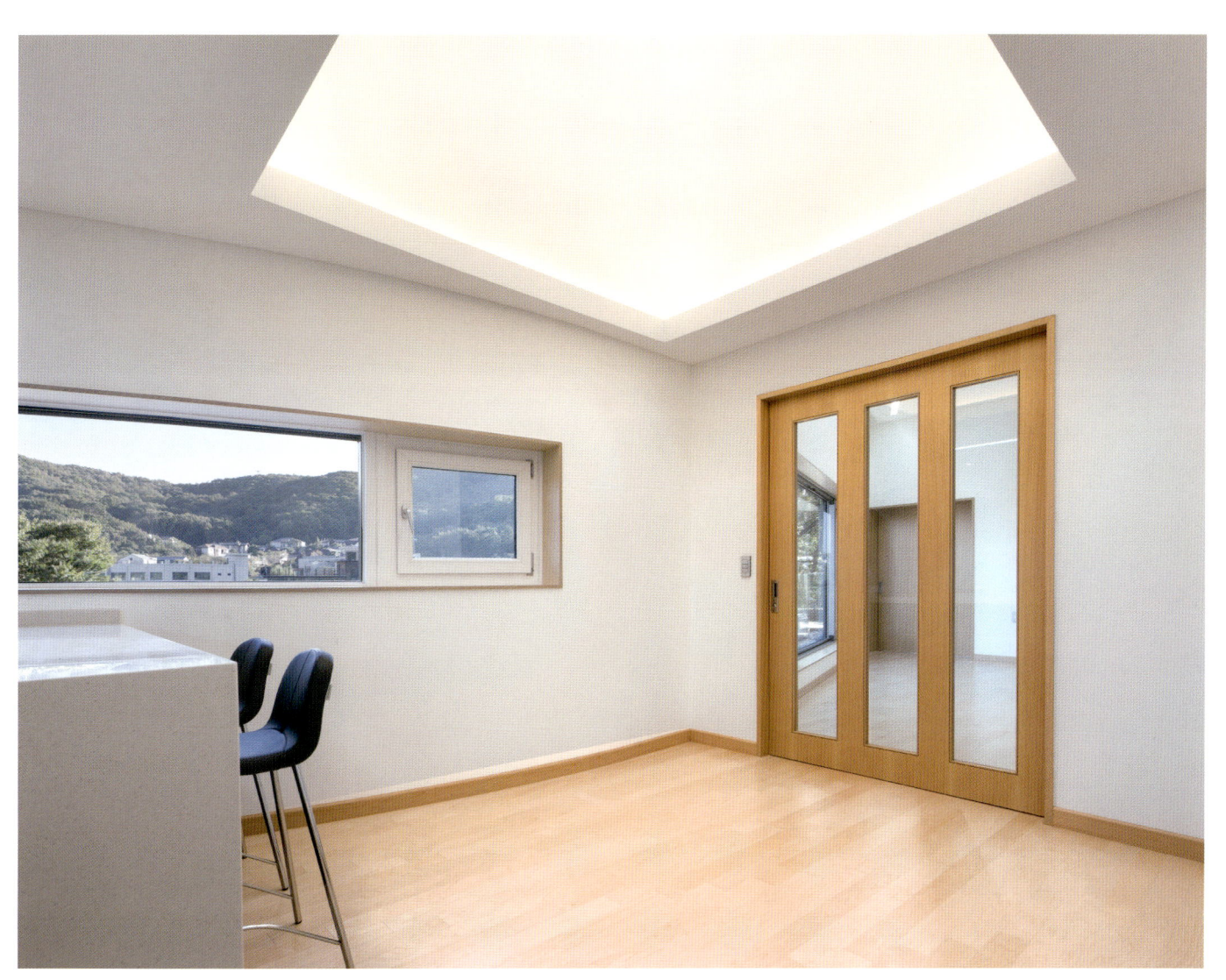

GROUND FLOOR PLAN

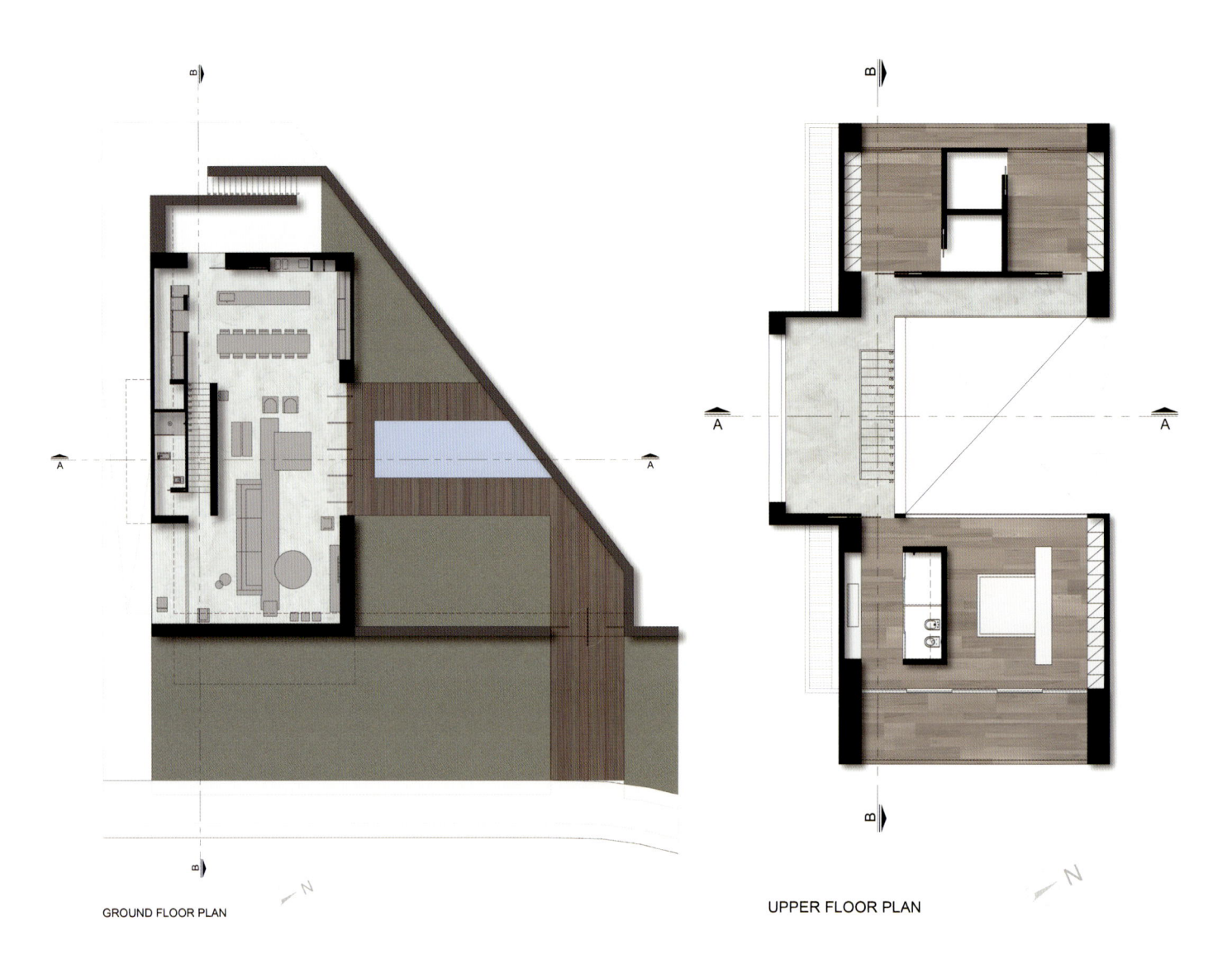

UPPER FLOOR PLAN

LA House
LA House breaks paradigms and does away with traditional spaces and partitions.

Studio Guilherme Torres
Londrina, Brazil
410sqm

The big wooden box commands the attention of everyone who sees it. The house abolishes traditional spaces and partitions.

The designers created a plateau foundation and built walls to surround the whole construction in order to give the owners privacy.

The core concept of breaking paradigms is evident at the entrance; the entrance leads past the pool to a double-height atrium. The living room, located on the first floor, works as a link between the inside and outside and features large pivoting doors.

The kitchen is fully integrated with the surrounding space and is equipped with a stove and barbecue. The dining area is fully integrated with the kitchen and living room. Even the bathroom is designed to work as a pool changing room.

The hall located by the stairs on the upper floor works as a small office. Its windows are protected by hollow concrete elements. Simple solutions and a generous use of a few materials give this home personality and a timeless touch while showcasing a simpler way of life.

Studio Guilherme Torres

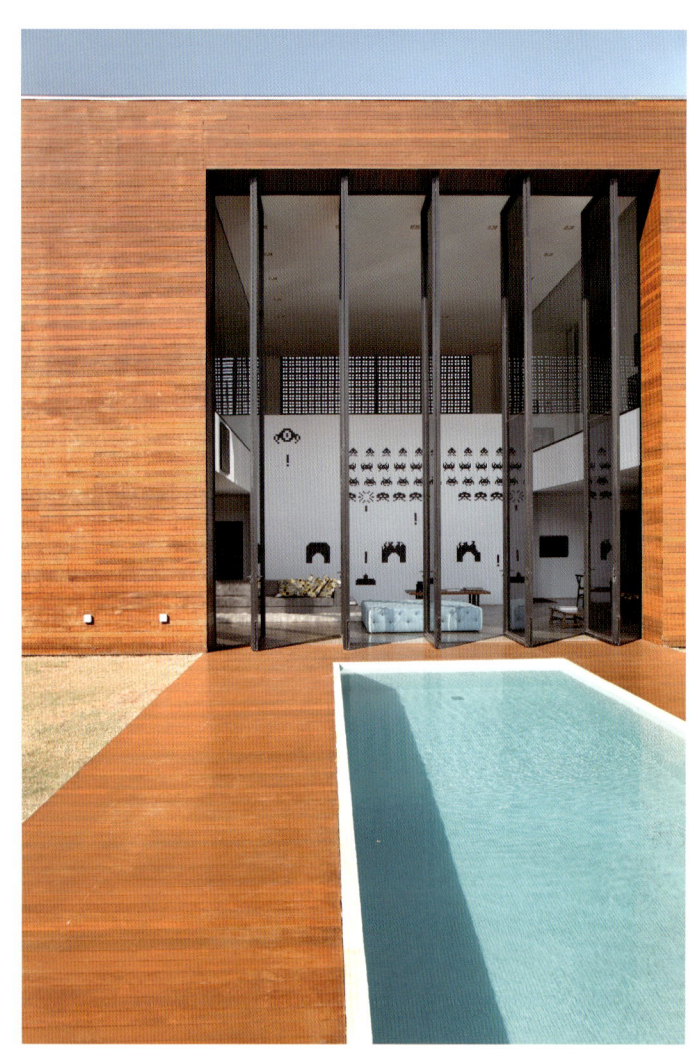

LA House

Studio Guilherme Torres

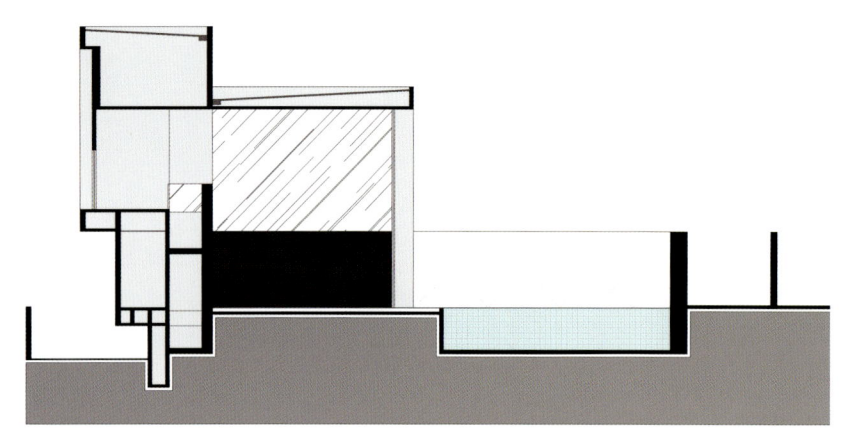

SECTION AA

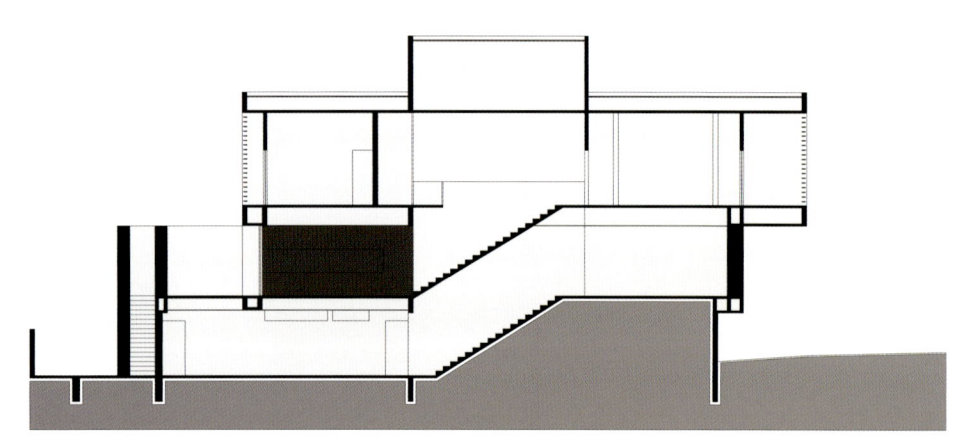

SECTION BB

LA House

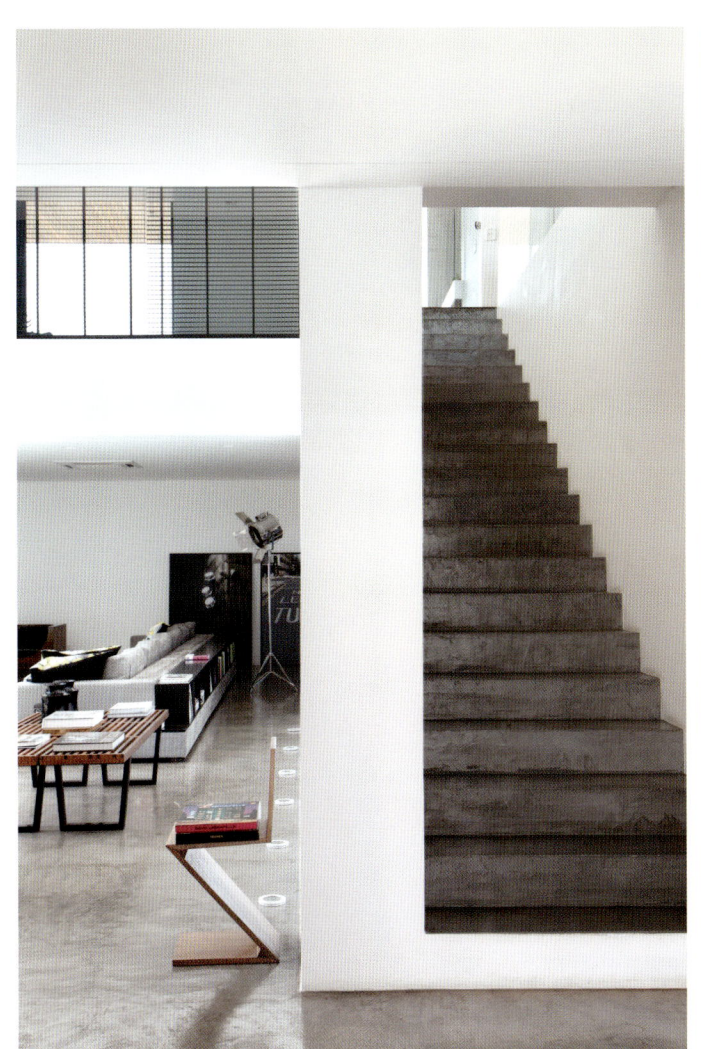

Studio Guilherme Torres

Villa SSK
Villa SSK gives one the impression that it was constructed according to a mysterious set of laws.

Takeshi Hirobe Architects
Chiba, Japan
105sqm

This house sits near the calm and tranquil waters of Tokyo Bay. It was designed to connect the surrounding mountains to the sea.

A tiled central courtyard serves as an outdoor living room where guests can gather and mingle. Water can be allowed to flow into the courtyard where it will reflect the subtle nuances of light and the wind.

Timber panels and trusses were used to create a structure that connects the ocean-facing side of the house with the mountain-facing one. Placing the walls at oblique angles prevented the building from becoming oppressive.

Architecture ought to be rooted in the place it occupies. The architectural form of this building emerged during the long process of analyzing and studying the location. The finished building gives one the impression that it was constructed according to a mysterious set of laws.

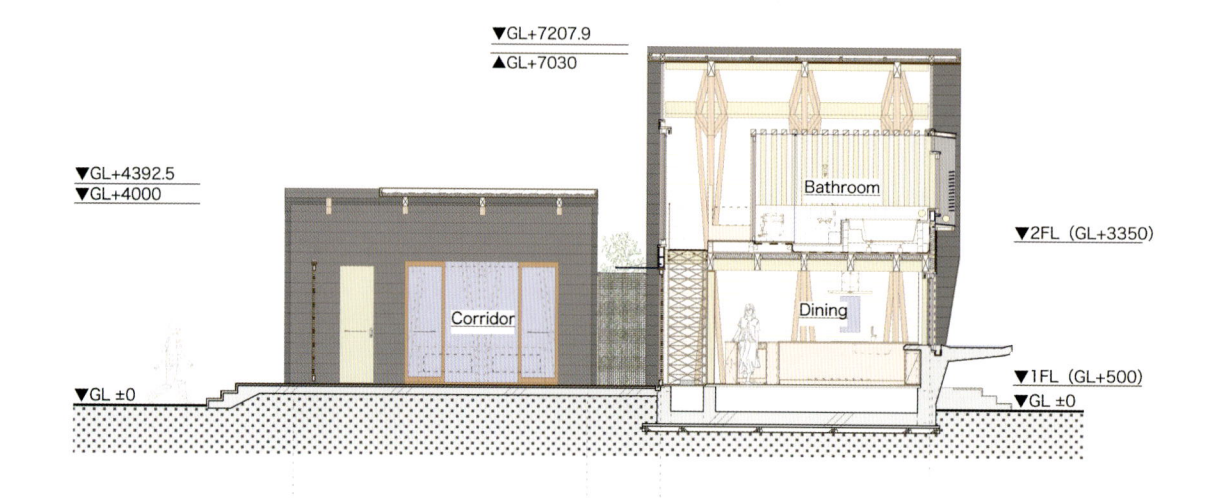

Takeshi Hirobe Architects

Villa SSK

Takeshi Hirobe Architects 187

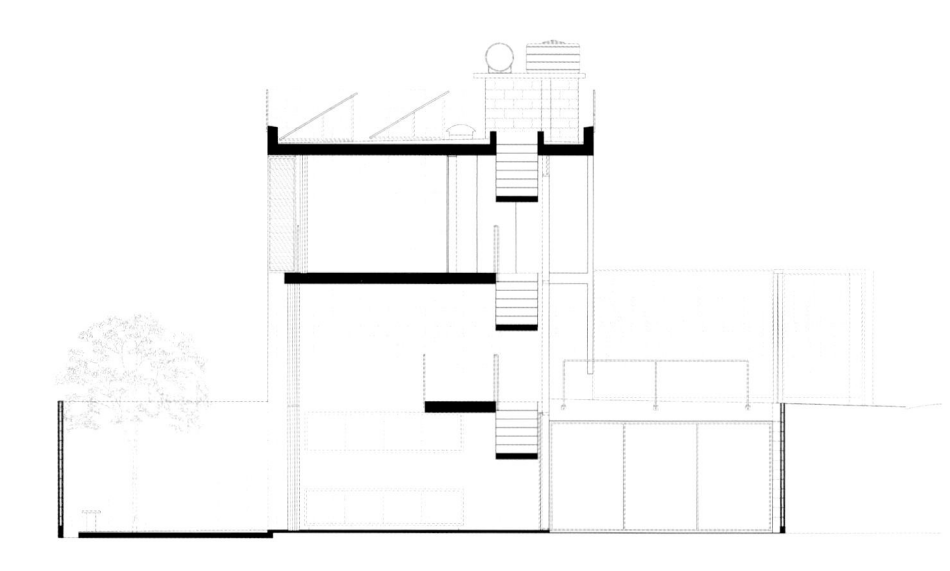

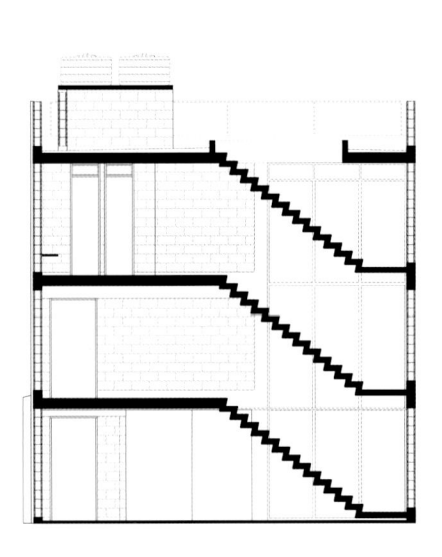

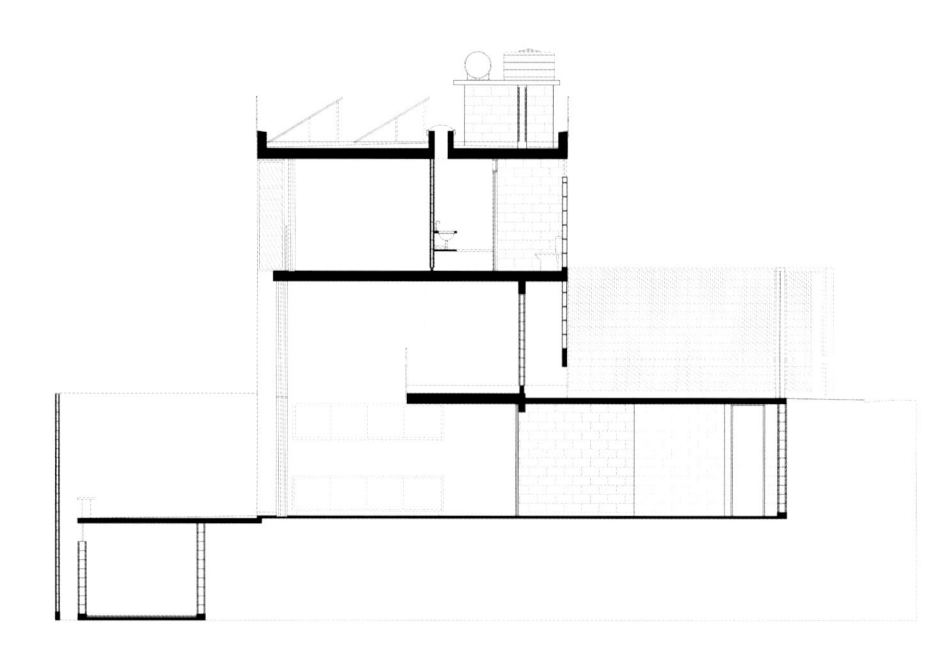

Maracanã House

Maracanã House reveals a new option for narrow lots made possible by a series of horizontal and vertical paths.

Terra e Tuma Arquitetos Associados
São Paulo, Brazil
185sqm

The jarring geometry of this house stands in contrast to the surrounding traditional houses. The house fully occupies its lot, creating a sense of continuous space.

The house reveals a new possibility for narrow lots. A series of horizontal and vertical paths make a different spatial organization possible.

The entrance is located behind a ceramic mural painted in black, white, and red.

A series of stairs lead through the house. The social and service areas are downstairs while the private areas of the house are located upstairs. Light enters the house through massive glass openings that contrast with the strength of the concrete walls.

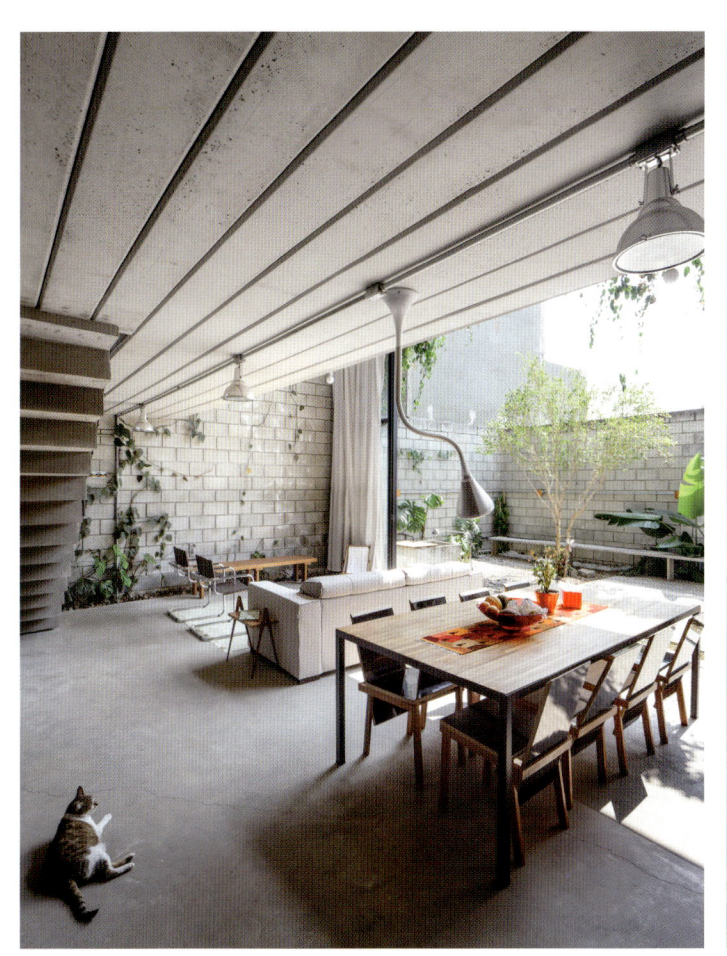

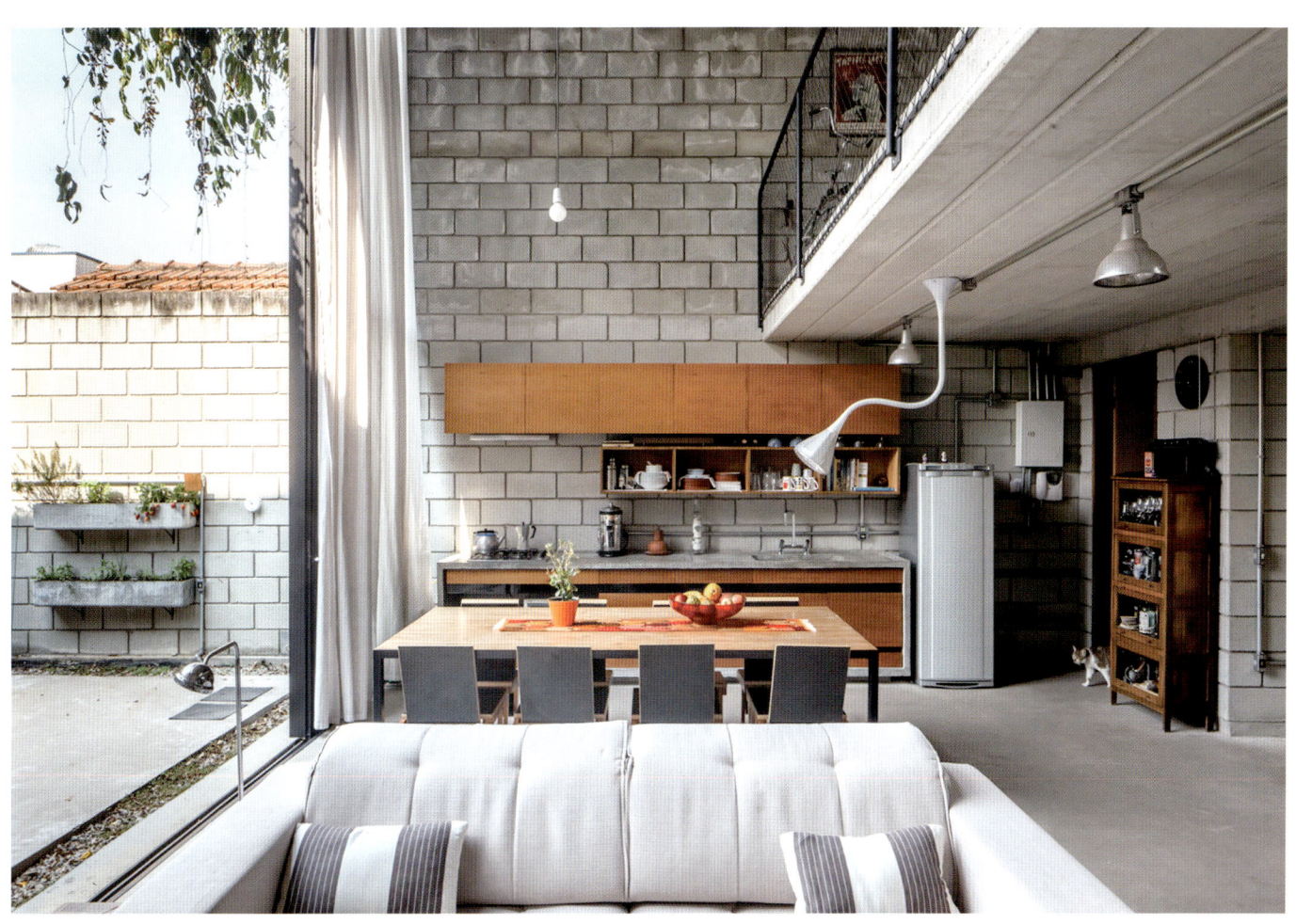

Terra e Tuma Arquitetos Associados

Maracanã House

The entrance opens onto a mezzanine floor. Concrete staircases lead up to the first floor bedrooms and down to the open living room and dining room. Large glass doors open the living room out to the courtyard garden beyond, while a second sunken courtyard is positioned at the front of the house beside a tall window that stretches all the way up to the roof.

Terra e Tuma Arquitetos Associados

Whistler Residence

Whistler Residence's thoughtful allocation of program results in a strong but unimposing home that is extremely private without compromising access to daylight and panoramic views.

BattersbyHowat Architects
Whistler, Canada
540sqm

Located in a growing neighborhood of large-scale homes on the slope above the resort community of Whistler, British Columbia, this house occupies a restricted yet prominent, site in the development. The visual mass of this large volume is minimized by strategic use of the terrain and careful blasting of the bedrock. A substantial portion of the house appears below grade. The thoughtful allocation of program results in a strong but unimposing home that is extremely private without compromising access to daylight and panoramic views.

In the often garish context of Whistler vacation homes, the designers focused on a structure and experience that captured the essential qualities of the ski lodge archetype but without the typical formal and stylistic constraints. The lowest level has a maze-like disposition and consists in a collection of private and communal spaces. Exposed concrete walls bracket seamless wood lined alcoves that provide access to the sleeping quarters and service spaces located on this level. The main floor is a large open room animated by multiple natural light sources and varied views of the forest and mountains beyond. As on the first floor, the walls extend past corners obscuring the space's sense of containment. On the exterior, the walls operate in a similar manner by extending the perceived limits of the interior and cropping views to control exposure and privacy.

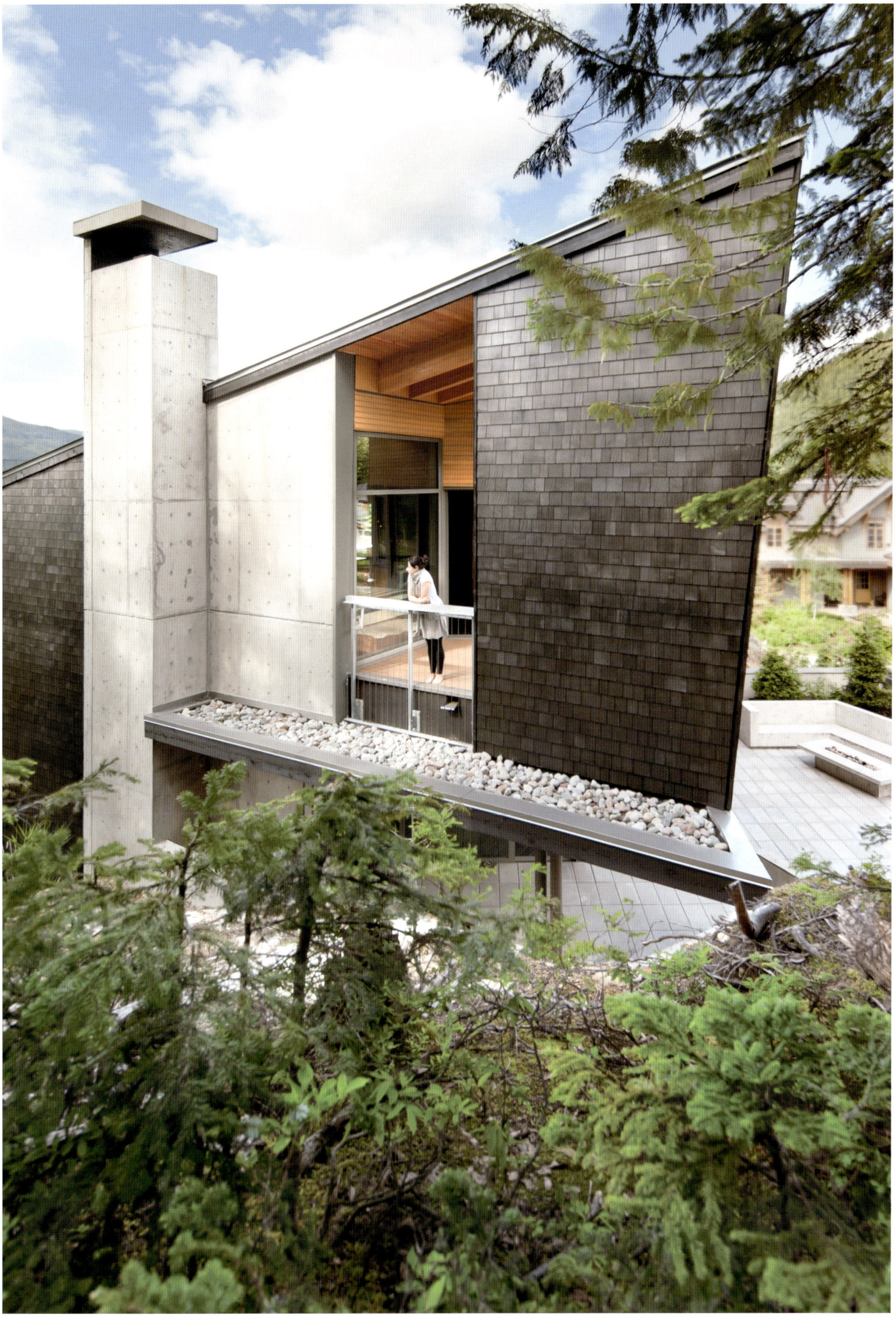

Whistler Residence

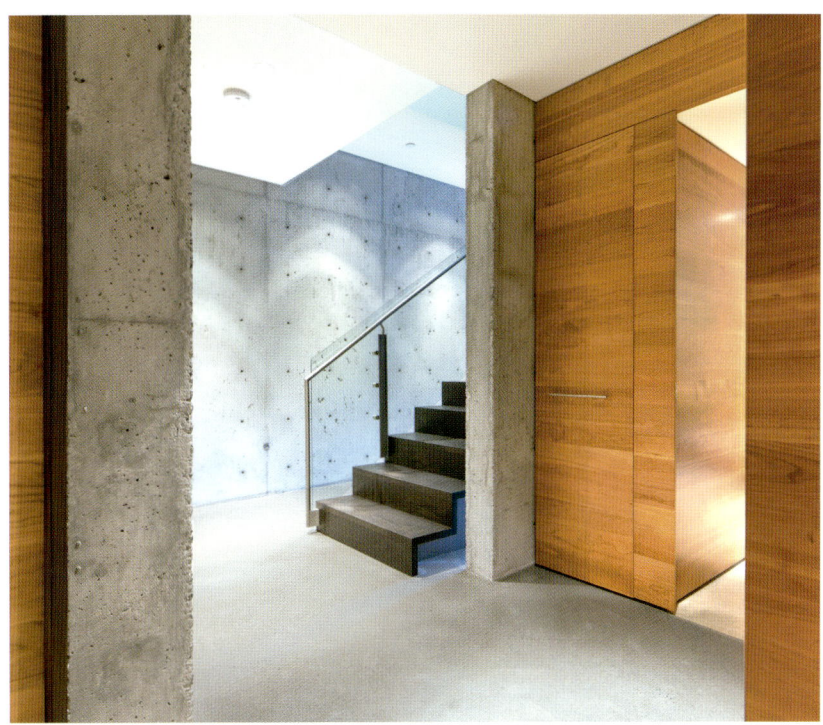

This house was designed for clients who appreciate the timber structure characteristic of a Whistler chalet, but desired a unique family home for seven that would capture this ambience without its typical organization and aesthetic.

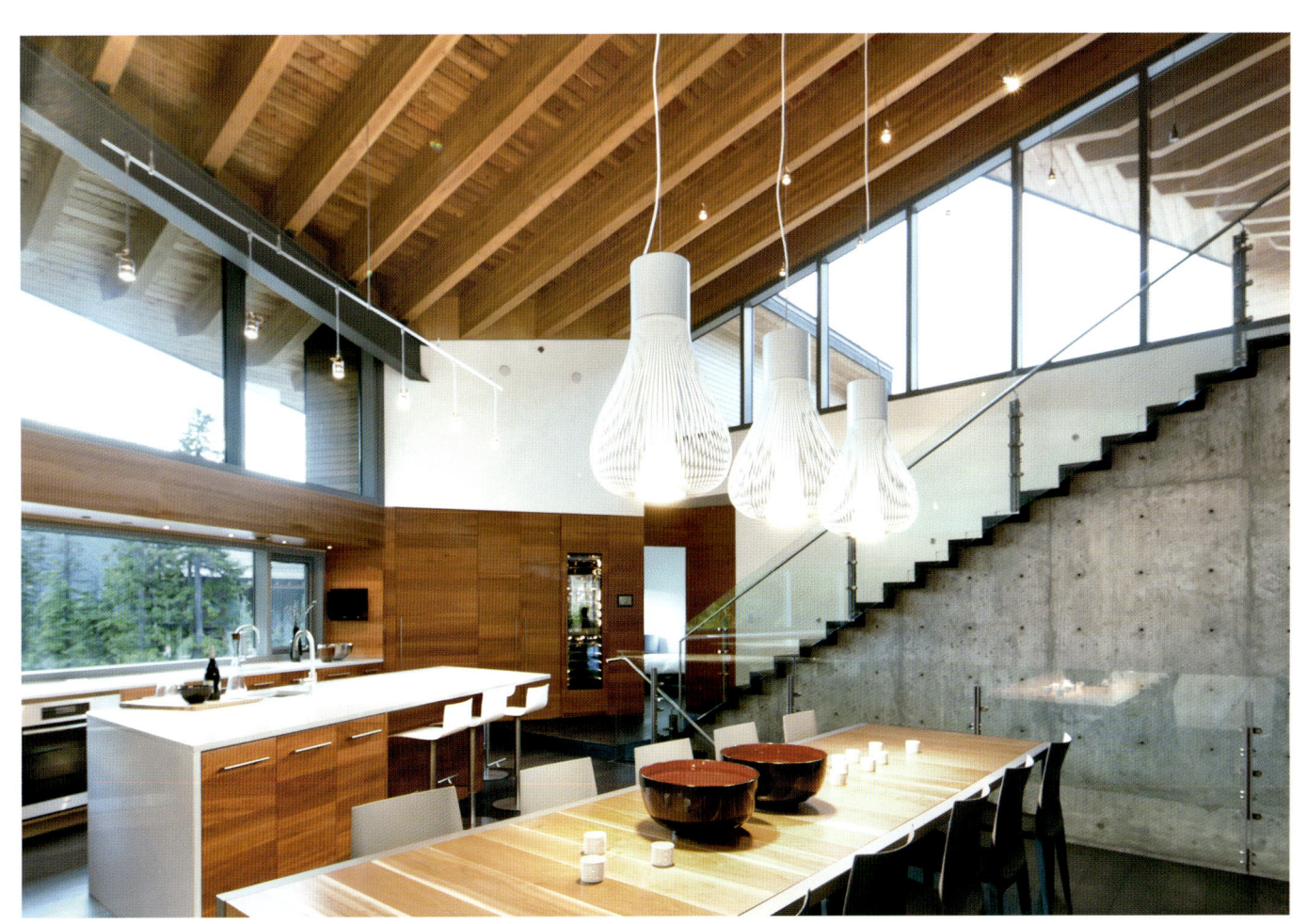

BattersbyHowat Architects

Whistler Residence

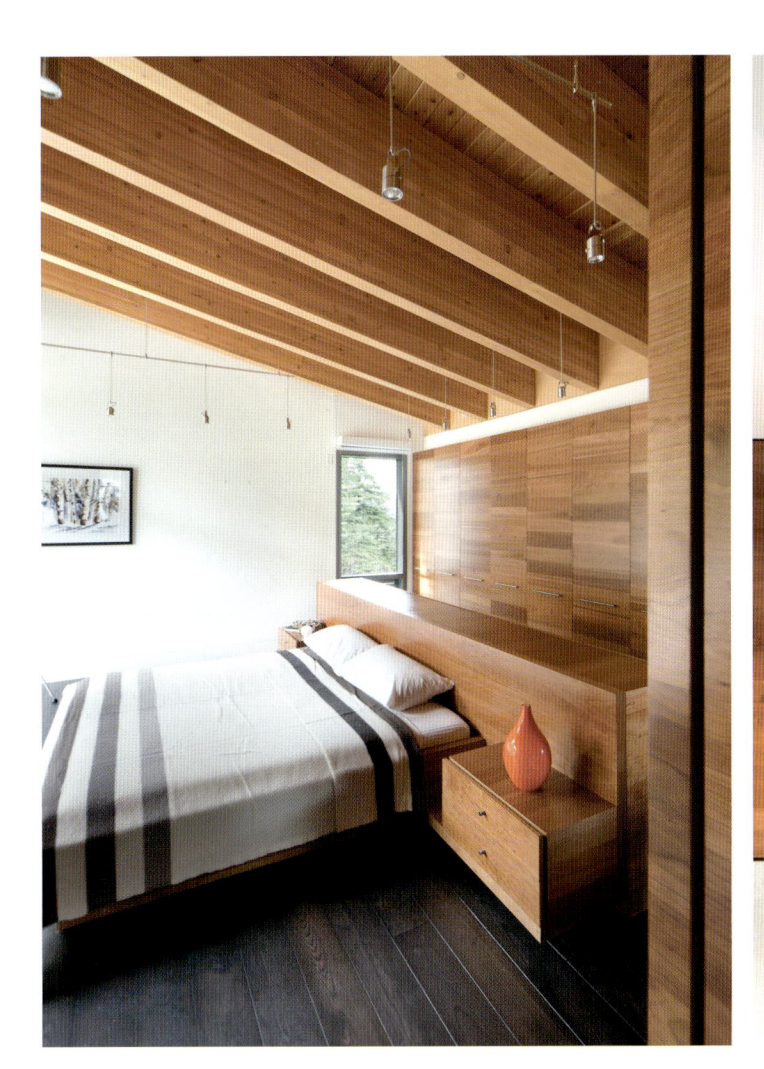

BattersbyHowat Architects 197

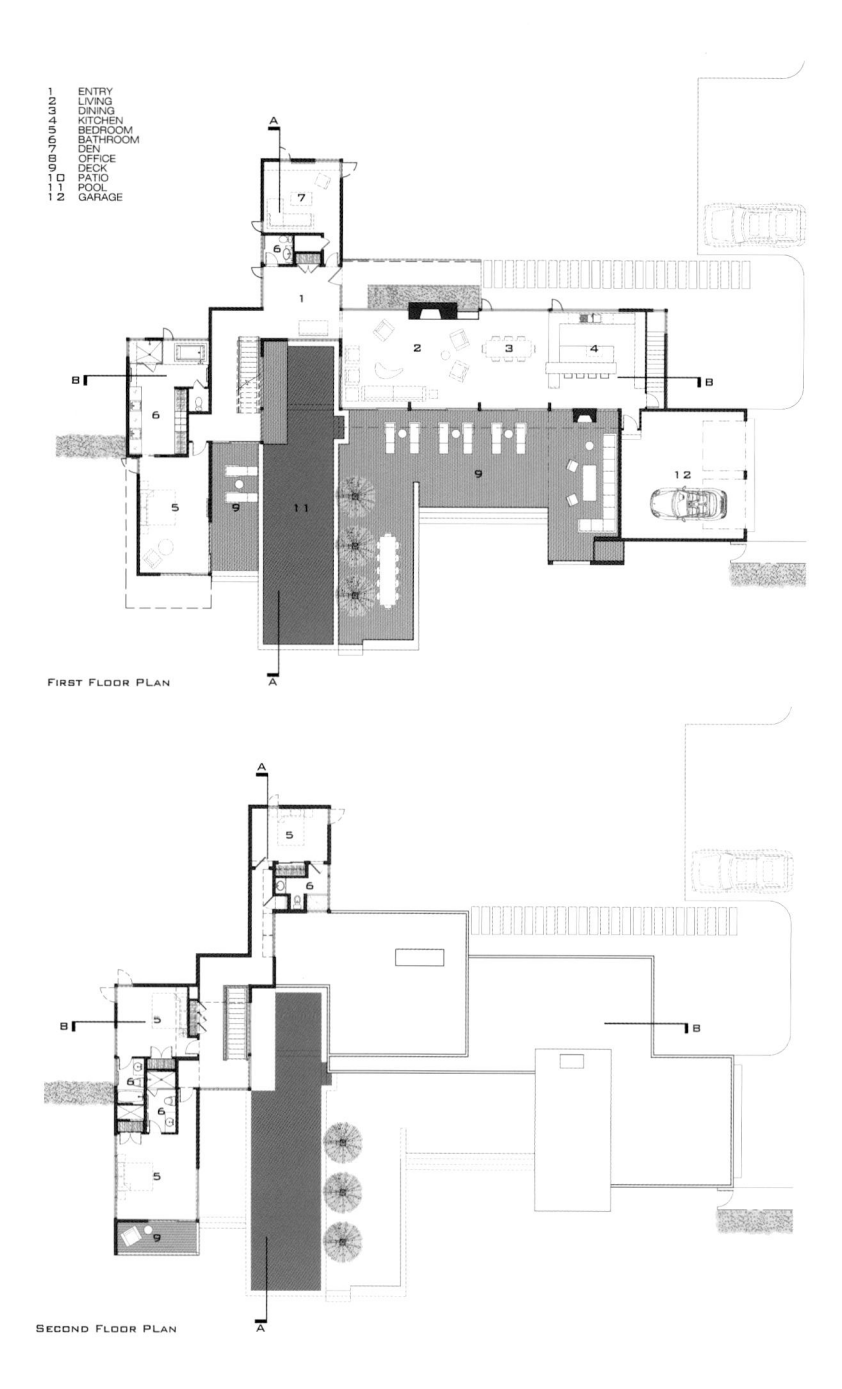

1 ENTRY
2 LIVING
3 DINING
4 KITCHEN
5 BEDROOM
6 BATHROOM
7 DEN
8 OFFICE
9 DECK
10 PATIO
11 POOL
12 GARAGE

FIRST FLOOR PLAN

SECOND FLOOR PLAN

Fieldview House
Fieldview House has three primary volumes arranged in a "C" that look out toward the adjacent agricultural reserve to the south.

Blaze Makoid Architecture
East Hampton, USA
371.6sqm

Located on a flat, one acre flag lot with neighbors close to the front and side yards, this 4,000 square foot house has three primary volumes arranged in a "C" that look out toward the adjacent agricultural reserve. This view serves as a backdrop for the interwoven composition of interior and exterior spaces.

The entry is located in a glass void on the northern side of the house and is reached by a raised stone walk covered by an uplit canopy. The foyer divides the house with the public space to the left and the private two storey bedroom wing to the right. An open floor plan that contains the living room, dining room, and kitchen stretches along the length of the central outdoor patio. Large expanses of south facing glass help to dissolve the barriers between the interior and the exterior. The glazing on the windows facing north, east, and west help maintain privacy and regulate temperature.

The design features intimate indoor and outdoor spaces that can serve various functions throughout the day.

Blaze Makoid Architecture

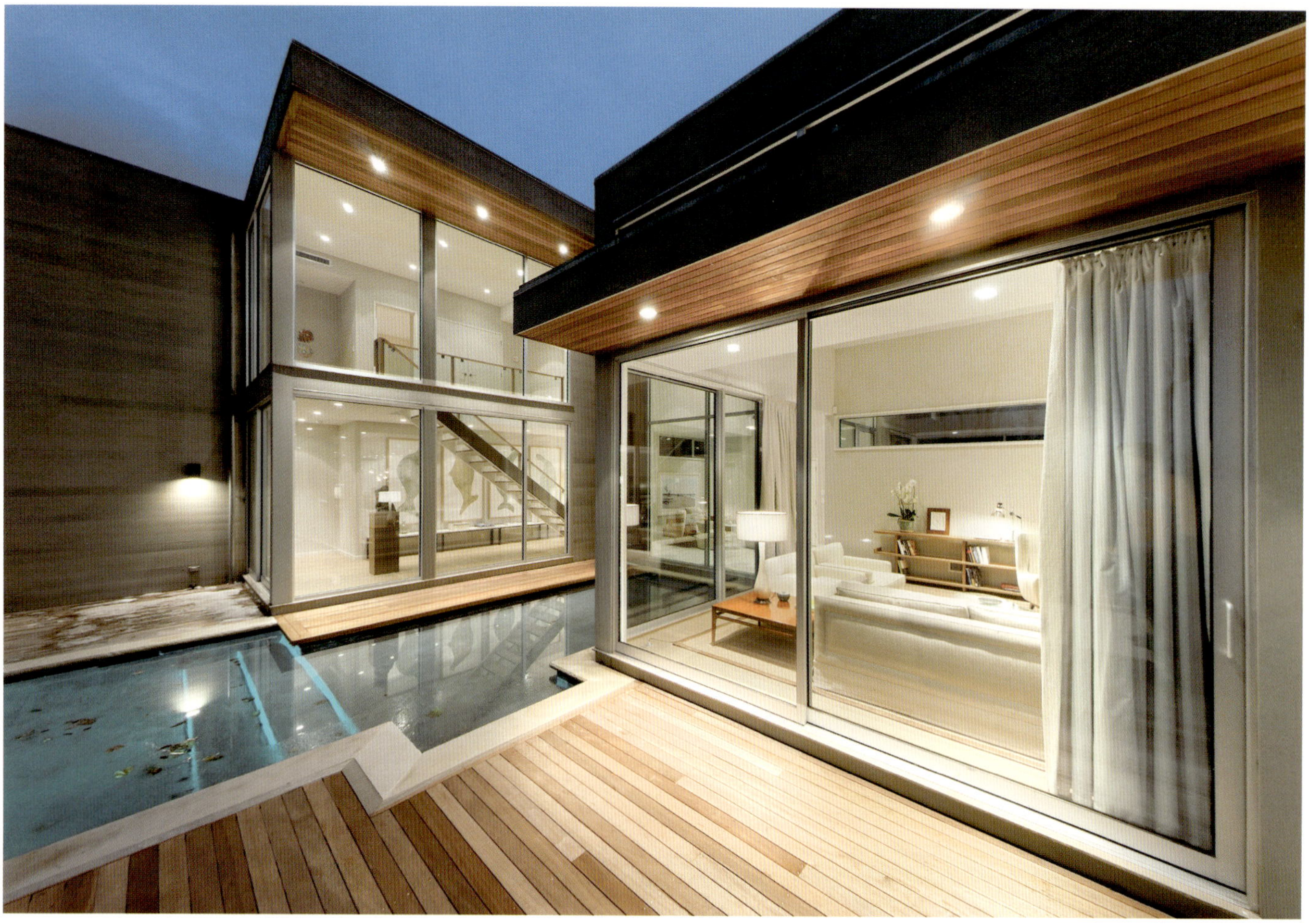

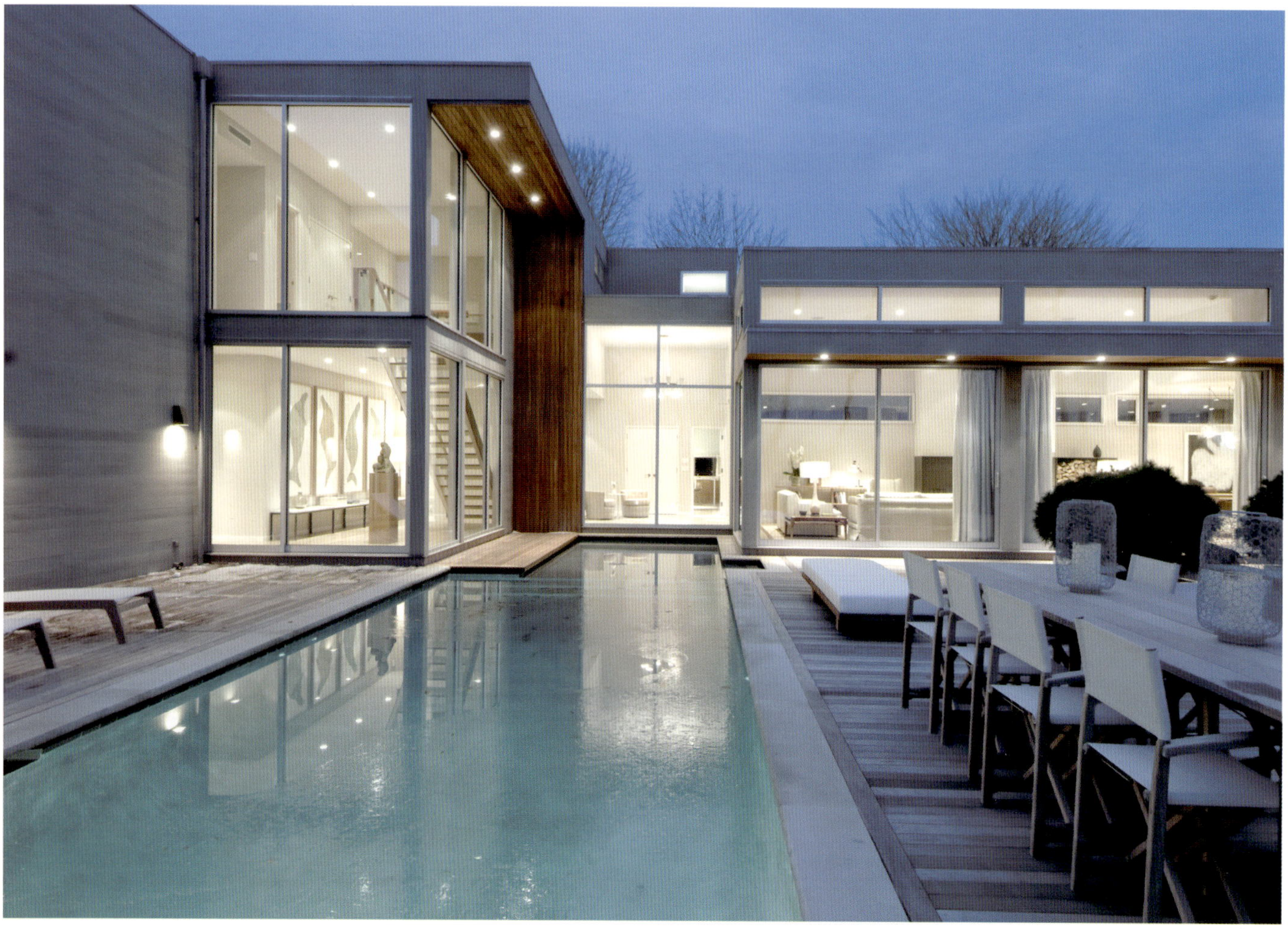

Blaze Makoid Architecture 201

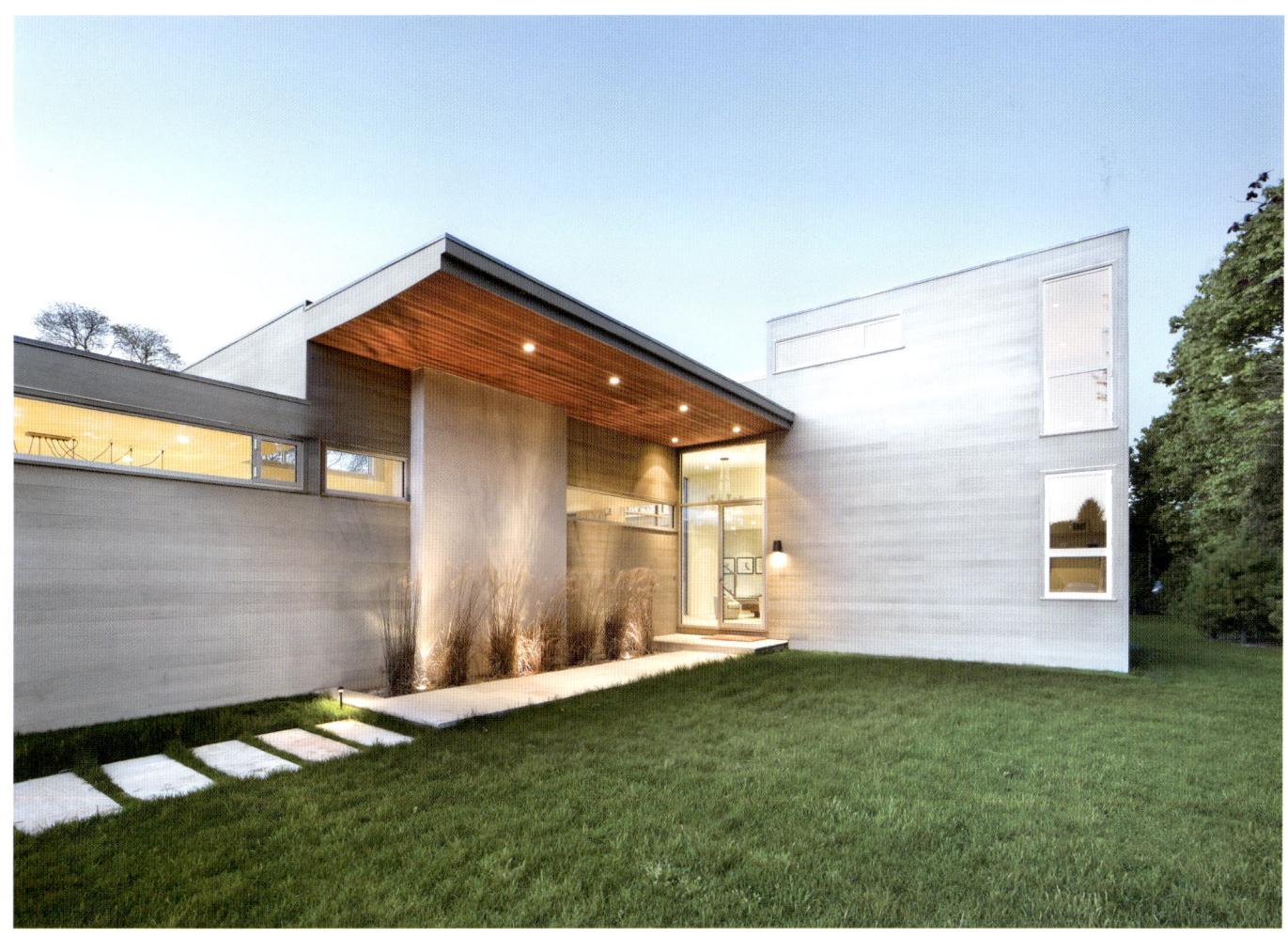

House VMVK
House VMVK is a reshaping of the archetypal rural house.

dmvA
Sint-Katelijne-Waver, Belgium
506sqm

dmvA started designing by reshaping an archetypal form with a hip roof. Extensive form-studies led to an amorphous form with a warped hip roof. The unusual angles and the cutout on the roof give the house its sculptural form.

The garage, entrance, office, bedrooms, and bathrooms are all located on the ground floor. A monumental white straight staircase leads up to the second level, which houses a living room, an open kitchen, and a storage area. The loft-like living room has marvelous windows with views of the green neighborhood. A spiral staircase leads up to a multi-purpose room located next to the extraordinary intimate roof top terrace.

The lacquered zinc roof and walls give the house an iconic look.

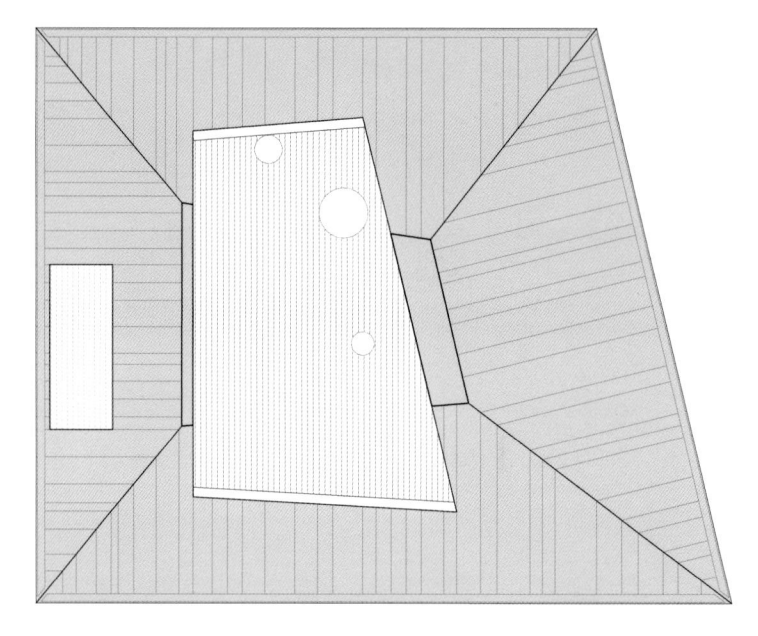

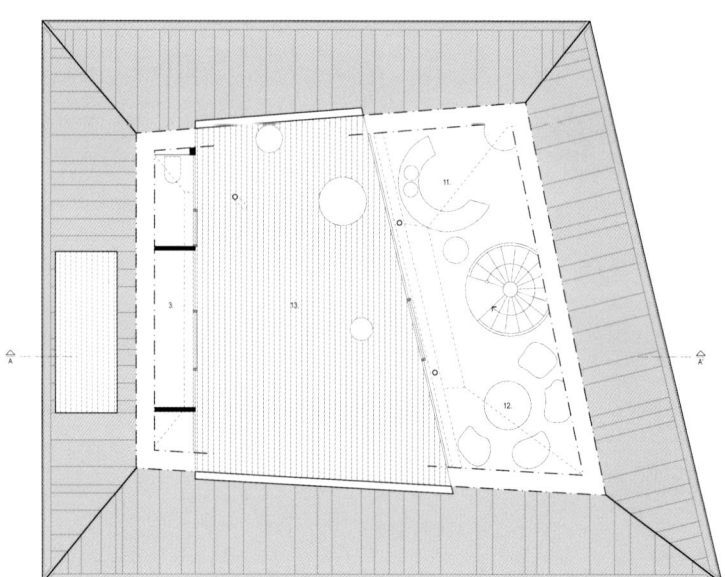

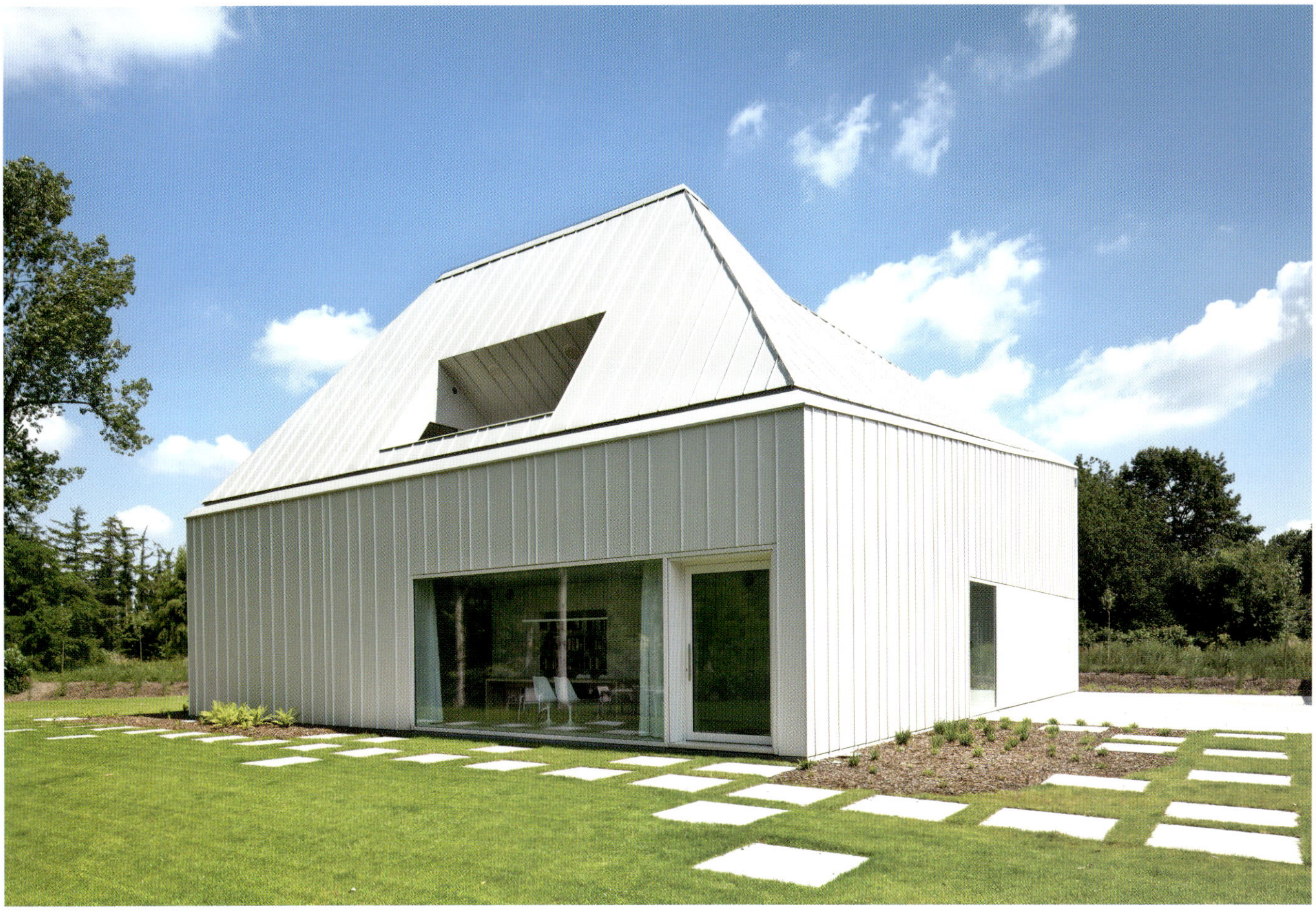

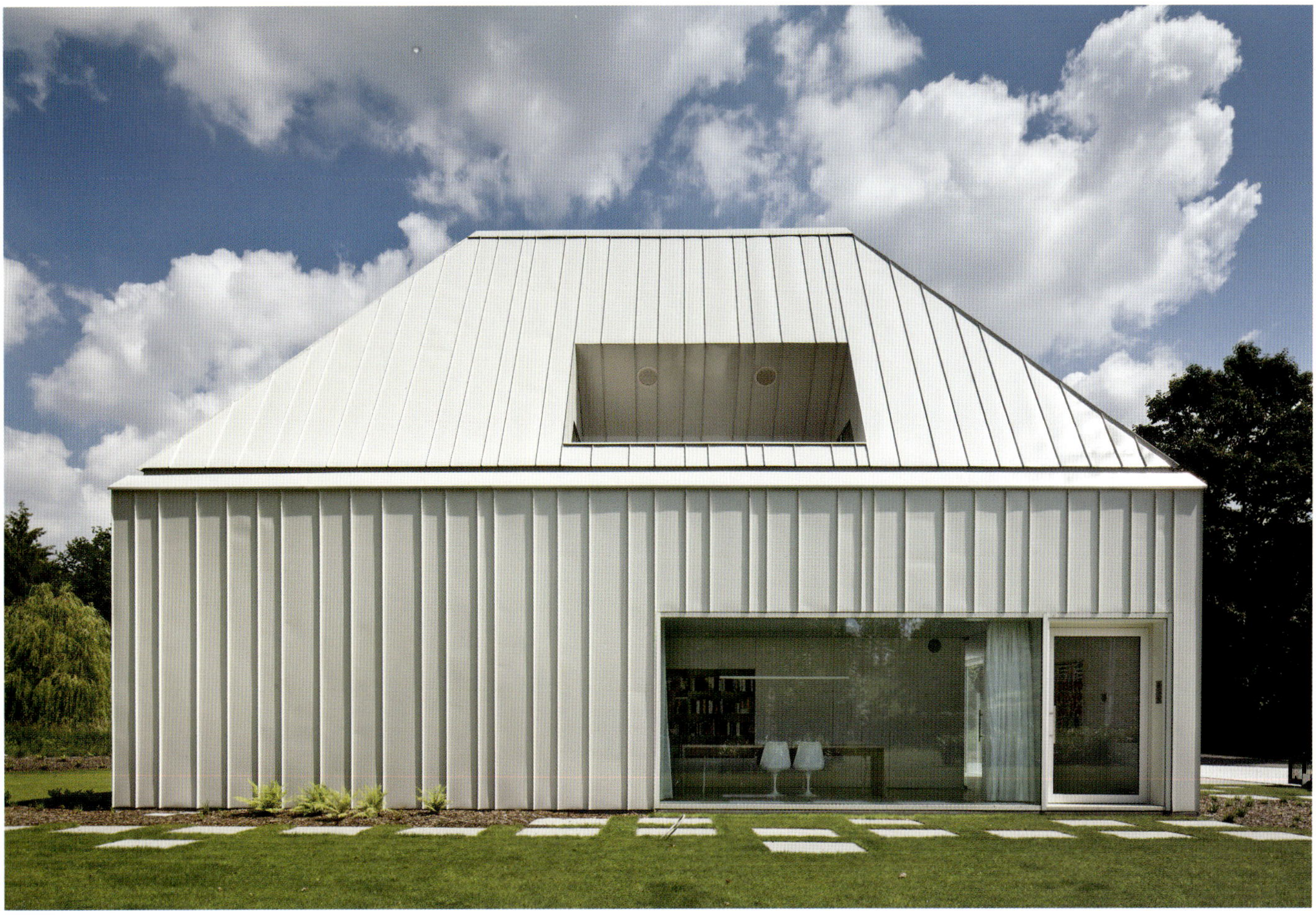

House VMVK

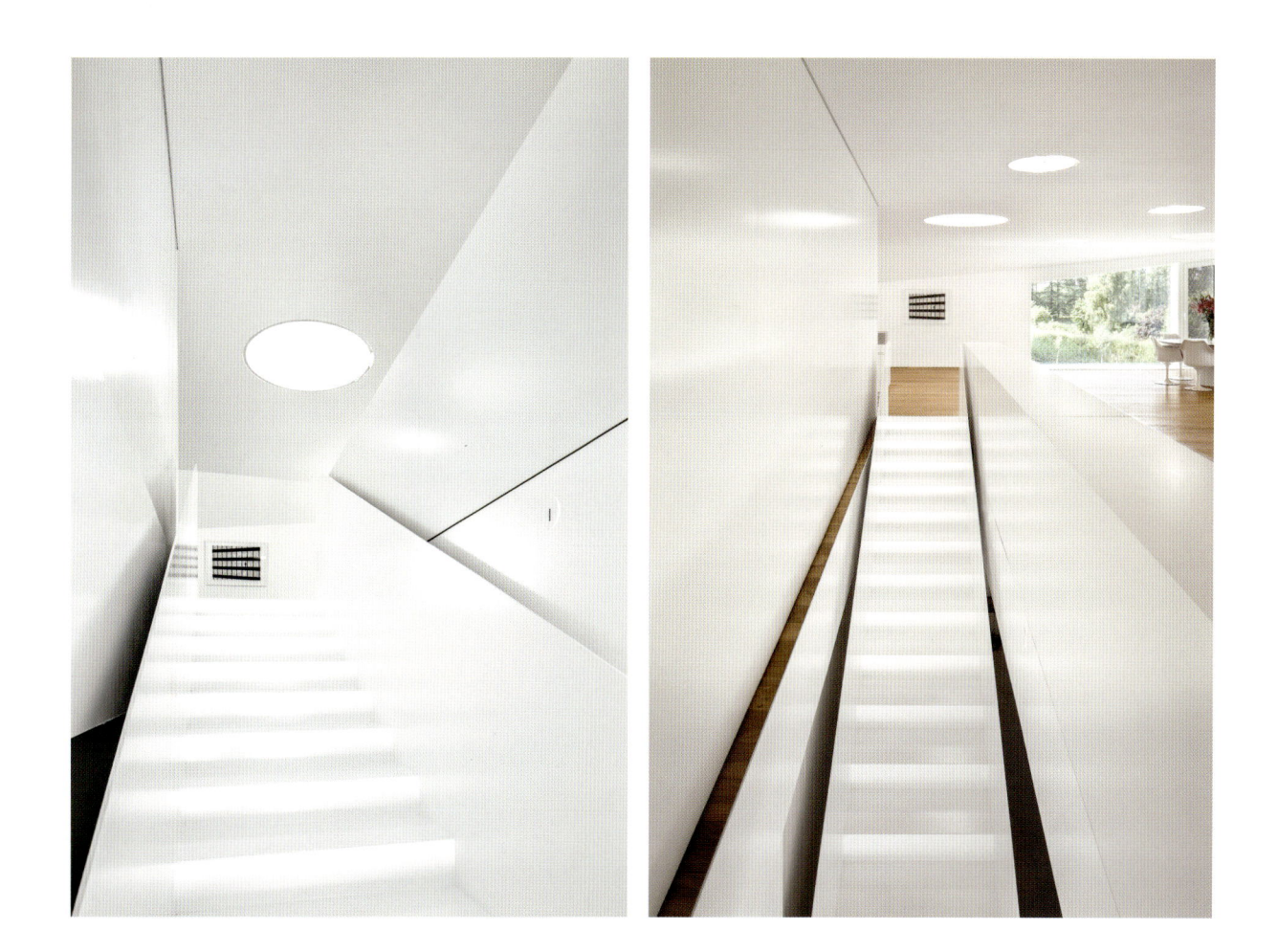

dmvA

205

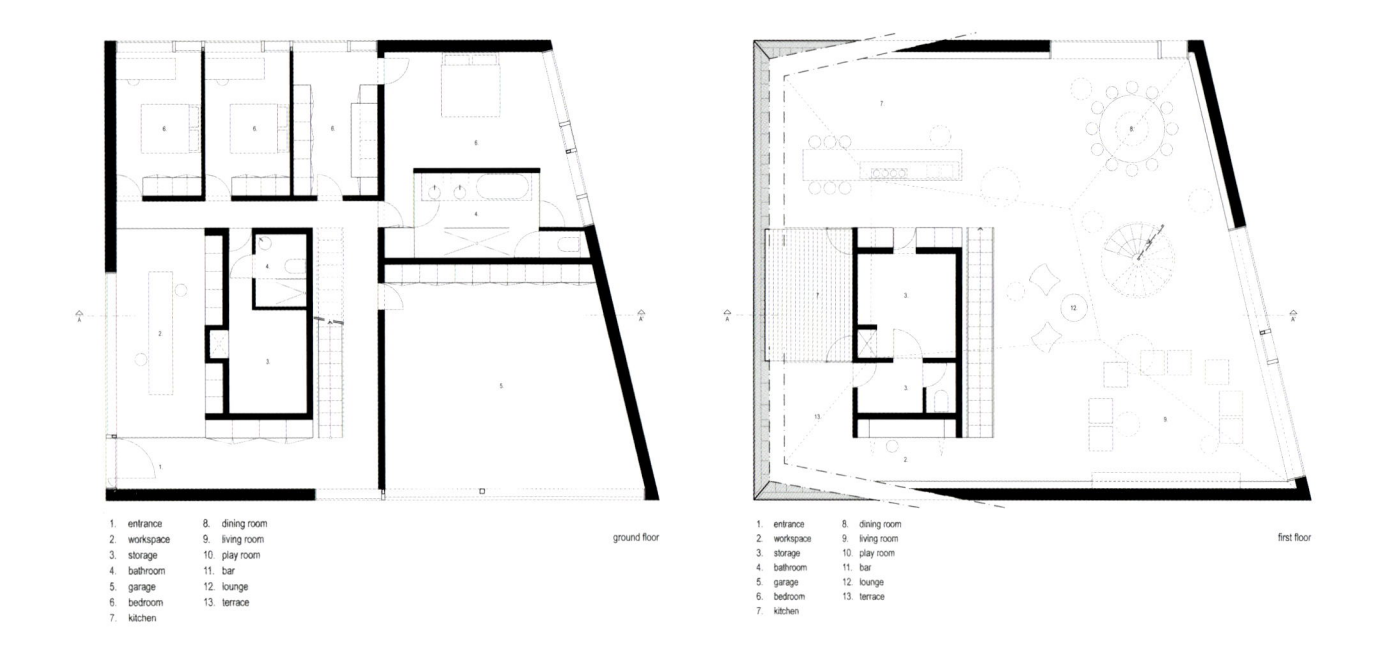

1.	entrance	8.	dining room
2.	workspace	9.	living room
3.	storage	10.	play room
4.	bathroom	11.	bar
5.	garage	12.	lounge
6.	bedroom	13.	terrace
7.	kitchen		

ground floor

1.	entrance	8.	dining room
2.	workspace	9.	living room
3.	storage	10.	play room
4.	bathroom	11.	bar
5.	garage	12.	lounge
6.	bedroom	13.	terrace
7.	kitchen		

first floor

House VMVK

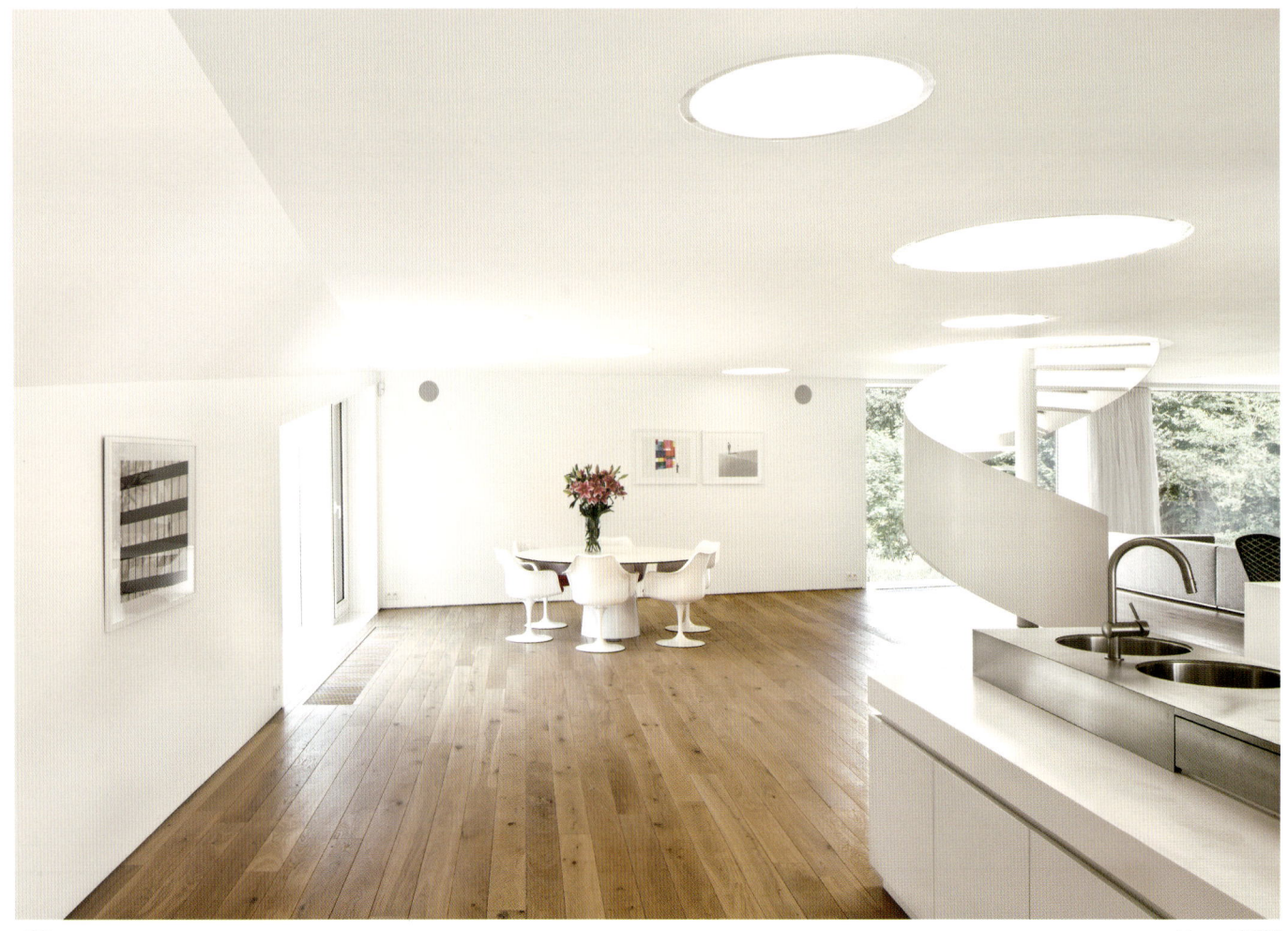

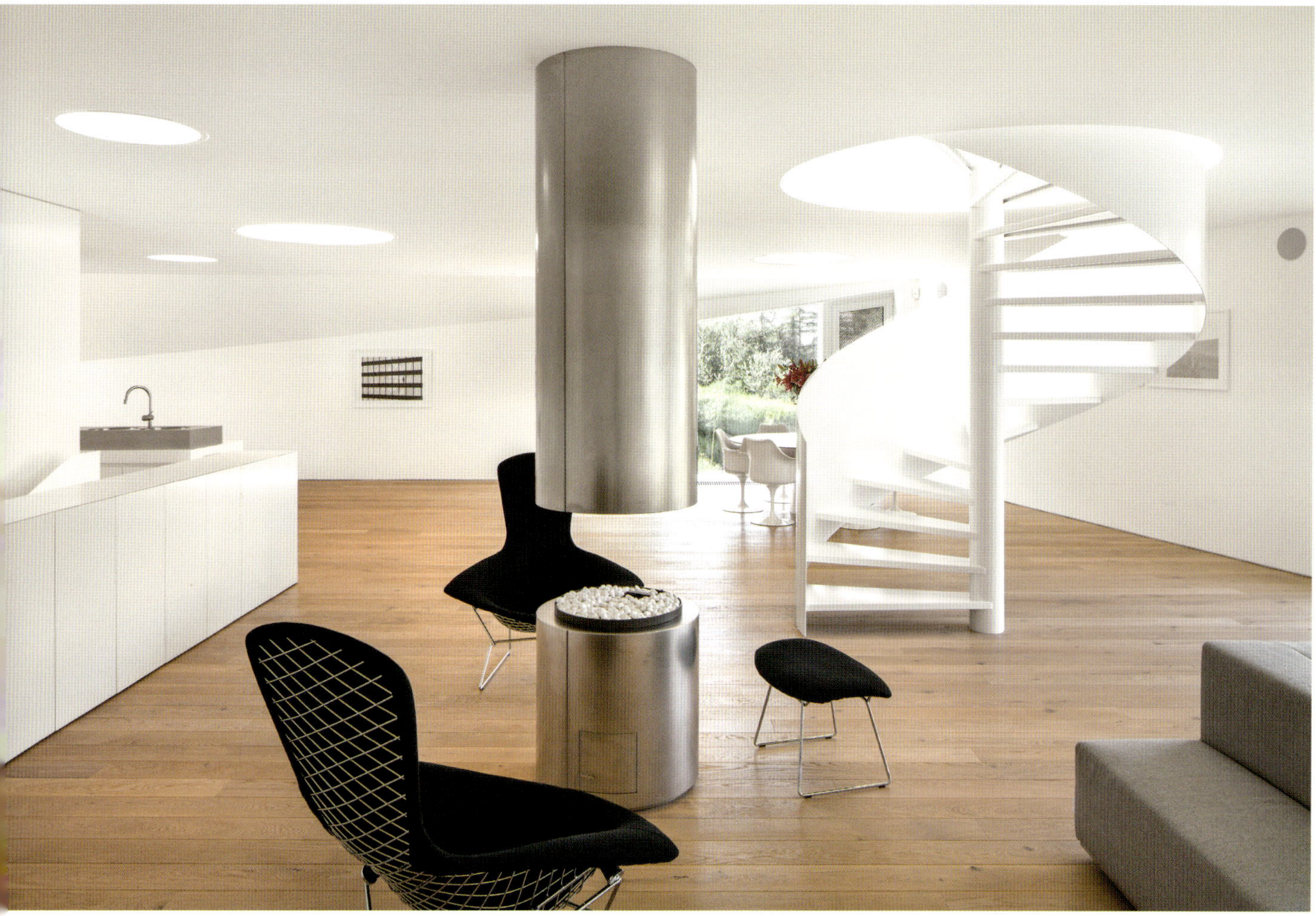

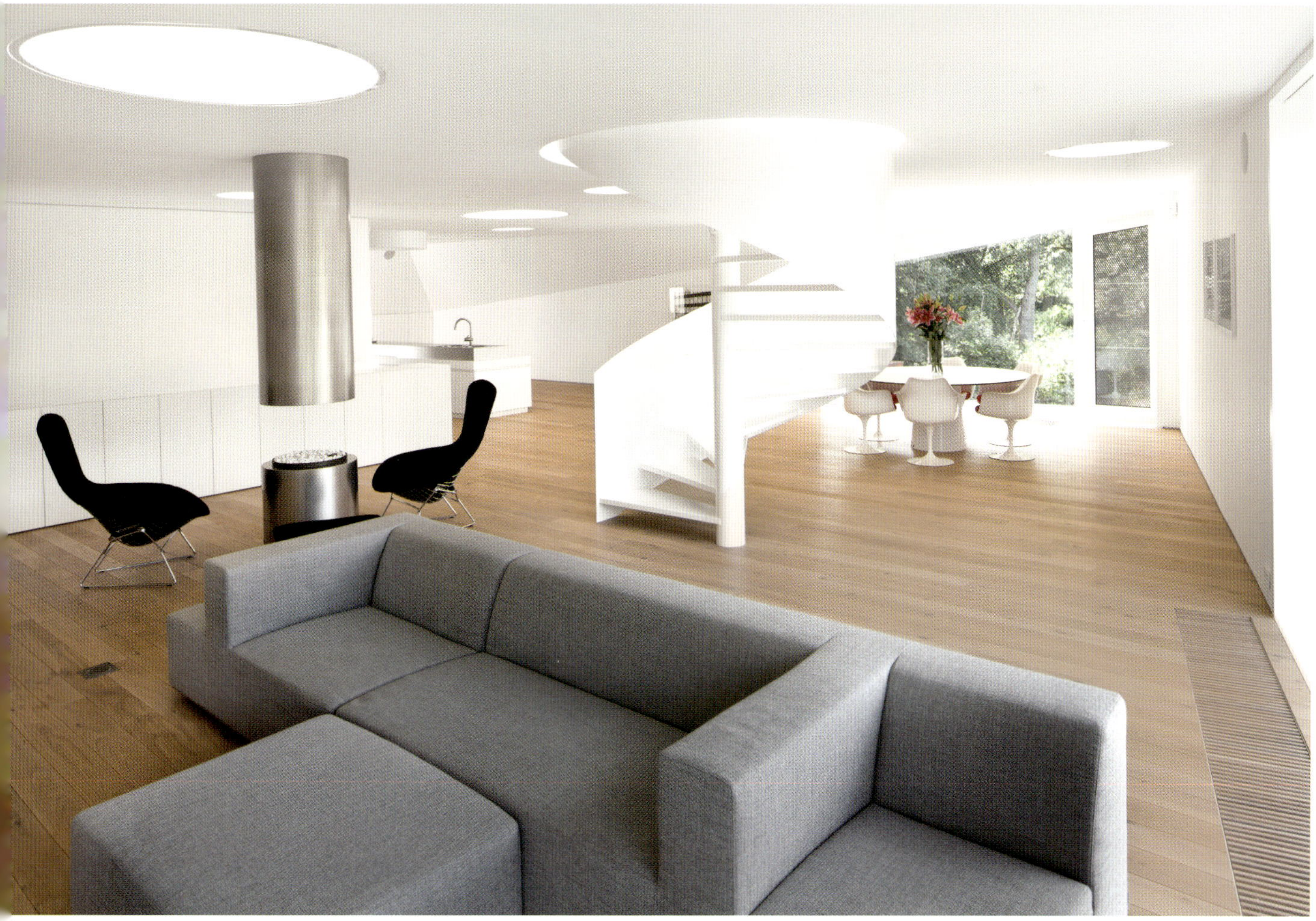

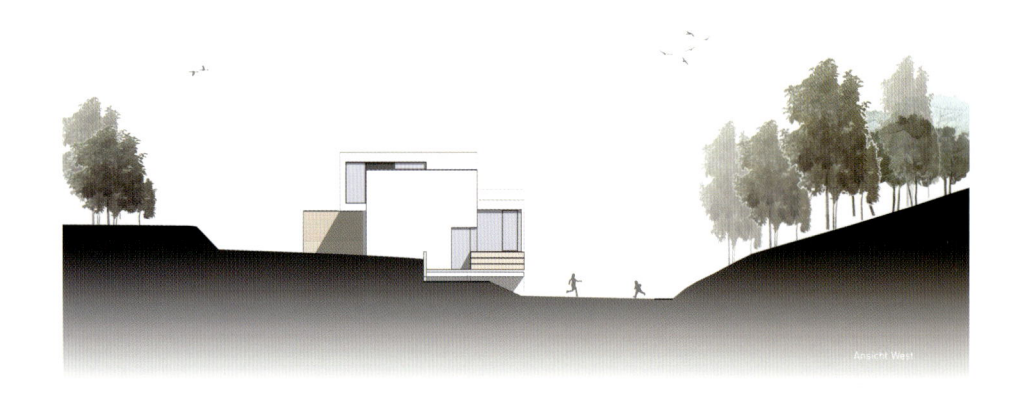

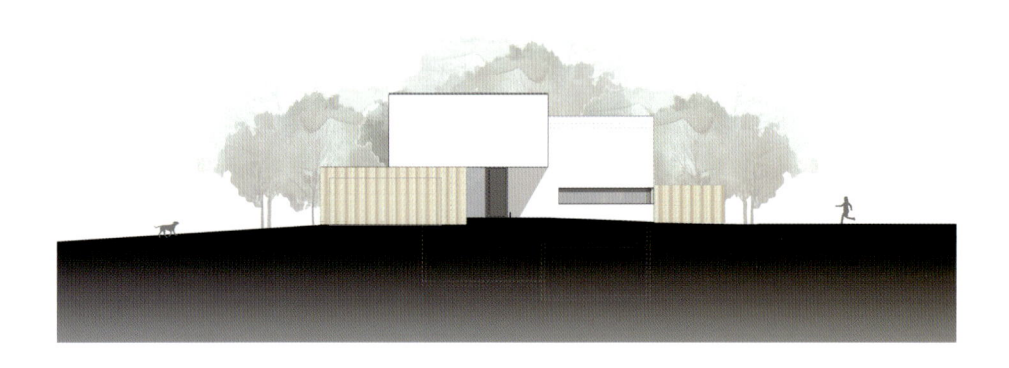

Aalen-Zochental House

Aalen-Zochental House is situated in the middle of a town and is yet peacefully alone.

L/A Liebel/Architekten BDA
Aalen, Germany
201sqm

Because the site is located in a valley with a steep slope on the southern side, many interested buyers thought it would be impossible to build on it. The slope shields the site from the outside world, making it possible to open the house up toward the south, giving every room a beautiful view of the countryside.

The client wanted there to be a harmonious connection between the house and the garden. The challenge of the topography led to a split-level design. The house is a unique and personal living space that features panoramic views and welcoming transparency. Large steps playfully join the different levels of the house.

The windows allow a breathtaking experience of light as it changes throughout the day and with the seasons. All the openings were carefully placed to guaranty privacy while still providing a sense of openness. The building's north side is almost without windows, thus causing the neighboring buildings to seem to recede into the distance. Each room was designed to be flexible and work for many different living situations. The parents and children currently sleep on the first floor, while the lower level contains guest rooms and workspace. Both floors have bathrooms and separate entrances. This design will allow the parents to occupy the lower level once the children are older.

L/A Liebel/Architekten BDA

Aalen-Zochental House

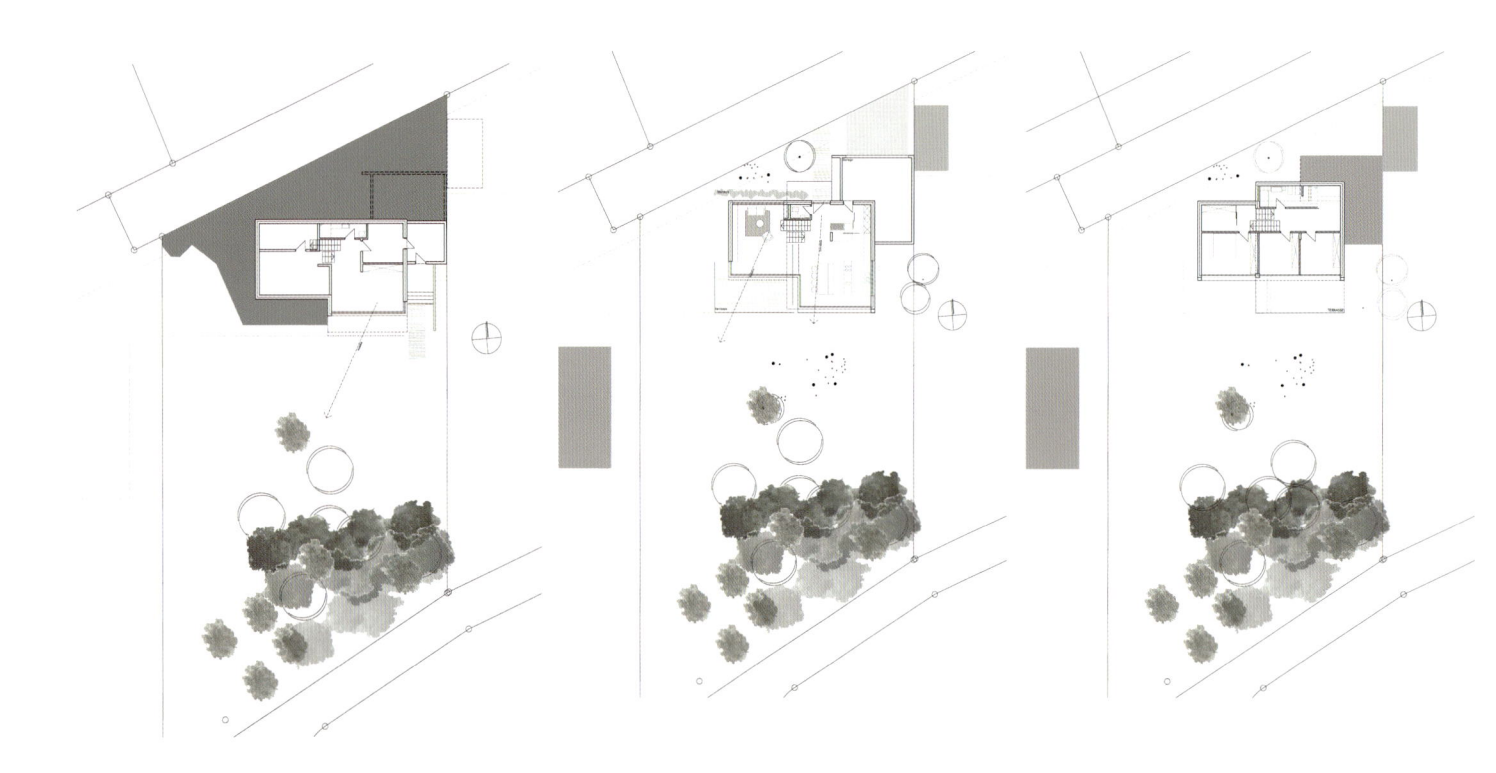

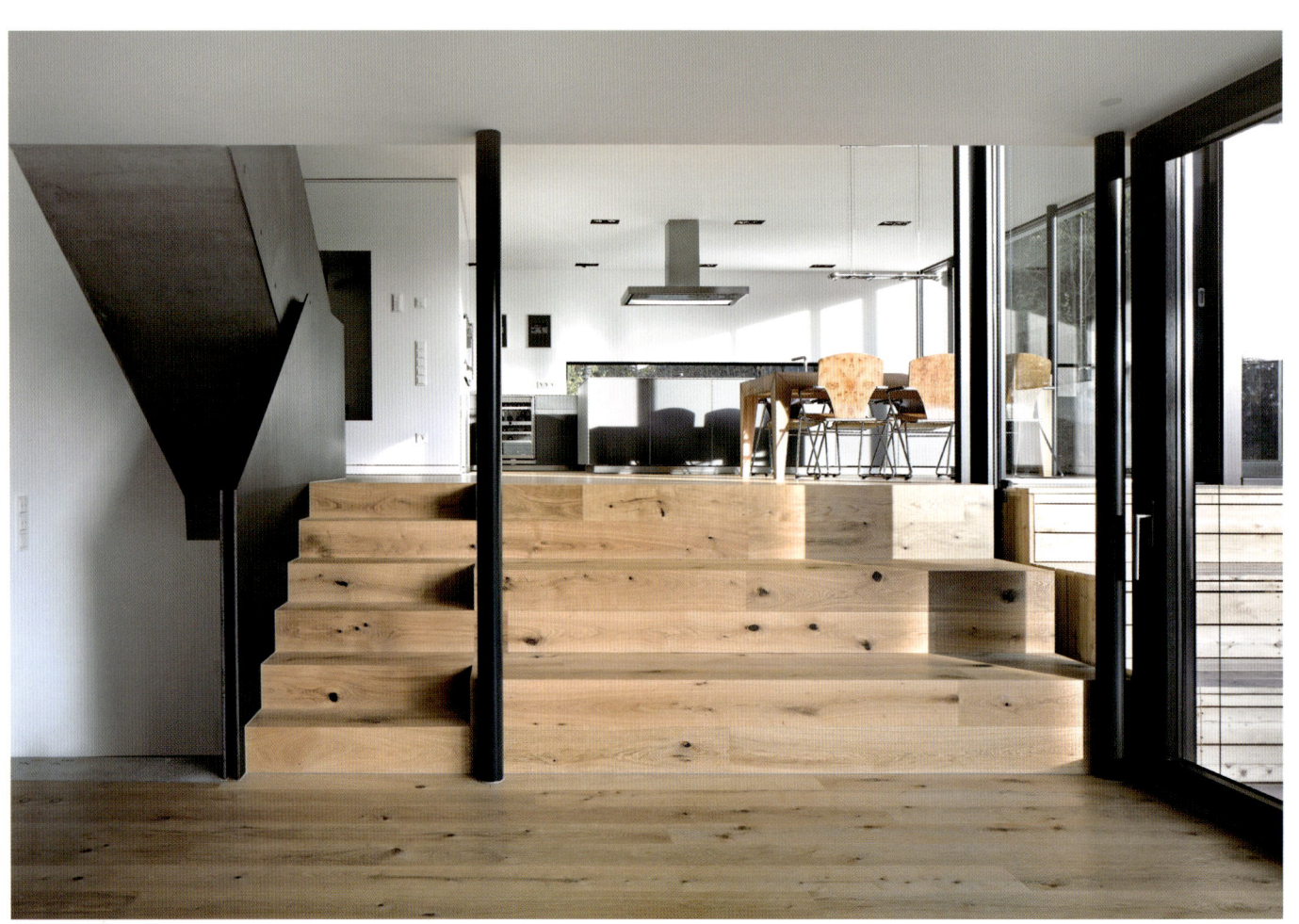

L/A Liebel/Architekten BDA

House in Ayukawa

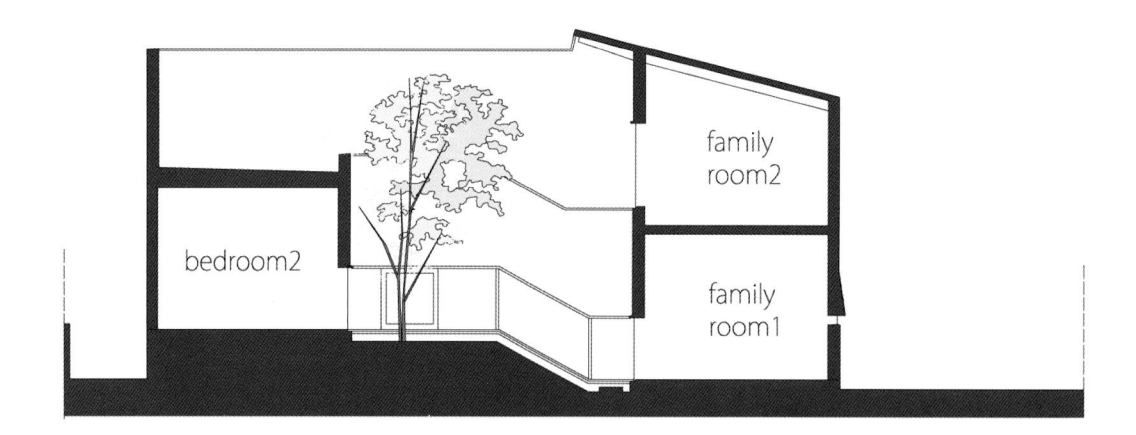

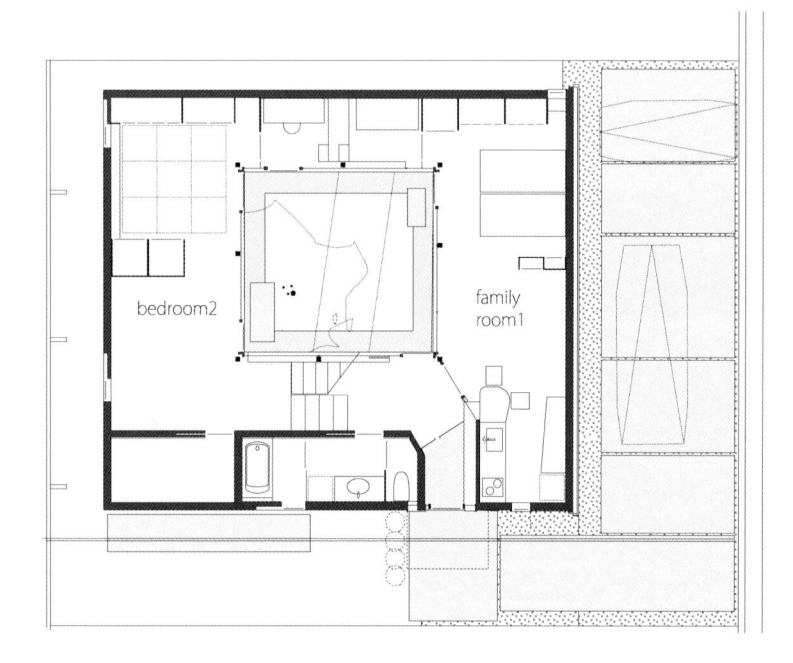

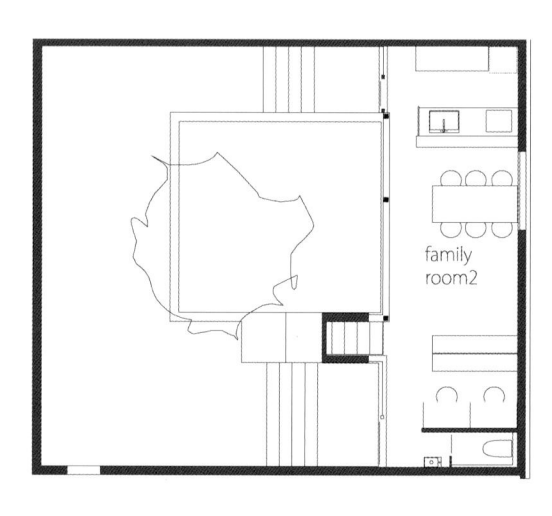

House in Ayukawa is a multi-family house that was designed so that it could be adapted for single-family use.

Dai Nagasaka/Mega
Osaka, Japan
123.6sqm

Although it is currently a two-family house, the spaces surrounding the courtyard will give the building continuity when it is converted into a single-family residence. The neighboring buildings shelter the house and lot.

The courtyard design was chosen to ensure privacy for this outside space. The design has the added benefit of allowing a great deal of light to enter the interior. The house also features a comfortable rooftop terrace.

The exterior walls are silver and the interior ones are white.

The lower part of the first floor provides space for the parents and the upper part contains a space for a couple and children. The second floor houses a family room.

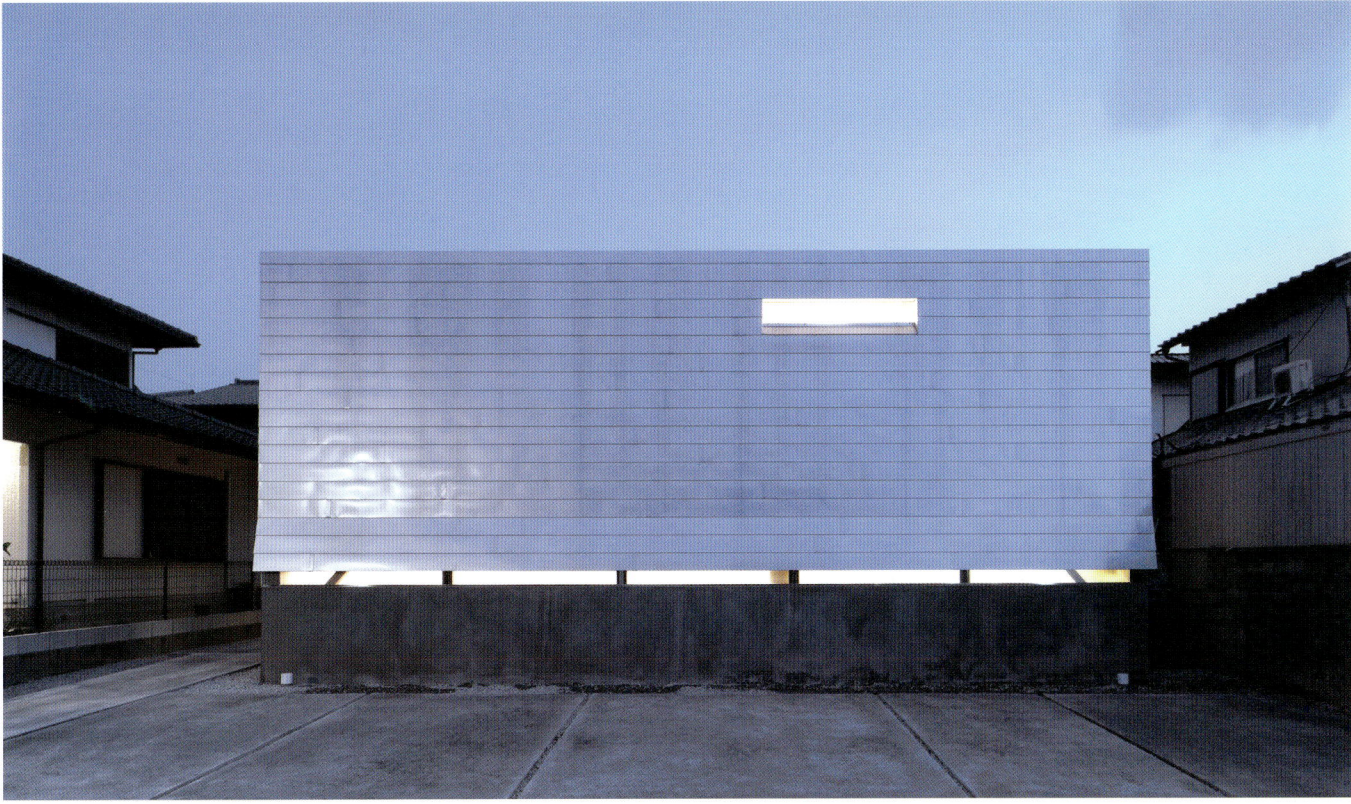

Dai Nagasaka/Mega

House in Ayukawa

Dai Nagasaka/Mega

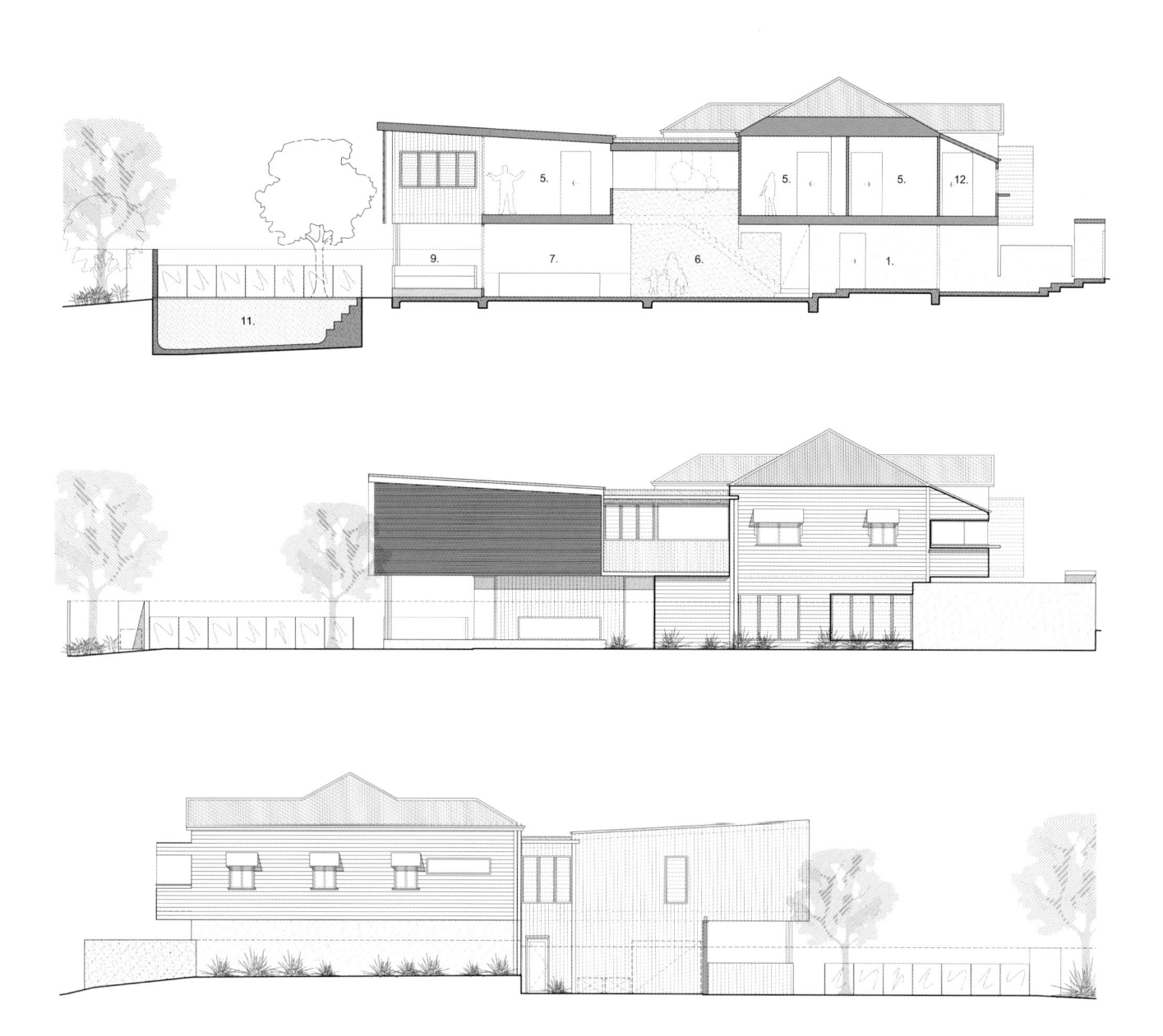

105 V
105 V was created by extending and renovating a pre-war home.

Shaun Lockyer Architects
Brisbane, Australia
350sqm

The house is a contemporary renovation and extension of an original pre-war cottage in New Farm, Brisbane.

The design incorporates a dramatic screening device designed to offer sun protection, privacy, and intimacy of space.

A large central void joins the new and the old parts of the house and allows for north sun to flood the living space.

The house has a deliberately minimal and restrained material palate with a highly articulated timber and steel bridge as a feature within the space.

Shaun Lockyer Architects

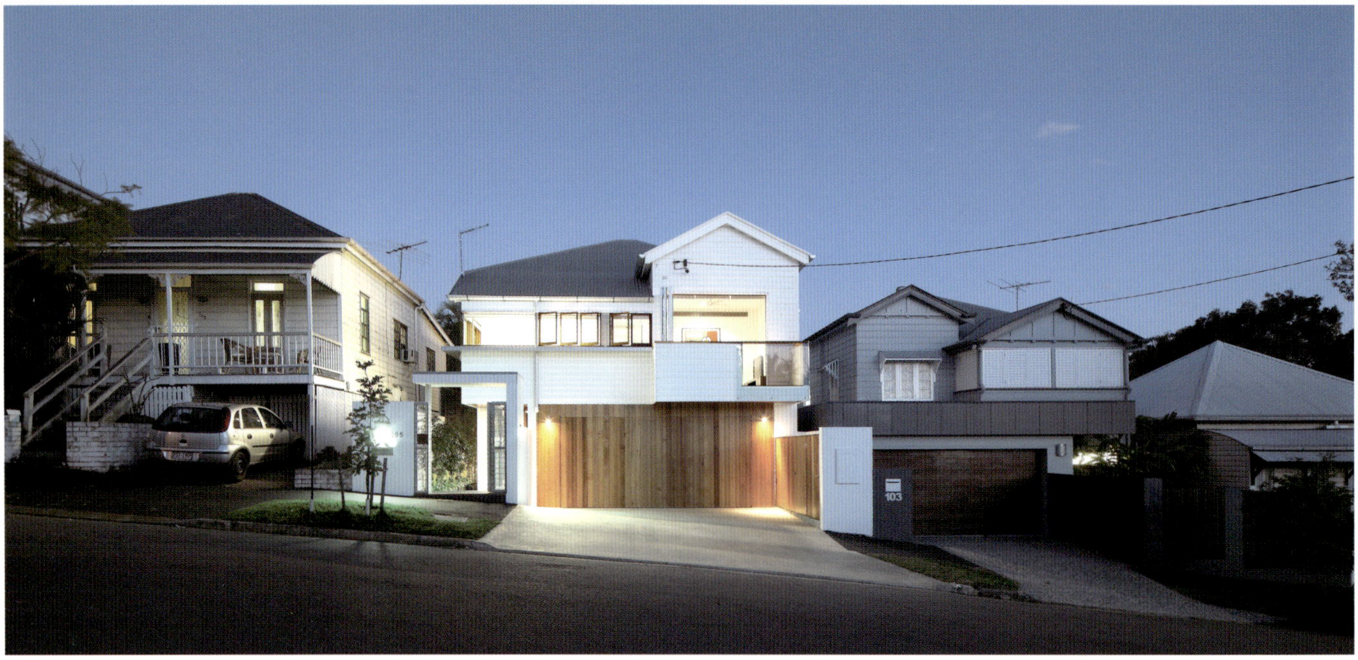

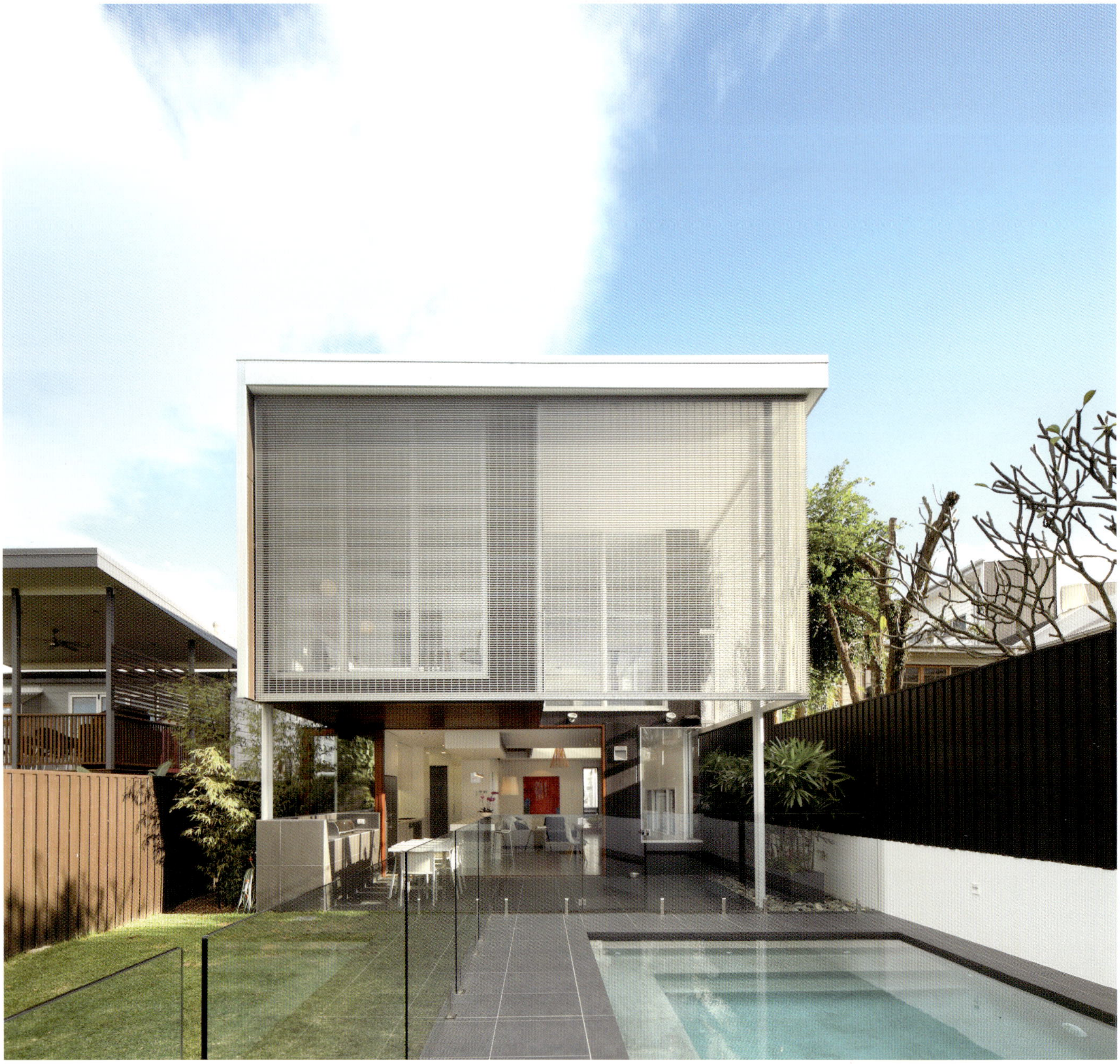

A large central void joins the new and old parts of the house and allows sunlight from the north to flood the living space.

Shaun Lockyer Architects

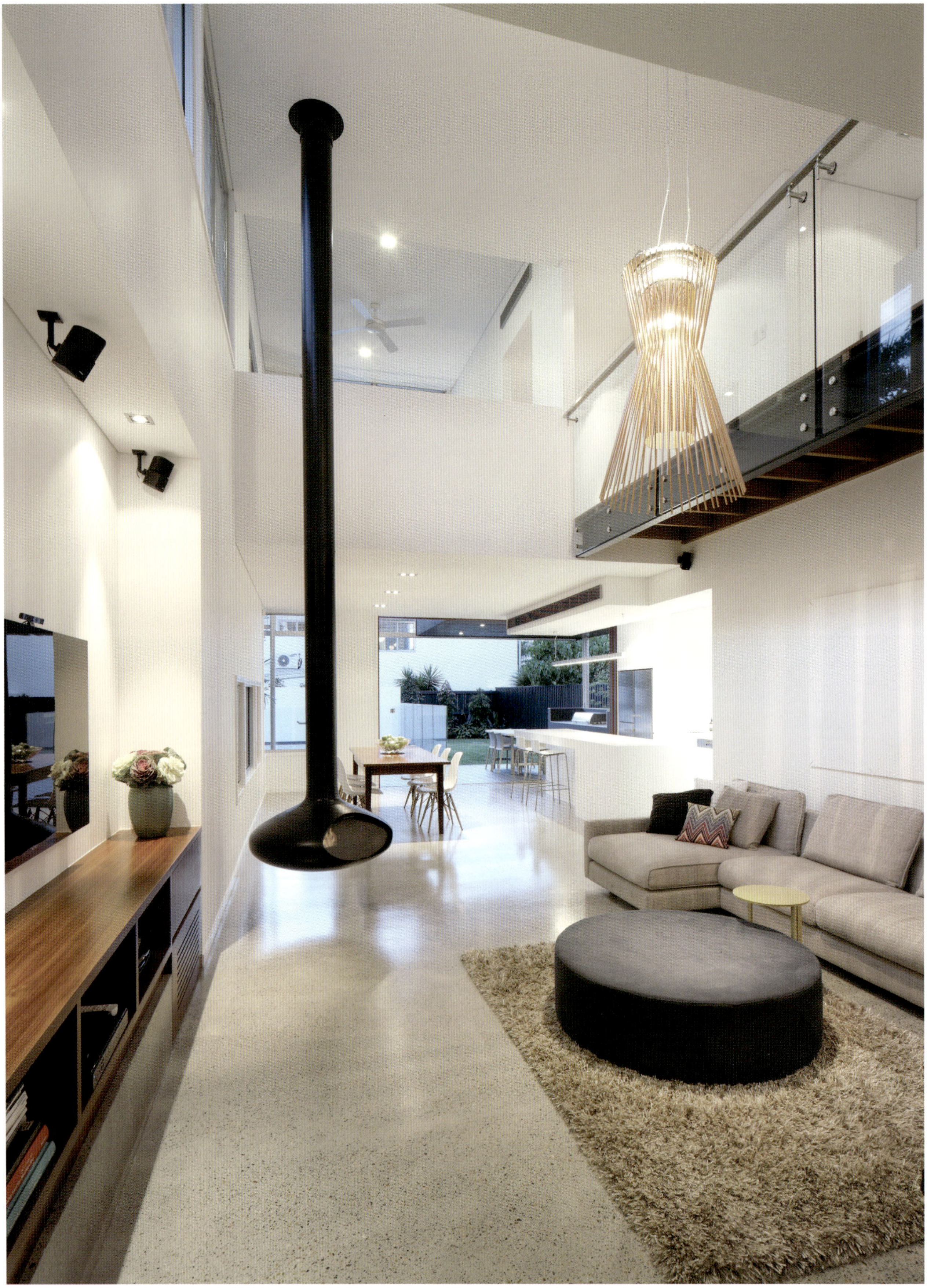

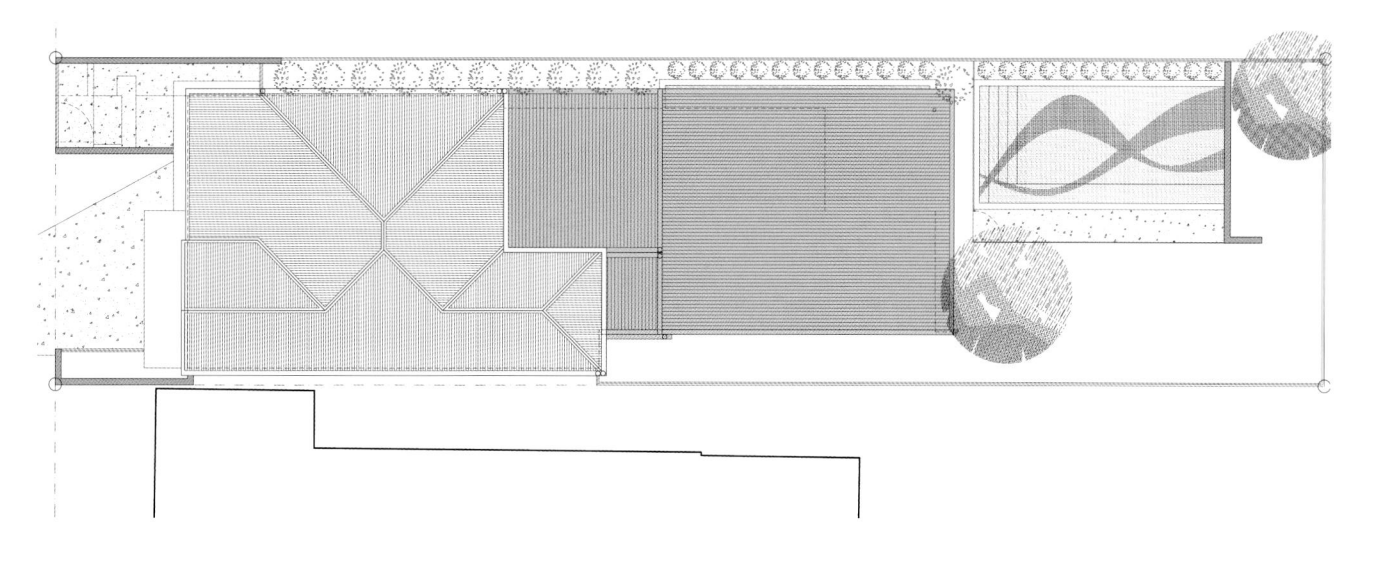

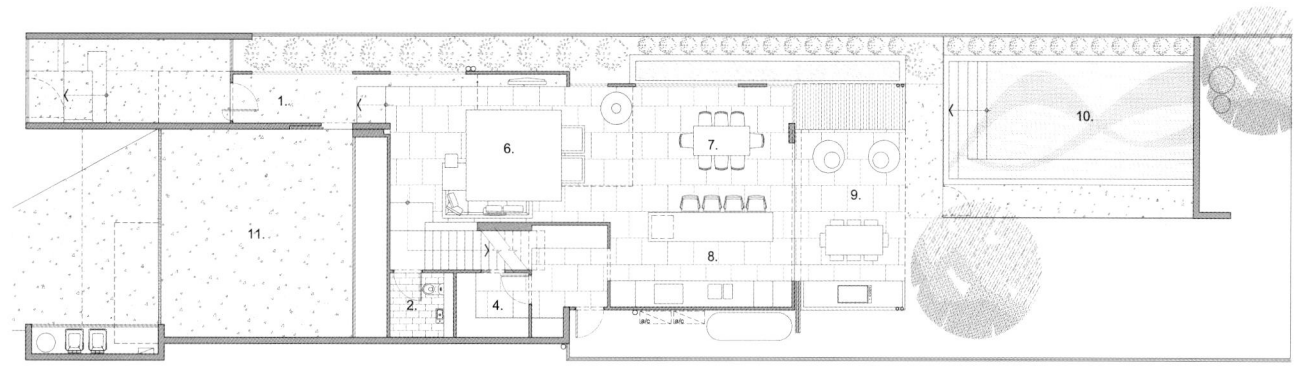

Shaun Lockyer Architects 221

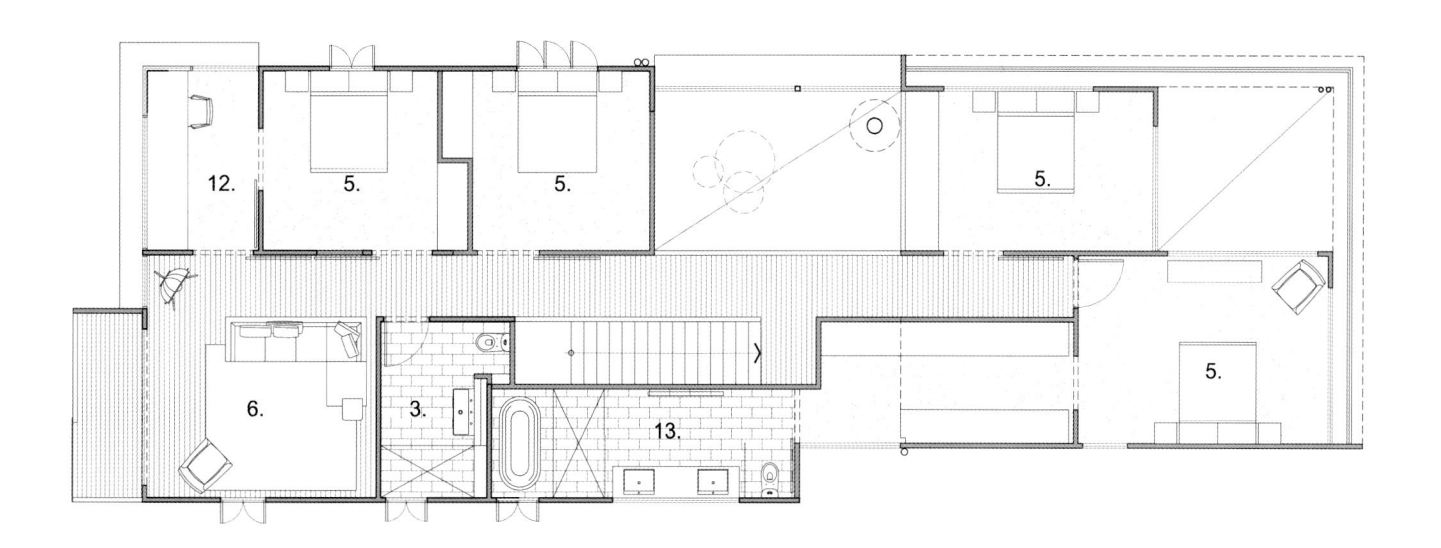

Tusculum St. Residence

Tusculum St. Residence offers extraordinary spaces complemented by confident forms, understated design, and exquisite detail.

Smart Design Studio
Sydney, Australia
325sqm

This exciting renovation and extension of a turn-of-the-century terrace house in Sydney's Potts Point focuses on a grand and gracefully spiralling stair that forms the pivotal junction of the old and new parts of the house. The staircase, spanning the width of the building, features delicate fan-like steel treads cantilevered from the central steel post that wind their way past six split levels. The stair was conceived as the element that grafts the contemporary and new minimal structure to the refined, trimmed, and formal older portion of the dwelling.

Spacious living areas and private zones open out from each side of the stair with one area per level, alternating between the old and new building. The formal and informal zones of the house maintain a natural sense of privacy from each other through the offset in level, yet they maintain a sense of interconnection in the openness and movement created by the stair.

Internally, finishes in the old portion of the house are contemporary and elegant in a stripped classical style. They include deep flush skirting boards, mannered panelled doors, and wide timber floorboards, all of which are a glossy white and offset by richly coloured set plaster walls. In contrast, the mainly white extension with the same gloss white floorboards features a black stained timber-boarded joinery element across three levels. Bronze window frames, ironmongery, and trims unite both portions of the three-storey home.

Externally, the connection to the outdoors is accentuated through a 13m clear span wall of sliding doors that overlooks a pocket garden. In addition to this, the bi-folding doors are concealed by joinery to provide a seamless connection to the tiered rear garden that showcases a mature pepper tree.

Smart Design Studio

Tusculum St. Residence

Smart Design Studio

225

House in Quinta Patino

House in Quinta Patino takes a simple and effective approach to create a comfortable modern home that incorporates the landscape.

Frederico Valsassina Arquitectos
Estoril, Portugal
700sqm

The rectangular design arranges the living spaces within a modular arrangement of compartments and openings, integrating outdoor courtyards into the internal configuration. Placing all of these habitable spaces inside the four perimeter walls makes structure appear larger than it actually is. Rectilinear voids within each of the elevations extend the interior rooms to the outside zones. Multiple windows, patios, and doorways are cut out of the simple rectangular box design of the home.

There are several mature trees on the property and vegetation walls are positioned within the void spaces. Large wooden shutters shield the interior and the courtyards are equipped with wooden doors that may be closed for privacy. The wooden elements contrast with the gray concrete walls of the exterior.

An entry path leading to the home terminates within the courtyard. A hall leads to the living and dining area and the bathroom on the western side of the plan. The service spaces and kitchen are positioned across a courtyard. A flight of stairs leads to the upper floor, which contains the master suite, an office, closets, and bathrooms.

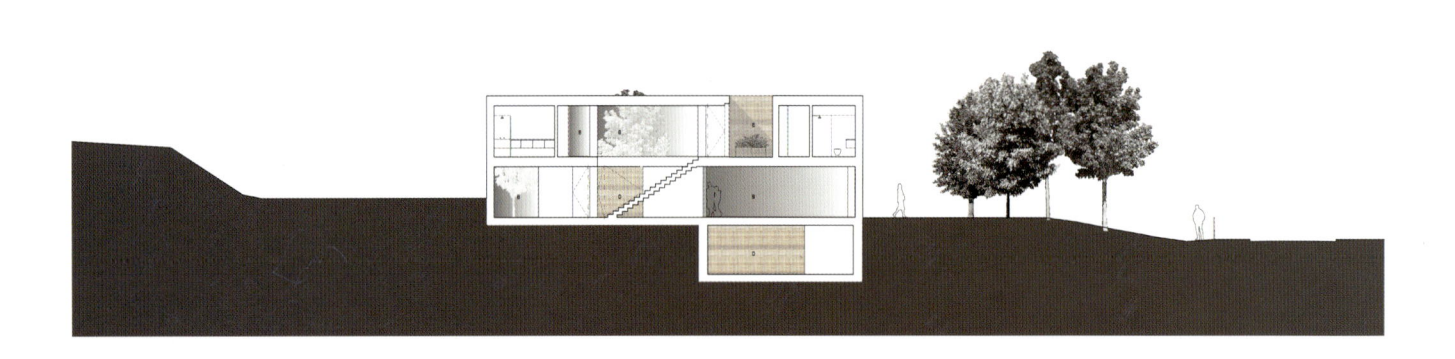

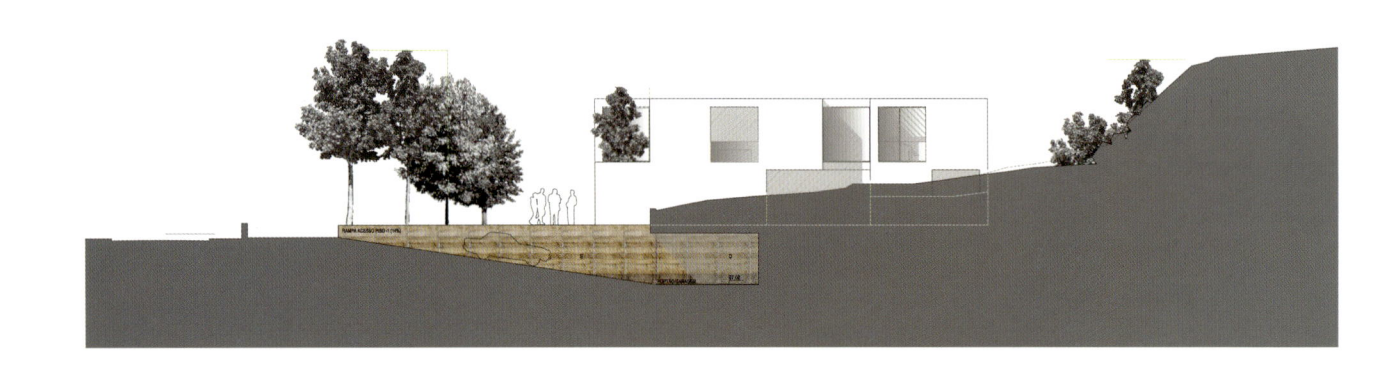

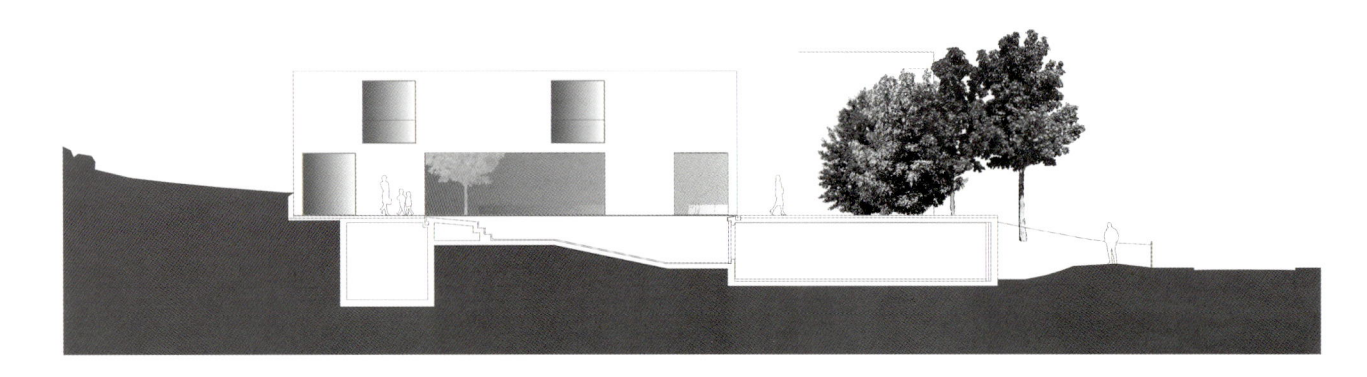

Frederico Valsassina Arquitectos

House in Quinta Patino

Frederico Valsassina Arquitectos

House in Quinta Patino

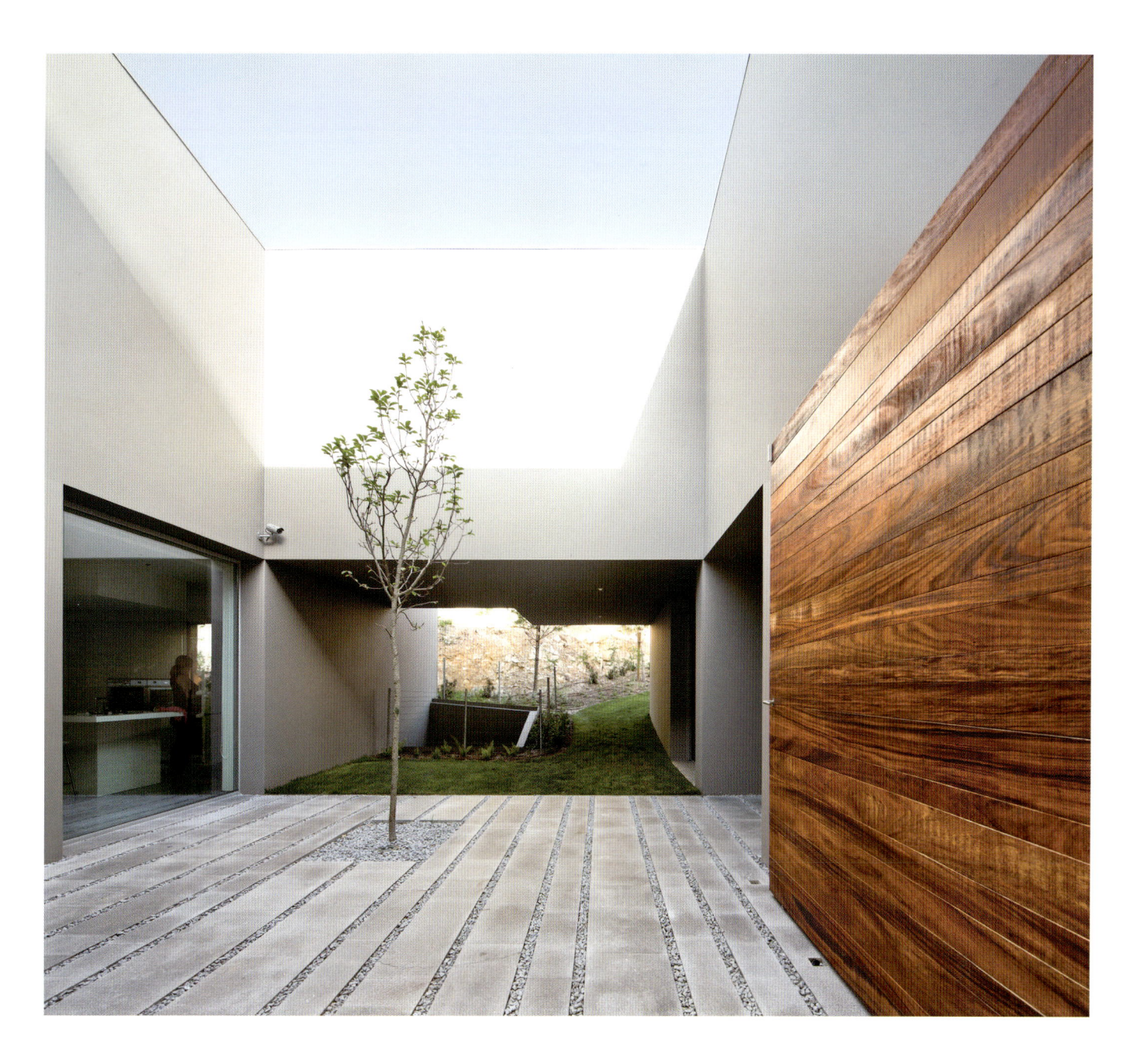

Minimalist details create a soothing and relaxing environment while a carefully manicured lawn allows for optimal outdoor recreational activity. The outdoor patio is home to a living wall that is taken over by plants. Outdoor lights illuminate the surrounding trees at night.

Frederico Valsassina Arquitectos

INDEX

123DV P76

The Netherlands www.123dv.nl

123DV was founded in 1999 by Mr. Liong Lie (1961). The current team consists of ten international architects, project managers, and interior designers whose goal is to design and realize homey modern villas. 123DV Modern Villas focuses on both architecture and interiors from product design to realization. Their disciplines include architecture and interior design from kitchens to furniture. A modern villa does not consist merely in an exterior. The connection between the inner and outer world is crucial. Therefore, the design for the interior is often included. 123DV also designs lighting, sound, and security. Sustainability is not treated as a trend, but as a matter of course.

Photography: Christiaan de Bruijne

314 Architecture Studio P20

Greece www.314.gr

314 Architecture Studio was founded in 2002 by architect and civil engineer Pavlos Chatziangelidis. It specializes in developing contemporary residences, private houses, and block apartments. The firm employs a large number of associate architects, engineers, and designers.

Photography: 314 Architecture Studio

Arch. Gabriel Rivera + Arch. Cristina Vargas P90

Ecuador www.gabriel-rivera.com www.cristina-vargas.com

Cristina Vargas and Gabriel Rivera are two independent architects who combine their skills for the development of architectural projects in Ecuador. Both strive to bring Ecuadorian architecture to the highest levels of design. They seek to create "architecture with identity" that reflects the needs of the customers and responds to the characteristics of the environment. Clean lines, clear volumes, warm materials, and respect for nature are the main elements of their work.

Photography: Sebastian Crespo

Ayutt and Associates Design P164

Thailand www.aadprojects.wordpress.com

Ayutt has successfully completed many projects that include not only architectural design, but interior, lighting, and landscape design as well. Past and current projects include commercial, residential, hospitality, exhibition, institutional, mixed-use, and interior projects. Ayutt's design philosophy rests on the belief that each project is unique and that the design should evolve through the particular characteristics of each project. He believes in allowing each project to speak with its own voice and to evolve around a set of objectives and strategies that emerge from within the project requirements, the client, the site, and the climate.

Photography: Piyawut Srisaakul

BattersbyHowat Architects P192

Canada www.battersbyhowat.com

Established in 1996 as a design firm and more recently in 2010 as a full service architectural practice, BattersbyHowat Architects Inc. is a partnership between David Battersby and Heather Howat. With combined degrees in architecture, landscape architecture, and interior design, the practice offers a truly holistic approach to design. Their work has been recognized with national and international awards and publications including the Canada Council's Ron Thom Award for Early Achievement in Architecture, two Canadian Architect Awards of Excellence, and the Interior Design Institute of BC Award of Excellence.

Photography: Sama J. Canzian

Blaze Makoid Architecture P198

USA www.blazemakoid-architecture.com

Blaze Makoid has practiced architecture and design since graduating from the Rhode Island School of Design in 1985. Prior to establishing his own firm, he worked for the internationally known design firms of Kallmann, McKinnell & Wood and the Hillier Group where he was the design director for their Philadelphia office. His designs have been exhibited in New York City, Boston, and Philadelphia. He has received numerous national and international design awards including the 2008 Long Island AIA Commendation for Outstanding Achievement in Residential Design, the Boston Society of Architects' First Citation, and the Philadelphia AIA Honor Award for Excellence.

Photography: Marc Bryan Brown

Dai Nagasaka/Mega P212
Japan www.mega71.com

Dai Nagasaka established Mega in 1990. Mega's focus is the design and supervision of architecture (including residences, collective housing, shops, restaurants, offices, museums, halls, schools, hospitals, factories, hotels, etc.), landscape, interiors, exhibition, furniture, and products. The designers at Mega think that everything is connected and part of the sphere. Architecture is, of course, a part of this interconnected world. Instead of defining the work of architecture as creating, the designers view it as a change in terrain. When working on a new design, the designers look at the terrain and think about the potential for change in it.

Photography: Kei Sugino

Daniel Redolat + Marià Castelló Architects P136
Spain www.m-ar.net

The studio was founded in 2002 and its first projects were public and private ones in Formentera. Formentera Island is experiencing rapid urban development and large numbers of low quality buildings are being constructed. These buildings contrast with the exceptional value of the natural substrate and the characteristic architecture. Formentera has historically opted for a model of sparsely scattered residences, and in this context the isolated family home has been the most common program to solve. The studio has worked with publishing projects and exhibitions in order to broadcast both the background of the property on the island as well as the well-thought-out contemporary interventions.

Photography: Estudi Es Pujol de s'Era

DAR612 P80
Croatia www.dar612.hr

DAR612 is a family-run architecture studio that designs contemporary living and work spaces. Their creative process, continuously present from the first design assignment to the building construction, is to merge their architectural knowledge and experience with their personal aesthetic. By being intensely involved in projects, DAR612 builds a trusting relationship with clients, ensuring that their aspirations and needs, along with office's design visions, are met in the most successful and creative way.

Photography: Robert Leš

dmvA P202
Belgium www.dmva-architects.com

dmvA was formed in 1997 by Tom Verschueren and David Driesen. Both architects want to express themselves through architecture, which is what the Dutch abbreviation dmvA stands for (door middel van Architectuur). Together with their team of architects, they have completed several private and public projects. Several of their projects have been nominated and have won awards both nationally and internationally.

Photography: Frederik Vercruysse

EANA P118/124
Japan www.eana.jp

EANA is an architecture practice based in Kanagawa, Japan, and is composed of two architects. Their focus in architectural design is the relationship between objects because spaces are measured by the relative value of things. Since these relationships are able to produce an infinite number of different spaces, the architects carefully assess conditions and environments first. After this initial evaluation, they propose new values for the architectural space.

Photography: Koichi Torimura

Elías Rizo Arquitectos P112
Mexico www.eliasrizo.com

The design goal of Elías Rizo Arquitectos can be summed up in one simple idea: create beautiful spaces that improve the client's everyday life. It's about fulfilling the client's needs with a commitment to honesty, service, and quality. It is essential to understand, learn, and create despite the risks. Nothing can be gained without risk. The firm is committed to those who are willing to experience both the good and bad that architecture represents. Elías Rizo Arquitectos is confident that through architecture, one can transform fantasies into reality.

Photography: Marcos García

Empty Space Architecture P8

Portugal www.emptyspace.pt

Empty Space Architecture is an architecture office for those who wish to construct buildings and spaces that are architectural pieces with unique identities and images.

Photography: João Morgado

Enrico Iascone Architetti P14

Italy www.iasconearchitetti.it

Enrico Iascone Architecture Studio (EIA), founded in 2001 by Enrico and Carlotta Menarini, operates in the field of architectural design with a particular sensitivity to environmental and energy issues. EIA pays special attention to landscaping and uses sustainable technologies.

Photography: Daniele Domenicali

Fran Silvestre Arquitectos P142

Spain www.fransilvestrenavarro.com

Fran Silvestre Arquitectos is an architecture office in Valencia, Spain, founded by Fran Silvestre in 2005. Architecture can be a tremendous feature as well as a subtle detail, if each brief is taken as an opportunity to realize a great project.

Photography: Diego Opazo

Frederico Valsassina Arquitectos P30/226

Portugal www.fvarq.com

FVA Architects is an office that works effectively and with professionalism. The team produces architecture with a contemporary image that transcends its time and space. The architects use new materials and technologies in their projects.

Photography: FG+SG Fotografia de Arquitectura

General Design Co., Ltd. P102

Japan www.general-design.net

General Design was established in 1999 by architect Shin Ohori. Shin was born in Gifu in 1967 and graduated with a master's degree in architecture from Musashino Art University in 1992.

Photography: Daici Ano

Hans van Heeswijk Architects P158

The Netherlands www.heeswijk.nl

Every assignment begins with a question. Hans van Heeswijk Architects likes to take the time with clients to formulate this clearly before starting to design. To be successful, good architecture not only requires a capable architect, but also an inspired client. The approach of the office is to combine its solid experience in a wide range of work with attention to detail. What is the answer? Most of all: clarity. Above all, architecture should be light.

Photography: Imre CsanyDAPh

Hironaka Ogawa & Associates P106

Japan www.ogaa.jp

Hironaka Ogawa & Associates was established by Hironaka Ogawa in 2005. Hironaka Ogawa was born in Kagawa in 1975. He completed the master course at the Department of Architecture at Nihon University in 2000. He is currently a lecturer at Toyo University, Kagawa University, and Nihon University. He has received numerous awards. His work unites materials with new technologies and a sophisticated aesthetic, thus suggesting new possibilities for architecture.

Photography: Daici Ano

IDIN Architects P94

Thailand www.idinarchitects.com

An acronym for Integrating Design Into Nature, IDIN Architects was founded by Jeravej Hongsakul in 2004. They interpret the word "nature" in two ways. Firstly, the word can be defined as the ecology around us. Secondly, it can also refer to different mannerisms and personalities. IDIN's design philosophy and concentration is to merge these two senses of the word with their architectural aesthetic. This merge is done through the process of analyzing and prioritizing the different needs and requirements of each project. In addition, the Thai word "idin" is used to describe the natural phenomenon when soil releases a beautiful scent after rainfall. This symbolizes Thailand's tropical climate, something all IDIN designs aim to respond to.

Photography: Spaceshift Studio

IROJE KHM Architects P130
South Korea www.irojekhm.com

Architect HyoMan Kim, a Dankook University graduate, is the principal of IROJE KHM Architects. He has won the World Architecture Community Award, the ARCASIA (Architects Regional Council of Asia) Award, the Architectural Culture Award of Korea, the Architectural Award of Seoul, and the CRI-AC Award to name a few. He is also a concurrent professor at the Graduate School of Architecture at Gyeonggi University and an editorial adviser for CONCEPT Magazine. He has exhibited his works in many countries including the USA, Italy, and Japan.

Photography: JongOh Kim

JOHO Architecture P172
South Korea www.johoarchitecture.com

JOHO Architecture is based in Seoul and was established by Jeonghoon Lee in 2009. JOHO Architecture endeavors to reinterpret traditional Korean spaces through the use of various patterns and repetitive units composed of affordable and readily available raw materials. Mr. Lee strives to create new features and identities based on form and façade that harmonize with context of the site. The studio's major works include The Curving House, Namhae Choe-ma House, and Herma Parking Building. JOHO Architecture is one of the top up-and-coming architecture studios in Korea and is currently working on several new projects.

Photography: Sun Namgoong

L/A Liebel/Architekten BDA P208
Germany www.liebelarchitekten.de

L/A Liebel/Architekten was founded in 2000 by Bernd Liebel and is based in Aalen, Germany. There are a total of 16 architects working on residential, commercial (bank and factory), educational, and sports projects. The practice of L/A Liebel/Achritekten has received numerous international awards. Many projects are the result of successful competition submissions.

Photography: Michael Schnell

Mário Martins Atelier P148
Portugal www.mariomartins.com

Mário Martins was born in Lagos, Algarve, Portugal in 1964 and graduated from the University of Architecture of Lisbon (Arquitectura da Universidade Tecnica de Lisboa) in 1988. He has worked in Lagos in his architectural office, Mário Martins - Atelier de Arquitectura, Lda, since 1989. He has designed public sector buildings, tourist developments, and private houses mainly in the south of Portugal. His work has been featured in various publications in the media and at conferences.

Photography: Fernando Guerra (FG+SG)

Miguel Ángel Aragonés P64
Mexico www.aragones.com.mx

Miguel Angel Aragonés was born in the city of Mexico in 1962. The self-taught architect has been doing rich and original architectural work for over two decades. Miguel has been an exhibitor and speaker at many universities in Mexico and abroad. His monograph on the work of Aragones published by L'arca has been circulated in France, Germany, Italy, Norway, England, the United States, China, etc. His work has been published in hundreds of magazines and publications in countries such as Russia, Italy, Spain, France, Germany, the U.S., Argentina, Brazil, and Mexico among others.

Photography: Joe Fletcher

monovolume architecture + design P68
Italy www.monovolume.cc

monovolume has been working in the sector of architecture and design and piloting projects that go from urban design to interior design and furnishing since 2003. The monovolume team is constantly looking for challenges. Architecture and design mean much more than just creating forms. It is important to question traditional beliefs and habits and look at them from other points of view in order to create something innovative. The goal that represents the label monovolume is to create intelligent architecture with audacious design that reacts to the environment and takes advantage of its characteristics.

Photography: M&H Photostudio

Nelson Resende Arquitecto P152

Portugal www.nelsonresendearquitecto.com

Nelson Resende has been an architect at F.A.U.P. since 2000. He leads a small architecture office located in Ovar, Portugal.

Photography: FG+SG Fotografia de Arquitectura

Nico van der Meulen Architects P72

South Africa www.nicovdmeulen.com

Nico van der Meulen Architects is one of the most prominent modern architectural practices in Africa. With more than 40 years of experience, the studio specializes in contemporary home design and modern luxury residences. At Nico van der Meulen, designers work closely with all the clients to ensure optimal satisfaction and outstanding results.

Pitágoras Arquitectos P48

Portugal www.pitagoras.pt

Pitágoras Arquitectos is an architecture firm based in Portugal with 20 years of experience. The growing team is now made up of 14 people and is led by its four partners Fernando Sear de Sá, Raul Roque Figueiredo, Alexandre Coelho Lima, and Manuel Vilhena Roque. In collaboration with external partners, it creates an interdisciplinary team that works in all architectural fields: from interior design to ruban planning, including residential, health, and equipment for the private and public sectors.

Photography: José Campos Photography

Renato D'Ettorre Architects P98

Australia www.dettorrearchitects.com.au

Renato D'Ettorre Architects draw inspiration and references from areas as wide as possible. Each project presents an opportunity to explore aspects of phenomenology and the challenge of bestowing specificity. Once these hidden forces are discovered and the design direction becomes clear, the architecture has the potential to achieve a meaningful presence. The object is to create architecture that is evocative, attempts a sense of place and beauty, satisfies the human need for textural expressions, calms or stimulates the senses with light and shade as well as space and materiality, while reducing complexity to achieve clarity and simplicity, thus emphasizing the ephemeral elements that good architecture can generate.

Photography: Francesca Giovanelli

Robert M. Gurney Architect P24

USA www.robertgurneyarchitect.com

The office of Robert M. Gurney, FAIA is dedicated to the design of modern, meticulously detailed, and thoughtfully ordered residential and commercial projects sensitive to site, program, and budget. Materials are employed with honesty, integrity, and ecological awareness. Regardless of project size or budget, our office is committed to producing buildings and spaces that strive for design excellence.

Photography: Maxwell MacKenzie Architectural Photographer Anice Hoachlander (Hoachlander Davis Photography)

Shaun Lockyer Architects P84/216

Australia www.lockyerarchitects.com.au

Shaun Lockyer Architects is an award-winning Brisbane architecture firm. Formed in 2010, SLa focuses on modernist architecture that connects people and place. Inherent within each project is a desire to craft memorable, sustainable, and efficient design solutions that add value to the inhabitants' lives. SLa engages in various types of projects including residential, institutional, commercial, and interior design. Working with private and public clients who value a collaborative and transparent design process, each SLa commission employs a versatility and passion that transcends scale and budget.

Photography: Scott Burrows (Aperture Photography)

Skinotechniki P36

Cyprus www.skinotechniki.com

Georgios Papadopoulos is an architect and scenographer. He graduated from the London University's Bartlet School of Architecture with first degree honours. He obtained the Diploma in Architecture and became a member of RIBA, ARCUK, and ETEK. He studied under such architects and teachers as James Stirling, James Gowan, and Phylip Tabor. In 1992 he formed the company Skinotechniki to provide his clients with a complete package that includes design and construction of sets for the stage, television and film, exhibition stands, museums, and architecture.

Photography: Andy Soteriou

Smart Design Studio P222

Australia www.smartdesignstudio.com

The philosophy of Smart Design Studio (SDS) can be distilled into three simple words: excellence, innovation, and collaboration. The SDS team consists of 30 staff members. We have been operating for over 13 years as a successful practice with the capacity and experience to undertake a broad array of projects. Our efforts focus on getting great buildings built. We apply our experience in design to each project we undertake, while striving to introduce innovation and new concepts to continually invigorate our work. This approach creates a unique quality for each project and encourages continual growth in the studio.

Studio Guilherme Torres P178

Brazil www.guilhermetorres.com.br

Guilherme Torres is a perfectionist. It says so on his arm. Not in many words, but via the daft punk quote that graces both his skin and the walls of his studio. This unofficial motto describes a work ethic and commitment to quality that is readily apparent in his work. The crisp forms, minimalist details, and rich but reserved material palettes that characterize his designs are consistently applied across his works. A certain playful levity can be found in his interior design projects that balances the rigorous aesthetic of his architecture. The stark forms and subtle surfaces provide an appropriately quiet backdrop for the lively furnishings within, while the thoughtfully arranged spaces benefit from an astute attention to natural light. Taken together, his portfolio of work is an exceptional achievement, especially for someone so young.

Photography: Denilson Machado (MCA Estúdio)

Studio MK27 P42

Brazil www.marciokogan.com.br

Studio MK27 was founded at the beginning of the 1980s by Marcio Kogan, an architect who graduated from Mackenzie University in 1976. Today the studio is made up of 20 more architects as well as collaborators located in various parts of the world. The studio's architects develop the projects from start to finish. The architects at Studio MK27 value formal simplicity and always take great care in the details and finishing. Marcio Kogan and the team are great admirers of the Brazilian modernist generation and strive to undertake the difficult mission of giving continuity to this line of production.

Photography: Reinaldo Cóser

Takeshi Hirobe Architects P184

Japan www.hirobe.net

Takeshi Hirobe was born in Kanagawa Prefecture, Japan in 1968. He graduated from College of Science and Technology, Nihon University in 1991 and established Takeshi Hirobe Architects in 1999. He is currently an adjunct lecturer at Nihon University and Meiji University. Takeshi believes that a building moves in the same way music does. The structure is firmly fixed to the earth, but as the earth itself moves over the course of the day, different kinds of light flood in. As seasons progress other changes also occur. When people spend time inside, these changes can be sensed, and people are reminded that we too are part of the earth.

Photography: Koichi Torimura

Taller Héctor Barroso P54

Mexico www.tallerhectorbarroso.com
Taller Héctor Barroso is dedicated to the development of all kinds of architectonic projects, no matter the scale or type. In each project, an investigative method is used to find the most adequate solution in order to ensure the client's satisfaction. The firm maintains an open dialogue and looks for new ideas to exchange with each client in order to enrich each project. The multidisciplinary workshop works with engineers, landscape designers, interior designers, and other professionals and always looks to improve each project. The team believes that people's quality of life can be changed through architecture and design.
Photography: Yoshihiro Koitani

Terra e Tuma Arquitetos Associados P188

Brazil www.terraetuma.com.br
Architects Danilo Terra and Pedro Tuma Terra Tuma established Terra e Tuma Arquitetos Associados together. The studio specializes in residential projects and furniture design.
Photography: Pedro Kok

Vitor Vilhena Arquitectura P58

Portugal www.vitorvilhena.com
Born in Lagos in 1971, Vitor Vilhena graduated from the University Lusíada in Lisbon in 1997. Between 1996 and 1999, he collaborated with architects Jorge Gonçalves and Paulo Simões (Aupera), Henry Albino, Margarida GomesSimoes, and Vitor Lourenço and developed works of all kinds. In 1999, he started to work alone and created Vitor Vilhena Architect Atelier.
Photography: João Morgado Photography

ACKNOWLEDGEMENTS

WE WOULD LIKE TO THANK ALL OF THE DESIGNERS INVOLVED FOR GRANTING US PERMISSION TO PUBLISH THEIR WORKS, AS WELL AS ALL OF THE PHOTOGRAPHERS WHO HAVE GENEROUSLY ALLOWED US TO USE THEIR IMAGES. WE ARE ALSO VERY GRATEFUL TO MANY OTHER PEOPLE WHOSE NAMES DO NOT APPEAR IN THE CREDITS BUT WHO MADE SPECIFIC CONTRIBUTIONS AND PROVIDED SUPPORT. WITHOUT THESE PEOPLE, WE WOULD NOT HAVE BEEN ABLE TO SHARE THESE BEAUTIFUL WORKS WITH READERS AROUND THE WORLD. OUR EDITORIAL TEAM INCLUDES EDITOR SU JINGLAN AND BOOK DESIGNER CHEN XINWEI, TO WHOM WE ARE TRULY GRATEFUL.